THE
FICTITIOUS
COMMODITY

Recent Titles in
Contributions in Labor Studies

THE
FICTITIOUS
COMMODITY

A Study of the U.S. Labor Market, 1880–1940

Ton Korver

Contributions in Labor Studies, Number 30

GREENWOOD PRESS

New York • Westport, Connecticut • London

Library of Congress Cataloging-in-Publication Data

Korver, Ton.
    The fictitious commodity : a study of the U.S. labor market,
1880–1940 / Ton Korver.
        p.   cm. — (Contributions in labor studies, ISSN 0886–8239 ;
no. 30)
    Includes bibliographical references
    ISBN 0–313–27338–3 (lib. bdg. : alk. paper)
    1. Labor market—United States—History.   I. Title.   II. Series.
HD5724.K64 1990
331.12′0973—dc20   90–2717

British Library Cataloguing in Publication Data is available.

Library of Congress Catalog Card Number: 90–2717
ISBN: 0–313–27338–3
ISSN: 0886–8239

First published in 1990

Greenwood Press, 88 Post Road West, Westport, CT 06881
An imprint of Greenwood Publishing Group, Inc.

Printed in the United States of America

The paper used in this book complies with the
Permanent Paper Standard issued by the National
Information Standards Organization (Z39.48–1984).

10 9 8 7 6 5 4 3 2 1

CONTENTS

TABLES

ACKNOWLEDGMENTS

In writing this study I was fortunate enough to receive help and encouragement from many people. Albert Mok was a stimulating guide throughout the time-consuming conception of the book and did not even lose confidence when the pace of progress was dismally slow. Also, I benefited from his wide knowledge on the economics and sociology of labor markets as well as from his many remarks on the subject of scientific management.

A series of drafts preceded the completed book. Lily Clerckx, Michael Kraetke, Pieter Pekelharing, and Jannie Veltman read one or more of the drafts. Their comments have led to several changes in the text and its construction.

Rypke Sierksma read the chapter on Taylor and prevented me from confusing principles of optimization and maximazation. Veit Bader, Mino Carchedi, and Michael Masuch read drafts and parts of the final manuscript. Their stimulating criticisms have led to several clarifications in the study.

Many thanks are due to Michael Hanagan, whose report was sent to me by Greenwood Press. It was of great help in reworking the manuscript.

Finally, I want to thank Jac Christis. He read and criticized most of the drafts and the final or almost final versions, gave valuable advice, and provided support and friendship throughout the project.

I disclaim the usual disclaimer on the family. They are as happy as I am that the work is finished.

1

RECRUITMENT AND MOBILITY

A study of the American record in the history and development of labor markets is a challenging enterprise. It is also a hazardous affair, and it seems best to start with the hazards and the ways and means employed in this study to cope with them. The difficulties and uncertainties connected with the study of labor markets reside in the poverty of the dominant theoretical and conceptual instruments. Partly, this is due to the lazy habit of using heuristic and sensitizing concepts as theoretical ones. The concept of power especially seems prey to this faulty procedure. Partly, we have to blame the insufficiency of the ruling concepts of markets and contracts. Although one finds ample recognition of the fact that labor is, indeed, an odd commodity, only rarely is the very concept of labor as a commodity put to the test. Instead, it is asserted that labor is a peculiar member of the series of commodities— peculiar, but a member all the same.

The issues are connected. Markets and purposive contracts can be analyzed in terms of power and its unequal distribution and vice versa. Markets, contracts, and power, however, are not up to the major task in the analysis of the labor market, the labor contract, and the respective powers of demand and supply. This major task is the explanation not of relations of power but of relations of authority. The law is explicit on the matter: The labor contract establishes above all the legal authority of the employer to direct and command the employee. In reverse, the employee does not sell capacities and even less his powers. He sells, in the celebrated words of J. R. Commons, "his promise to obey commands" (Commons, 1924: 284). Accepting authority, then, is of the essence in the labor contract, and this state of affairs defeats the usual discourse on markets and contracts. Also, the legal definition is, for excellent reasons, silent on matters of power. Power is, on any microlevel of negotiations between individual employers and employees, an unstable balance of conflicting interests. Such a balance may at times explain conflicts between employers and employees, but it cannot explain the routines of everyday labor and management.

It may be objected that the routines derive from nothing but the strategic behavior of the parties in the employment arena. Often they do, but this is completely besides the point. Strategic behavior relates to the motivation of actors; authority, on the other hand, is the prior question of differential, legally defined or bolstered statuses. Statuses take behavior as given. Motivation, on the other hand, takes behavior as a variable. It is obvious that authority and motivation are interdependent. It should be as obvious that, for all their interdependence, they do not belong to the same equation (Littler, 1982). They have their own histories, causations, and rhythms of change. Indeed, much of the discourse on markets (and in the past few decades more generally on decision making) is an attempt to underpin the motivational aspects of rational economic behavior. Yet influencing motivation in capitalist economies has to stop short of relations of authority. That, in the end, is the primary difficulty.

POWER AND AUTHORITY

Strategic behavior may be found under widely differing systems of authority, be they traditional, charismatic, or rational. On the other hand, the system of rational authority, as developed by Max Weber, holds a special difficulty for market societies. The difficulty is that although markets do spell relations of power and are themselves objects of power, they are silent where authority is concerned (Gouldner, 1954: 162–165). Indeed, the thing about markets is precisely that they are beyond authority. The market is the realm of the impersonal where relations are established and dissolved for purely instrumental reasons. Moreover, it is never the person who is enveloped in market transactions but always the goods or the services. What counts are prices and qualities, not persons and their reputations. Economic reasoning depends on the innocence of the market as to skewed relations of authority. The law of "indifference," as W. S. Jevons (1871: 137) called it, characterizes the market—indifference, that is, as to ascribed qualities of status like place of origin, gender, and ethnicity. The stronger in the market may have power; they have no authority. They influence the scope of action of the less powerful, but that, again, is a far cry from a relation of authority.

Power, in the classical sense of control over critical resources—echoed in the early meanings of capital as an advance and a stock—does not create commodities or services. The routines these demand to get produced at all rely on predictable and stable parameters of behavior. In this respect, the attempt of Michel Foucault to close the gap by inflating the concept of power to include both authority and motivational and even physical malleability is a mere denial of the problem. The panopticon is not a market, and the invisible eye is not the invisible hand. Indeed, markets are failures in inducing behavior that is both predictable and stable, and this is not because markets are immune to power but precisely because they consist of nothing else. Historically, no doubt, predictability was one of the major ideological strongholds of behavior in markets, as opposed to an unpredictable political rule (Hirschman, 1977). Yet markets do not produce anything; they merely coordinate what is produced elsewhere. Theoretically, the neutrality of market exchange as to relations of authority has led to a mode of depicting the production function as the market-determined combination of inputs, whose internal relations, once their price is determined, are a matter of technology. Organizations, as a form of economic coordination distinct from the market, fall beyond the scope of such theorizing. So do forms of authority.

To enter a labor contract, then, is to accept a non-negotiable status. The regular purposive contract is neutral to status, for it regards it as a datum of the transaction at hand. The labor contract, in contrast, first defines the status of employers and employees as those who may issue and enforce orders and those who have to obey. The duty to obey is a personal one. An employee cannot let himself be represented by someone else. However interchangeable and substitutable the job that the employee has to perform may be, the worker himself is contractually bound to an individual, nonsubstitutable responsibility for his indistinguishable task. For the employee there is no intermediate zone between being there in person and quitting. For the employer, therefore, it is important to know, and the more so the less interchangeable and substitutable the job to be performed, how good the "promise to obey," actually is. Recruitment and selection, given the personal nature of the labor contract, always involve more than a check on competencies and credentials. Competencies and credentials can be ascertained in a nonpersonal manner. The market for services is the appropriate example. But what the employer, tapping the labor market instead of the market for services, needs to know is the person, for it is the person who defines the employee side of the contract.

There is a very real predicament here. The authority of the employer holds good only for the given contract. The authority is meaningless beyond it. If the costly lesson of welfare capitalism proved anything, it was, indeed, this. Within the labor contract there is no discretionary zone controlled by the employee. What the employee controls is what I, for want of a better concept, call his discretionary mobility. The employee may move from job to job, employer to employer, and he may move beyond the labor market as such. Like the fear of unemployment, the discretionary mobility is an essential characteristic of the modern definition of wage dependency. For the employer, it is imperative to be informed about typical patterns of discretionary mobility. In the field of recruitment and final selection of employees the employer, consequently, will behave like an insurance company, and the labor contract takes on the appearance of an insurance policy.

There are objective probabilities regarding the patterns of workers' mobility. The literature on statistical discrimination in hiring presents the evidence. But the objective probabilities are only half the story. The other half is best described by the concept of "moral hazard." If the labor contract is looked upon as an insurance policy, the moral hazard is that the policy "*might itself change incentives and therefore the probabilities upon which the insurance company has relied*" (Arrow, 1970: 142; emphasis in the original). As a result, the employer will refuse to shoulder unpredictable risks and, more generally, screen employees, including the "resort to direct inspection and control, to make as certain as he can that the insured is minimizing all losses under the latter's control" (Arrow, 1970: 143).

The nature of the losses, in the case of labor markets, is threefold. First, there is the information cost. Since the information has to be personal, and the person cannot be trusted to be the best source of information about his behavior after contracting, information will have to be supplied from elsewhere. Henry Ford used the clergy as the best proxy for reliable information before entry and the Sociological Department after entry. If recruitment usually takes place in a given community and foremen are part of such a community or control strategic links with its leading members, hiring can remain a stronghold of foremen long after other aspects of the employment relation have become extensively bureaucratized (Jacoby, 1985). Even trade unions may serve a similar function, as may padrones, clubs, fraternities, and the like (Granovetter and Tilly, 1988: 192; Korver, 1988a). Second, there are the motivational problems of converting labor power into effective labor performance. Third, and most pertinent in our case, are the potential losses on account of discretionary mobility. The motivational problems can be identified by observing any organizational system of penalties and rewards, that is, in the effects of membership. The problems of discretionary mobility and the limits on the employer's authority that they represent can be identified in terms of the entry and exit of organizational membership. Rewards and penalties "discipline"; they play on behavior; entry and exit influence the parameters of behavior. Entry and exit influence and are influenced by discipline, but that does not make them identical. Entry can be difficult and expensive; the same holds for exit. Probationary periods with comparatively low pay and intensive screening are an example of the former; loss of accumulated seniority rewards (pensions, for instance) are an example of the latter. In a related vein, entitlements to unemployment compensation reward "loyalty" and punish voluntary exit (on entry, exit, and "loyalty," see Hirschman, 1970: 77ff.).

Although strenuous, there is a feasible analytical relation between the system of membership payoffs and the usual criteria of productivity and efficiency. That the relationship is sometimes hard to establish stems from the type of task to be performed. Many tasks have idiosyncrasies (Williamson, 1975, 1985) prohibiting direct and individualized measurements of productivity. Rewards and penalties in such instances are incentives, neutralizing the possible adverse effects of idiosyncrasy and therewith the moral hazards of membership. Although I believe that the measurement problems are much more formidable than Williamson acknowledged, the real difficulty lies elsewhere.

The difficulty is that the rewards of membership tend to include the effects of entry and exit. The case is most obvious in the low pay of beginners, for this reflects entry costs, comparatively limited worker's productivity, and, possibly, training costs that the employer shifts in greater or smaller degree to the beginning employee. The point here, however, is that the item of entry costs cannot be strictly related to comparative productivity and efficiency, whether now or in the future. Entry costs insure for loyalty, and entry is therefore refused to those not worthy of that honor. It may be that those weeded out by the screening procedures are more productive than those allowed in. In certain instances higher productivity is even likely. Credentials, health, training capacity, and so on of young workers may be better than like characteristics of adult workers. Yet youth unemployment is almost an endemic feature of labor markets. Terms of entry cannot be translated into the language of productivity and efficiency, for they do not focus on competencies of persons but on those persons themselves (Osterman, 1980). By necessity, then, discretionary mobility is matched by discretionary recruitment, and it should be remembered that recruitment is a permanent process throughout one's career. The organizational criterion of merit in promotions, that is, recruitment to a higher position, combines rewards for membership with the more intangible valuation of loyalty, especially the estimated and sometimes even the explicit forsaking of the possibility of exit.

RECRUITMENT, TECHNOLOGY, ORGANIZATION

The endogenous change of incentives and preferences, as in the moral-hazard example, is very hard to reconcile with a concept of the market (Hirschman, 1982, 1983, 1985). The analysis of demand and supply takes preferences as given or assumes some exogenous source for their change. Changing tastes are an example. If raising the price for discrimination in the labor market whets the appetite for discrimination, the conclusion in terms of the market is not that the market is defunct but that tastes have changed (Friedman, 1962; for a critique see Marsden, 1986). The situation is different once we allow for endogenous change. Workers' preferences and incentives are not the same before and after the conclusion of the contract. They have changed because of it. The contract and the market are not neutral, that is, as to preferences. Crippling entry costs may make a preference for exit mute, instead of sharpening it. Low entry costs may do the reverse (Hirschman, 1970). Preferences, then, may appear both on the input and the output side of the equation. High penalties for discriminatory preferences can actually produce discrimination. The phenomenon of the "backlash" is one illustration. The thesis that economics cannot be separated from ethics is another.

In nineteenth-century America, labor was both scarce and expensive. The high price of labor did not lead to an adequate supply (Habakkuk, 1962). The constraint of scarcity was not lifted. It could even result in the very opposite. High wages did not make wage labor more, but rather less, attractive. The preference for wage labor was not enlarged but diminished. The opportunity costs of labor were simply to high to create equilibrium conditions in the labor market. The "frontier," in more everyday language, constituted the opportunity. The possibility of obtaining land free or at low cost made wage dependency a temporary station, especially when wages were high.

It has been pointed out repeatedly that the frontier in this sense had become an illusion for most Americans by the first quarter of the nineteenth century (Schlesinger, 1946; Degler, 1962; Strauss, 1971). This does not preclude that the promise of the frontier lent a distinct quality of indeterminateness to local labor markets. Unskilled labor, in particular, was hard to come by. The reasons are easy to understand. Unskilled labor, when compared to the skilled, was far more concentrated in factories. Skilled workers populated the many small shops, where factory methods were not even contemplated until the seventies and eighties of the previous century. Unique about the situation in the United States, then, was the high wage for unskilled labor but not the scarcity of unskilled workers relative to the demand originating from factories. In the United Kingdom as well, the rise of industrial capitalism was slowed because of the refusal of the "working poor" to accept factory work. Where wage dependency had extended its reach over several centuries before the advent of the industrial revolution, the combination of wage dependency and factory work provoked resistance on an unknown scale.

The English conditions, however, differed dramatically from those in the United States. The background in England was a structural oversupply of labor in the countryside that refused to spill over to the emerging world of the factory. Scarcity of labor, to observers of the time such as Adam Smith and Jeremy Bentham, was highly contrived. For that reason, the Poor Law came under attack, since it was assumed that the system of parish-bound outdoor relief prevented the mobility of labor. Karl Polanyi, therefore, quoted the Poor Law Amendment Act of 1834—in which outdoor relief was forbidden, the workhouse was to become a place of terror, and the destitute were bereft of their civil rights—as the birth of the modern labor market (Polanyi, 1944). Once the oversupply of unskilled labor had channeled to the factory, the critical bottleneck became skilled labor. English technology in the nineteenth century therefore became bent toward neutralizing dependence on the skilled worker. American technology, on the other hand, was not conceived that way. Instead of focusing primarily on skilled labor, it tried to make the most of the very restricted pool of unskilled labor. In fact, there were chronic shortages of unskilled labor combined with a more normal behavior in the market for skilled labor (Habakkuk, 1962; Rosenblum, 1973: 62; Gordon, Edwards, and Reich, 1982: 66).

A Poor Law policy of the English kind was administratively completely out of the question. More to the point, it would be utterly irrelevant for the problem. Instead, a liberal immigration policy was maintained throughout the nineteenth century. A constant inflow of new labor, on arrival more often than not without independent resources and therefore available for wage labor, was the result. For the major part of the century this option proved to be of temporary and limited avail only. Despite comparatively high wages, factory labor remained last in preference. In fact, employers had to rely to a considerable degree on persons with a weak citizenship status (children and women in particular) and on force. Even that was often a mixed blessing, for turnover was high (on England see Thompson, 1968; Habakkuk, 1981; on the United States see Thernstrom, 1964; Dawley, 1976; Gutman, 1977; Prude, 1983; for a comparative approach see Littler, 1982).

Recruitment and Technology

Recruitment histories demonstrate the intimate connection of population politics (from social policy to immigration) and labor-market developments. Moreover, recruitment histories have long-lasting effects on the shape of technology and organization. The shortage of labor in the United States in the previous century was translated in a capital-intensive technology of a peculiar type (Habakkuk, 1962; Rosenberg, 1972; David, 1975). In spite of a high rate of interest (Temin, 1973), a high ratio of capital to labor prevailed. Also, labor remained expensive: The new capital saved labor, but it did not substitute it. Rather, the development of capital-intensive technology made the most of the available small supply of labor. High wages, thus, reflected both scarcity and high productivity.

If we want to explain the path of American technology during the nineteenth century, we have to account for a high price for labor, a very low price for raw materials, and a high price for the means of production. From the employer's point of view all of these things are factors in capital outlay. The remarkable feature is the low price for raw materials. The English mid-century visitors to the United States applauded the efficiency of the American machines while questioning the enormous waste of raw materials, with timber being the usual example. Efficiency and waste, however, went together, for the deployment of mechanization in a standardized form initially could not be realized without a lavish use of raw materials. The scarcity and high cost of raw materials in England had precluded the mutual development of standardization and mechanization. The wide and cheap availability of land and its resources for industrial use in the United States enabled standardization. The high price of labor, furthermore, encouraged standardization since standardization raised the product and the productivity of the labor force.

There are elementary economic reasons, then, that the method of interchangeable parts, although not a unique American invention (Giedion, 1946), became so widespread in the United States that it soon was called the "American system." The essential role of interchangeable parts for the technology of mass production is well known. In the context of our argument, its effect on skill is noteworthy. For their production, interchangeable parts required highly skilled craftsmen. In their use, however, these parts made the complicated activity of fitting superfluous. Each man, in a sense, could be his own mechanic. This may have leveled some skills, but the more important aspect is that it standardized skill requirements for an increasing number of factory jobs. In fact, the very concept of unskilled labor acquired a new dimension.

Before the era of standardization, unskilled labor meant the work of women and children in factories and sweatshops. It meant the work in gangs of prison labor or practically purely physical labor employed in digging canals and waterways, the construction of roads and roadbeds, and so on. Next to women and children, Irish and Asian labor was almost automatically identified with work of an unskilled nature. Unskilled labor, therefore, was characterized by the low social and civil status of those performing it rather than by the technical nature of the work involved. Standardization did not change that, but it added a new element to the rank of the unskilled. The unskilled machine tender was not by definition frozen in that rank; the line separating the unskilled from the new and growing reality of the semiskilled worker was thin. Unskilled labor no longer by necessity entailed social and organizational separateness. The category of unskilled labor assumed split features. There is an hierarchy in unskilled labor even today in which those groups with a weak civil and social status (undocumented aliens, for instance, but also black and Hispanic minorities) perform unskilled labor of the "old" variety. They are at the bottom of the hierarchy, even if they are employed by a large employer. One example is the employment of blacks by Henry Ford in the twenties and thirties. They had jobs mainly in the foundry and the painting department as unskilled workers. Organizationally, therefore, they were separate from the core of the company: the assembly line. That did not mean that the assembly line was independent from unskilled work. It definitely was not. On or near the line, however, implied unskilled work that was organizationally, and often technologically, integrated into the core activities of the company. As for skill, it could not be readily distinguished from unskilled work of the old variety. As for organizational place and nomenclature, it could be, for often the workers on these jobs were designated immediately as semiskilled.

The crucial difference in ranking the unskilled has become one of differentiating jobs that do or do not promise terms of entry to a "ladder" of semiskilled stations. Those that do are on top; those that do not remain at the bottom. The difference tends to reinforce already existing patterns of social segmentation, provoking debates about social closure, balkanization of labor markets, and noncompeting groups within the total labor supply (Kerr, 1954; Bonacich, 1979, 1980; Burawoy, 1980; for the general argument see Parkin, 1979). For our argument here it suffices to conclude (1) that the shape of American technology in the nineteenth century was distinctly influenced by the chronic shortage of unskilled labor; (2) that the mark of distinction in this respect was the standardization movement, accompanying mechanization; and (3) that standardization led to a leveling of skills such that unskilled labor in terms of career prospects, organizational location, and supporting technology could at times be compared with work of other skill requirements. The problem of recruitment, then, matters. Yet recruitment, like standardization, is in the final analysis a question of organization.

Recruitment and Organization

Recruitment is, as we observed above, a practice for which the information of the market is insufficient as to reliability and completeness. It is an organizational task as such, for which, in the case of labor contracts, there is no ready market substitute. The point needs emphasizing because in the now dominant literature on economic theories of organization (Wachter, 1974; Williamson, 1975, 1985; Okun, 1982; for a critique see Perrow, 1986), organizational coordination is presented as the better alternative to markets in situations in which "asset specificity," "opportunism," and so on are important characteristics. This approach is very fruitful, but because of its strict adherence to the canons of efficiency and conventional economic rationality, it is of limited significance in the explanation of organizational recruitment behavior.

Economic theories of organization start from the elementary observation that market exchanges are but a small part of all of the relevant economic transactions that occur. Transaction, in the view of J. R. Commons (1951), is seen as the basic term, and the approach consists of attempting to prove that organizational transactions are rational when they, relative to market transactions, economize on transaction costs. Information in this respect is the most crucial variable. It is assumed that information—to get it, to process it, to select it, to evaluate it—is anything but a free convenience. Moreover, to obtain information about future events is often difficult or even impossible. This is of special relevance to the labor contract, for this is a conditional promise about future activities.

On account of bounded rationality (limits on the capacity to process information), opportunism (the danger that the source of information manipulates, withholds, or distorts information), and the costs one has to incur to lift the capacity constraint and to ascertain the truthfulness of the information source, it is predicted that the typical market exchange (many suppliers) will regularly give way to what is called "small numbers exchange relationships" (Williamson, 1975) or even "bilateral monopoly" (Williamson, 1985). One economizes on transaction costs by continuing one's relations with reliable suppliers. The market, then, is replaced. Many potential suppliers do not stand a chance because of a "first mover" advantage of a few. Next is a more direct hierarchical phenomenon, like satellite firms and mergers.

A comparable argument is presented for the labor contract. When labor tasks are idiosyncratic, management can save transaction costs by transforming the pure exchange relationship into an organizational one of, say, the internal market variety. That is, the original situation is one of many suppliers; the latter situation is characterized by fewer suppliers. The market is transformed into a hierarchy. As O. E. Williamson has it, entry screening of employees is no special problem (1985: 244). In fact, separate attention for screening is hardly worthwhile, given the assumption that the "workers employed under each mode are a random sample of the technically qualified population of which they are a part" (1985: 214). Two remarks, nonetheless, are in order. One is that when discussing cooperative endeavors of workers, Williamson is explicit about the insurancelike dangers newcomers present. The "random sample," then, is not without its exceptions (Williamson 1975, 1985: 228). Second, these insurance features are dropped once the labor contract has been introduced. But there is no argument. It is, as stated, a mere assumption and a bad one at that.

Given the tasks, assignments to the task follow the regular economic principle of least costs. On the other hand, economic organization theories are not very precise on the origin of task idiosyncrasies. The most explicit statement in this respect is made by Williamson (1985: 245ff.). The dimensions of idiosyncrasy are (non)separability and (non)specificity of assets. When nonseparability (the difficulty of measuring individual output or productivity) is combined with asset specificity (human assets are specific to the firm), task idiosyncrasy will be high. When individual output is easily measurable and human assets are nonspecific, task idiosyncrasy will be low. In the former case "relational contracting" may be expected; in the latter case the distance from "classical contracting" will be small (Williamson, 1985: 69–72, 245–248, 254–256). Relational contracting is comprehensive and relatively undetailed and relies on private ordering, in the case of conflict, rather than on independent third-party interference. Collective bargaining, including the grievance machinery, are examples. Classical contracting is limited and possesses no special governance structure. Both unskilled and professional workers "can move between employers without loss of productivity, and firms can secure replacements without incurring start-up costs" (Williamson, 1985: 245).

This example omits three factors relevant to the contract. One factor is that it identifies the labor contract for professional and unskilled work and a service contract. It would have surprised the Lowell girls, and it will surprise the Chicanos. The second factor is that it forgets that unskilled work can be both the waiting room for semiskilled, more specific jobs and the old-fashioned type. In the first case, as will happen with most jobs implying asset specificity, it pays to screen before hiring. Credentials and age requirements, for example, may be introduced that are hardly relevant for the immediate job at hand. These requirements, however, are useful as terms of entry and their costs, whose payoff will arrive at a future date, contingent on performance, merit, and, if the union has a say, also on seniority. The third factor is that the decision to call jobs unskilled does not depend on the technical nature of the job or on worker's qualifications. This decision is an organizational one and relates to the complex processes of job design.

Asset specificity is above all a consequence of the design of jobs and therefore should be discussed in terms of job requirements. The attempt to link asset specificity to worker attributes is doomed to fail. Professionals may have general qualifications, but that does not mean, from the point of view of the firm, that their value is not highly firm specific. Professionals sometimes face formidable exit barriers simply because their general skills are used on very specific and critical tasks. The point here is not that there are general skills but that the relation between tasks and performance is controlled by the firm in the case of unskilled labor and by the professionals in the case of professional work.

Job design is not technologically determined. Nor is it a "match" between technology and a worker's qualifications. As the examples above show, job design summarizes decisions on typical career paths, on the distance between skill requirements and available qualifications, and on the control over the relation between those two elements. The Taylorist strategy in this respect is noteworthy. F. W. Taylor, indeed, did plead for typical career paths, for establishing a distance between skill requirements and workers' qualifications (with the foreman as the teacher bridging the gap), and for complete managerial control of the distance established (1903: 141–147, 1911: 123–128). Job design and employment relationship, as Taylor well knew, are intimately connected. Taylor's attempt was to prevent any specific claims, or control, of specific workers on jobs and job skills. That makes Taylor a protagonist of bureaucratic organizations in which jobs are always defined in terms distanced from their incumbents. The distance leads to the necessity of training, a necessity of which Taylor was fully aware. Task idiosyncrasies, and their background in human asset specificity of the Williamson type, belong here too, not, however, as adapted human capital considerations but as consequences of job design.

The point needs underscoring, for the very possibility of the concept of a market for labor depends on it. If we follow the economic theories of organization, human capital arguments still rank high. This implies the assumption of an independent supply curve of labor, such that a "random" choice, proposed by Williamson, at least is feasible. Using this assumption, one has to suppress the peculiarity of the labor contract or restrict it to the realm of collective bargaining (Williamson, 1985: 255), but that is an error endemic in the field. Taking one's starting point in job design and proceeding on the assumption that job design is a managerial prerogative, on the other hand, leads to the denial of an independent supply curve of labor. In macroeconomics, this is part and parcel of the Keynesian approach (Korver, 1988b); in microeconomics, the point has been driven home also by L. C. Thurow (1975). Once demand for labor is dependent on jobs and their training requirements and costs, supply has to play on factors beyond its own control. In a sense, supply has lost its capacity to compete, since wage competition is out of the question. All one can do is to offer signals about trainability and (recurrence of) training costs. These signals, as Thurow emphasized, include a series of ascriptive qualities (gender, ethnicity, color, country of origin, and so on). These signals function as conjectures about discretionary mobility. Such "background characteristics," as Thurow baptized them, are hardly defensible in any notion of a "market" and "competition." At most, these signals may improve the likelihood of getting a job, but the usual predictability of results, given the market situation, has disappeared. A "labor queue," based on employer-determined estimates about training costs, replaces the independent supply curve and, therewith, the market.

We have returned, then, to recruitment. Both the technology adopted and the organizational responses in the field of job design and employment relationship are contingent on recruitment histories and discretionary mobility. Labor, accordingly, is not a commodity, not even a peculiar one. At most, it is, in the felicitous words of Polanyi (1944), a fictitious commodity.

AN OVERVIEW

The story of the American labor market will be told with three dimensions in mind. The first concerns the influence of the limited and unpredictable number of unskilled workers on the pace and shape of American technological and organizational innovation. We will hold that, as opposed to the so-called labor process approach, the bottleneck of American industrialization has been the position of unskilled labor.

The position of the skilled worker is our second dimension. The rapid industrial expansion after the Civil War, combined with the radical restructuring of unskilled work, created the necessity of a new definition of skilled work. The long fight over both Taylorism and vocational education and training reflects the new reality of skilled labor. The position of the American Federation of Labor (AFL) is noteworthy: Its attitudes toward vocational education and toward Taylorism changed at the same time and, one may infer, for the same reasons.

The third dimension is the relative strategic position of groups of employees in the corporate organizational structures that emerged since the late nineteenth century to dominate the economic scene thereafter. As indicators we use the selectivity of the system of welfare capitalism; the bureaucratization of the employment relationship and the rise of the internal labor market; the hotly debated issue on privately or collectively sponsored unemployment insurance; and, finally, the great changes in labor relations during the thirties and the rise of the Congress of Industrial Organizations (CIO).

The description of these dimensions is not strictly chronological. After a short exposé on railways and the development of standards and new organizational forms (chapter 2), chapters 3 and 4 address the issue of standardization in its relation to the structure of the supply of labor: Professionalism, vocational education, and the opening up of a virtually unlimited reservoir of unskilled labor since the 1880s are the themes. The last topic returns in chapter 5, dealing with the international migration to the United States during the period of predominance of the "new immigrants" and its immediate aftermath. The change in the pattern of migration since the twenties coincides with the extending bureaucratization of the employment relationship. This relation is sketched and, in chapter 6, illustrated through the perspective of the relevant developments in the American automobile industry.

In the seventh and eighth chapters it is argued that the at-first-sight radical political changes, effected in the field of employment and social security during the period of the New Deal, were not that radical after all. They were not a complete rupture with the social, political, and economic developments of the first three decades of this century but, rather, their logical conclusion. They embodied the factual recognition both of the disappearance of "exit" as the dominant possibility to escape a particular employment relationship, or even that relationship as such, and of the importance of "voice," and thus the promotion of labor unionism, even in the face of fierce resistance from employers. The period immediately preceding the Second World War, then, finally fixes the status of labor: that of a semipublic, neither fully private, neither fully public, and therefore fictitious commodity.

2

RAILWAYS AND TIMETABLES

The pace of economic growth in post–Civil War America was astounding. In 1865 the United States ranked fourth in the order of industrialized nations, after the United Kingdom, France, and Germany. At the end of the nineteenth century, not only had the ranking changed, with the United States on top, but the industrial product of the United States equaled that of the product of the other three countries combined. The "gilded age" was the metaphor Mark Twain coined for the period between 1865 and 1900. It was the glitter of tycoons; the huge profits—and losses—on speculation; the "robber barons"; and the conspicuous display of newly gained wealth, so much in contrast to the old wealth of the more sober, Bostonian style, that attracted attention and gave nourishment to the great myth of rags and riches.

The period is just as well described as the age of transportation, the material foundation of an emerging national market for goods, services, and, albeit much slower, labor. During this age, water transport was improved, electricity revolutionized inner-city transportation, telephone and telegraph captured the scene, and the rate of railroad construction skyrocketed. The map of the United States at mid-century shows a few black lines, indicating railroads, in the northeastern part of the country and a few hesitating traces in the South and West. A few decades later, half of the country was densely covered with railroad lines, with the number of lines sharply declining west of Texas in the South and west of Minnesota in the North (Faulkner, 1941: 403–406). This is not to state that the West was unimportant. Just like the passage through the Allegheny passes before the Civil War promoted the economic linkage of North and South, the conquest of the Great Plains after the war proved an enormous stimulus to the development of trade, industry, and commercial agriculture in the West as it did to the integration of the West in the national economy. Also, the relative decline of the Northeast in terms of shares of industrial production and total employment is partly an effect of the shift in activity enabled by the railroads (e.g., the going south of textiles) and the rise of industrialism outside the northeastern part of the country occasioned by the railroads (North, 1966: 115–116).

The first successful coast-to-coast telegraph cable dates from 1866, immediately after the war. By that time, the telegraph had already become a stock item in the daily operation of many organizations. In fact, the telegraph had been widely used during the Civil War, once the northern states had recognized that warfare created huge administrative and organizational problems. After 1862 the northern war department was completely reorganized, leading to a clear organizational division between civilian and military operations, responsibilities and competencies. Railway engineers and lawyers are attributed the successes of this reorganization, which soon produced the northern lead on the battlefields (Hall, 1984). After 1875 the telephone spread quickly across the nation, with the number of telephone receivers nearing 2 million in the nineties. Yet the railroads, in terms of economic importance, outdistanced all the other revolutions in transportation and communication. They had, compared to water transportation, the enormous advantage of being able "not alone to follow the natural routes of transportation but also to expand in all directions. It was here that man won his first great victory over nature" (Faulkner, 1941: 403).

After the Civil War it took three great leaps, and the railway system neared completion. Between 1866 and 1873, 30,000 miles were completed; between 1879 and 1883, 40,000 miles; and between 1886 and 1892, a record 50,000 miles (Hacker, 1970: 235). In the intervals between these peak periods construction slowed down and sometimes was stopped before completion. One gets a glimpse of the economic importance of the railroads by considering the fact that the peaks and troughs of construction coincide exactly with the economic cycle. The economic downturns of 1873, 1884, and 1894 all were precipitated by a drying up of the financial resources for the construction of new railways (Hays, 1957: 8). The railways employed more people than any other industry. Direct construction workers during the eighties of the previous century totaled more than 200,000 (Hays, 1957; 8). Despite the slowdown of new construction in "trough" years, the property investment in railroads continued unabated throughout the second half of the nineteenth century (North, 1966: 113, table 14). In 1893 the United States was proud to have 176,000 miles of railway, including four transcontinental lines and enough for a three-time encirclement of the globe. No other country could boast of a comparable network (see Huberman, 1947; Alexander, 1963).

The reason for the swift victory of the railway over the waterway after the Civil War is to be found in the technological and organizational advancements in the construction of railways, especially during the 1840s and 1850s. Technologically, the exploitation of coal as a source of energy in transportation and in the promotion of the production of iron and, later, steel, proved of critical importance. Coal lifted the constraint of water resources for the delivery of energy. The development of the machine tool industry in the United States during the 1840s and the upsurge in railroad construction of the same period are directly connected with the exploitation of cheap eastern coal and the concomitant expansion in the production of iron (Chandler, 1977: 75–78, 90). The progress of technology enabled the introduction of uniform methods of construction, grading, tunneling, and bridging. These methods were essential for fast, all-weather transportation (Chandler, 1977: 82–87).

The organizational changes of the pre–Civil War era in railroad construction are possibly of even greater importance. The organizational problem was that "safe, regular, reliable movement of goods and passengers, as well as the continuing maintenance and repair of locomotives, rolling stock, and track, roadbed, stations, roundhouses, and other equipment, required the creation of a sizeable administrative organization" (Chandler, 1977: 87). Development of the railroad and development of the first professional group of business managers were two sides of one coin. The problems the managers tackled were manifold and, at the time, new and unknown. Many of them related to the establishment of an auditing system, capable of guaranteeing a regular flow of information on unit costs, depreciation, use of capacity, performance of lines, and so on. This proved absolutely indispensable in the setting of standards for costs, markups, and rates. The separation of accounting from bookkeeping is one product of the managerial effort during the early age of railway construction. The emergence of statistics as the dominant and standardized form of data collection is another.

The second big set of problems derived from the necessity of creating an organization as such and thus a hierarchy of strategies, commands, responsibilities, information flows, and communication channels. The principle of functional differentiation and its integration via the expedient of a line-staff organization were developed during the fifties (Chandler, 1977: 99ff.; Chandler and Tedlow, 1985). Many of the principles of the bureaucratic machine found their first practical application in companies like the Baltimore and Ohio. These were radically new developments, prefiguring the rise of managerial capitalism at the end of the century. Market coordination was no guide, and the emerging administrative coordination had no practical example to build on.

Although the first managers of the roads had a background in civil engineering and many of them had been educated at West Point, the military fold was not copied. Besides West Point, the military academy established in 1802, the only other relevant institution for the training of civil engineers was the Rensselaer Polytechnic Institute of 1824. Then, during the 1850s and 1860s, in response to the growing demand for engineers emanating from the railroads, some leading institutes of higher learning like Harvard, Yale, Columbia, Pennsylvania, and Virginia started to offer specialized four-year courses in engineering (Chandler, 1977: 132; Hall, 1984). All the same, the response of the prestigious colleges was slow enough to provoke the founding of the Massachusetts Institute of Technology in 1861 (Noble, 1977: 21–22). Yet until the Morrill Act of 1862 and the associated promotion and subsidy of state agricultural and mechanical colleges, the engineering profession was heavily restricted in numbers and in social background. This holds for the civil as well as for the mechanical engineer, although the case of the mechanical engineer is less obvious. The first half of the nineteenth century shows the rise of the mechanic and the emergence of the mechanical engineer from its ranks. A number of mechanics institutes enabled craftsmen to widen their field of knowledge through courses in mathematics and natural science. The elite mechanical engineers, on the other hand, generally held degrees from the more prestigious universities. Their mechanical expertise had been learned by their serving as apprentices, usually in shops owned by people of their own class and social circle (Calvert, 1967; Nelson, 1980). The background of the students of the institutes, thus, and of the mechanical engineer in America was shop experience (Collins, 1979: 165ff.; Struik, 1962; Calvert, 1967).

Social differences separated the civil engineer and the mechanic. West Point and the Rensselaer Polytechnic had been shaped after the French example of the Ecole Polytechnique, an institution that combined technical with administrative expertise and kept aloof from commercial and industrial interests. Instead, it "emphasized their gentry status and avoided anything smacking of manual labor, and, to a degree, of commercialism as well" (Collins, 1979: 164). The polytechnics were meant to educate a new social and political elite. In France, the venture succeeded. In the United States, the civil engineers offered their expertise to the railroad companies. There they became full-time, salaried managers, more intent on strengthening their professional identity and autonomy than on acquiring an entrepreneurial status of their own. They started their own journals and, in 1867, revived the Society of American Civil Engineers. Here again the influence of the railroad professionals was unmistakeable, as it had been during the earlier attempt at professional organization in 1852 (Chandler, 1977: 132; Noble, 1977: 35).

After 1865, developments continued apace. Technologically, the introduction of steel on a large scale was a major innovation. The rise of steel and steel products as an industry is one of the more outstanding economic backward linkages of the railways. Steel locomotives and carriers enlarged the loading capacity of the trains elevenfold between 1865 and 1900 (Hacker, 1970: 239). The postwar period set the stage for the introduction of block signal systems, airbrakes, and automatic tractions. These things enabled more speed, safety, and efficiency in the connections between lines. The eighties and early nineties also were years of standardization. The steel rails adopted a standard gauge; standardized time zones across the country and thus standard times were introduced; and the signal systems, brakes, and tractions were standardized, as were the freight rates and accounting procedures (Hacker, 1970: 238; Chandler, 1977: 130).

The standardization of accounting procedures followed upon the example spelled out in the Interstate Commerce Act, one of the many government interventions in the field of transportation and communication. The federal right of intervention in commerce within a state was, constitutionally, very limited, but in interstate commerce the margin of action was much larger. Standardization was one of the more obvious areas of action. It promoted not just uniform treatment of the customers of lines, uniformity of safety regulations, and the flawless interconnection of lines (and thus the reduction of transshipment costs to practically nil), but it also effected a major restructuring of competition between the lines. It required definite qualities, an extensive system of administration, the facilities of checking upon and testing materials, and so on. It required also that the lines hired the experts to ensure that operations did indeed adhere to the imposed standard demands. All of this puts a premium on size and scale of operation. Standardization was soon recognized as an extremely useful weapon in the elimination of "wasteful competition" (Noble, 1977: 82). In the nineties, of the many railroad companies after the Civil War, not more than six had survived (Hays, 1957: 50–51). The creation of managerial capitalism, with oligopoly as the dominant type of market structure, was partly an effect of the heightening of entry barriers into the trade or industry, erected by standardization and the associated heavy-investment effort required. At the same time, standardization—prepared, introduced, and guarded by the expert—strengthened the hand of the scientifically trained professional, as it did of applied science as such.

The role of the government in the creation of the oligopolistic market should not be underestimated. The mode of operation of the Interstate Commerce Committee of 1887 soon acknowledged the gains to be made by cooperating with the railroad companies and, especially, the more representative ones among them. The representative companies went to great lengths in qualifying the irregularities of a too competitive market as the major culprit in the abuses of the railroad system, abuses that had provoked government intervention in the first place. Streamlining competition, mainly through standardization, was one outflow of this cooperation (Brock, 1984). The conjecture that it "was a critical sector of the railroads themselves that advocated and helped create the Interstate Commerce Commission in 1887, and directed it along the paths the railroads chartered thereafter" (Kolko, 1976: 10; see also Gordon, Edwards, and Reich, 1982: 36), seems only too justified.

In other respects, too, the government promoted the interests of the railroads. Land policy, no doubt, was the most obvious and important. The railroads were the grand winners in the free-land politics of the postwar era. The amount of free land granted to railways exceeded the total area of England, Spain, and Belgium combined. This policy destroyed the last vestiges of Indian subsistence and culture (Presser, 1965: 316ff.; Hovens, 1977: 76–82; Dinnerstein, Nichols, and Reimers, 1979: 197–205), but it was of extreme advantage to the railway companies. It saved them the investment in the purchase of the land and created in addition an extra source of finance, since much of the land that was not directly needed for the construction of the roads was resold. Next to the monetary gain, however, resale of the land to private citizens meant a cost-free security and a safeguarding of the lines, a plan that was more efficient and reliable than any other possible solution to the safety problem.

The railway tycoons made huge profits on their investments. Cunning undoubtedly was one of the common strategies. The gains they made, though, generally had a secure base. It proved sound business to invest in the west-ward movement. The commercialization of the West waited on its disclosure by railway transport. The same development created other business empires, sometimes by way of vertical integration. The Carnegie steel works, after its integration with the Frick Pennsylvania coal mines, is one reknown example (Hays, 1957: 8–9). It may even be said that the opening up of the West by railway transport determined the fate of the 1862 Homestead Act. The com-mercialization of agriculture followed in the wake of the possibilities of transportation. This necessitated both specialization and expansion of the minimal necessary acreage. For this, the act was inappropriate. The plots of land it promised were too small for commercialized agriculture. At the same time, the price of land, in view of its growing commercial potential, was driven up. Many claimants under the act, aware of the lacking administrative apparatus to enforce its clauses, demanded land with an eye on speculation. The act itself allowed resale of the land, already half a year after the original grant. It led to a speedy concentration of land ownership. The frontier did not find its limits in the ocean; it was dissolved by the same commercialization that made railway construction such a profitable enterprise (Commons, 1951).

The railroad companies were the early corporations, singular in some respects, typical in others. Their singularity resides mainly in their labor recruitment. The work force was characterized by a division in workers needed to keep the lines running and workers needed to construct the lines. In the early period the latter outnumbered the former. The railways were hardly interested in a permanent construction work force. The major parts of their construction jobs were contracted out. Local labor markets soon proved insufficient for the ever-expanding demand for construction workers. Large contractors took on the job, supplying not only labor but most of the materials and machinery. It was the beginning of the development of con-struction firms, with a strong foothold in railway construction and spreading out into urban construction: the paving of streets, the building of schools, and the construction of water and sewage systems. Most of their workers were immigrants, the Irish for instance, but these companies hired agents as well to procure for them the badly needed workers from Europe (Chandler,

1977: 93–94) and the Far East (Commons, 1907; Dinnerstein, Nichols, and Reimers, 1979).

It is the emphasis on administration and organization that earned the railroad company the reputation of first corporation. Partly, no doubt, this emphasis was a response to the public need for a reliable system of transportation. But there is more to it than public influence and scrutiny. The time span of railway projects, the amounts of fixed capital involved, and the interdependency of all separate decisions and activities encouraged a form of coordination for which the market offered no guide. A. D. Chandler dubbed it administrative coordination. Market coordination squares with the metaphor of the "invisible hand." The appropriate image for administrative coordination is the "visible hand."

Administrative coordination changes the status of the market. In general, the rule is that the longer the time span of projects, all other things being equal, the more the signals of the market lose their transparency. Instead of becoming coordinates they tend to become contingent events, to be mastered rather than merely obeyed. In short, in long-run projects, markets enhance complexity instead of reducing it. If a projected outcome in a long-run venture is to materialize, it must be certain that the possibly disturbing influence of changes in the market can be neutralized. This is what the new managerial executives of the railroads set out to accomplish: "What the new enterprises did was to take over from the market the coordination and integration of the flow of goods and services from the production of the raw materials through the several processes of production to the sale to the ultimate consumer" (Chandler, 1977: 11). More specifically, it led, in time, to relationships with suppliers, contractors, workers, and authorities in which negotiating and sticking to the negotiated rules contended for predominance with the shifting outcomes of the perennial unstable relations of force in the market.

Summing up, then, the era of railway expansion brought forth the twin forces of standardization and professionalism of, in terms of Max Weber (1978), expansion and closure, uniformity and particularism. Both were predicated on a specific articulation relative to markets. Standardization enormously broadened the scope of markets, as it contributed to their integration in one huge national market. It opened up new markets, consolidated old ones, and literally altered the geography of market society. In the same movement it changed the structure of markets and their mode of functioning. Standards as such must be resistant to influences of time and circumstance. Their imposition and acceptance presupposes an area of consensus formation in which criteria of efficiency, durability, and, especially, accountability and inspection loom large when compared to the relations of power in the market at any time. This is not to state that these criteria are neutral in their effects on market relations or, even, that they oppose the stronger interests. Imposition of standardization everywhere led to added outlays on organization, administration, machinery, and personnel. It thus erected entry barriers that discouraged potential competitors and heightened the minimum scale of operation, driving many existing companies out of the market. But the translation of the relations of power in the market into the vocabulary of standardization required a particular bias: the profession, in the case of the railways, exemplified by the civil engineer. Standards thus served not merely the interests of the employing organization; they reflected and expressed the interests of the profession as well. This was to prove of major significance for the organizational structures and internal divisions of power in the decades to come.

3

STANDARDIZATION I: TAYLORISM

The lion's share of early mass production consisted of producer goods: tools, raw materials, metals and metal products, agricultural implements, precision machinery, and, since the second half of the nineteenth century, electrical equipment. The producer initiative in creating uniform demand stimulated the standardization of output. It permitted the customer, even if hundreds of miles away, to order and receive exact qualities of known products. Large agricultural implements could be shipped in cases, each item bearing its own code number, and assembled at the place of reception. Items to be replaced could easily be identified, ordered, and made to fit, with only limited mechanical ability required (Faulkner, 1938). Second, and for our present purposes the more decisive issue, it blended and mutually furthered the advancement and intertwining of mechanization and standardization. Given the magnitude of demand, once a product is perceived as an aggregate of distinct parts, one may standardize the parts, the prescriptions for their assembly, and, ultimately, the skills needed for assembling them.

The promise of interchangeable parts was the possibility of transforming processes of production, contingent on complex skills, into a series of steps in a construction kit. The obstacles in producing parts and materials adequate to the promise, however, were formidable. The applicability of interchangeable parts would remain severely limited unless measuring equipment became available with the capacity to read to minute fractions of the inch or centimeter. Also, to gain currency within the precision industry, the equipment would have to be relatively inexpensive. The spread of interchangeable parts was in fact hampered by the lack of such equipment until the early fifties. Then, around mid-century, the "vernier caliper" appeared on the market, the first inexpensive and very precise tool for exact measurements, a tool so accurate in fact that it was still in use in the 1920s (Williamson, 1951). It gave an enormous boost to precision manufacturing in the United States, as it did to the development of the mechanical shop engineering profession. The possibility of the production of parts fitting exactly into a mechanism had come a huge step nearer. As an important method of production, therefore, the rise to prominence of interchangeable parts practically coincides with the 1851 world exposition during which the "American system" had attracted so much attention.

TAYLOR AND THE ENGINEERING PROFESSION

Interchangeable parts and thus the immediate sphere of influence of the mechanical shop engineer do not embrace the whole of nineteenth-century American technology. Large parts of electrical, civil, and chemical engineering followed a different course and cannot be included in the history of interchangeable parts. On the other hand, the role of the mechanical trades in the development of American mass production is not just a forerunner of the role of later forms of engineering, such as in electricity and chemistry; the shops of the mechanics were absolutely essential in the invention and application of the new tools and machinery that ultimately formed the technological base of mass production. Indeed, the factories emerged from the shops; without them, the machine era in the United States could not have come about at the time and in the form that it did.

The crux of good management, according to F. W. Taylor, was the combination of low labor costs and high wages. The "trust" had appeared on the scene in the last quarter of the nineteenth century; yet the organization of the labor process lagged behind considerably relative to the growing size and complexity of the company as a whole. The Taylor system, dominating the managerial debates between roughly the 1890s and the First World War, promised a solution in the essential and conflict ridden area of the labor problem. Although hotly debated, Taylor's management system seldom was completely adopted by the companies that hired his services. The manufacturers of precision instruments (Remington typewriters, for instance) and of continuous-flow products (at Bethlehem Steel, for instance) were among his more prominent clients, the former by far outnumbering the latter. As if to underscore the highly personal nature of the elite of shop-culture engineers, most of Taylor's clients came from the Northeast, including Taylor's home town, Philadelphia. Many of these companies were still relatively small, numbering from a few dozen to a few hundred workers. Bethlehem Steel, in fact, was one of the larger clients. Estimates about the number of firms that put the Taylor system into practice differ according to the strictness of the criteria used. Conservative estimates do not exceed two to three dozen. More lenient estimates add up to about 120 companies (Nelson, 1975, 1980; Calvert, 1967; Stark, 1980; Meiksins, 1984).

Through his background and apprenticeship at the Enterprise Hydraulic Works in Philadelphia (Nelson, 1980: 27) Taylor had grown accustomed to the metal industry. His four-year apprenticeship taught him the trades of machinist and patternmaker. Immediately thereafter, in 1878, Taylor acquired a job at the Midvale steel company in Philadelphia. The Midvale company specialized in steel castings for railroads and, later, gun forgings for the navy, leading eventually to a growing proportion of defense contracts in the total output of the company. Taylor soon found himself in a subordinate managerial position in the machine shop of the company and started his experiments on metal-cutting machinery.

The manufacture of precision instruments entailed a continuous improvement along the lines of the method of interchangeable parts, whereas the production of metals, forgings, and alloys resembled more the "organic" type of manufacture. Drawing on the concepts of Marx (1867: 461–462), Taylor's background and his later experiences as a management consultant introduced him to both "heterogeneous" and "organic" manufacture. The *heterogeneous variety* involves the mechanical assembly of independent parts (the clock is the usual example), and the main organizational problem is internal transportation of parts, tools, materials, and people; the *organic variety* involves a series of combined processes and actions, and the main organizational problem is the optimal technical integration of the interconnected range of processes and activities. An interruption in the process of producing a clock would imply a growing heap of unfinished products; an interruption in the production of steel would lead to the complete standstill of the process as a whole.

We propose to look at Taylor's activities as markers in the organizational transition from heterogeneous to organic manufacture. It must be emphasized that the transition was organizational. Technically, Taylor had a foothold in both types, in productions depending on and furthering the interchangeable method as well as in more continuous-flow operations. But organizationally, the organic type was on the move. The newly created corporations integrated in their operations a large flow of interdependent activities, whose streamlining, as we saw in the case of the railways, required huge organizational efforts. The newer industries as well—like those in steel and electrical appliances and, somewhat later, that classical example of technical heterogeneity, the automobile—strove to streamline their operations to achieve an "organic" effect. Finally, the mass market for heterogeneous as well as organic products promised much more; not just the output but also the labor process could be standardized and made to function like a machine.

Strictly speaking, Taylor is not part of the machine era. His achievements were in the design of jobs and labor processes, such that continuous production would be the result. We find his method best exemplified in the procedure Taylor followed at Bethlehem (Nelson, 1980). There, as usual, Taylor employed his differential piece-rate, the "labor problem," as a starter.

Almost immediately, however, he took up the task of reorganizing and standardizing the tool room and the administration of inventories. The object was to acquire an overview of the work sequence, the materials and tools used, and the several factors and locations of costs. This was one stock item in the Taylor approach. After that came the main operation: the planning of an uninterrupted process of production. This required exact knowledge of the technical properties of the process, and it is here that Taylor's thousands of experiments with high-speed steel fit in with the main thrust of his activities. It was at Bethlehem, by chance in fact, that Taylor made his major discovery in the "art of cutting metals." But the necessity of the art itself was contingent upon the need for continuous, reliable, and precise machine operations and, thus, upon the organizational need of an exact planning of operations and activities.

The planning department was to become the place where the design of the organization of production was conceived, its implementation prepared, and its execution controlled. There, decisions were to be made about the scheduling and routing of work, the work methods (via instruction cards translated to the direct worker), the control of the process, and the analysis of output, performances, and costs (Taylor, 1903). This department was the "cockpit" of the enterprise. Through its very existence it would curtail traditional managerial discretion and, thus, incompetence. But in general, the introduction of a continuous-flow organization would also mean, especially in the technically heterogeneous lines of production, a reduction in managerial prerogative to the advantage of the technical, more objective capabilities of the engineer. This, in the end, was the logical consequence of the organizational transition to organic principles.

Reduction of managerial discretion in Taylor's system coincided with the introduction of experimentally established standards for the flow of production as a whole, for labor, and for the conditions of work. What Taylor called "scientific" was nothing but the substitution of tradition and custom by experiment. This held for managers and workers alike; both groups would have to go through a "mental revolution." Both groups were supposed to give up the standard of habit for the standard of experimentally tested norms. Higher management would stand to lose discretionary power, to the exact degree that the responsibility for production shifted to the planning department. Lower management, the foreman in particular, would be split up according to function, leading to a form of "functional foremanship" of specialists on aspects of production, coordination, control, and analysis. The foreman was to be the lowest echelon of management, completing the separation of managers and workers. It was with respect to the position of the foreman, in Taylor's days still usually combining managerial and direct production tasks, that Taylor uttered the much quoted words that "all possible brainwork should be removed from the shop" (1903: 98). The organizational location of the foreman as junior member of management was the means to this end. Brainwork, Taylor's sloppy expression for what he understood to be work of a clerical nature, did not belong in the shop.

It is obvious that for a systematically integrated flow of production the effort of the worker could not be treated as a datum but as a part of the production problem. Time study had been introduced before Taylor went about it. The novelty of Taylor on this score was that he insisted that timing in itself was meaningless, unless it would have a follow-up in the shape of new output norms, ready to be inserted in the total design of production (Littler, 1982). The customary standards of a fair day's work were destined to give way to standards that, taking the physical constraints of the human body into account, would lead to an economy of movements and efforts within the process of producing the optimum output.

The differential piece-rate was part of the project. It is an early theme in the writings of Taylor. His first paper to the American Society of Mechanical Engineers (ASME), in 1895, already addressed the subject, and his "Principles of Scientific Management," of 1910, still accorded it a large role. The differential rate had three functions to fulfill. It had to reward those workers that complied to the standards of performance, it had to interest the workers in optimizing output, and it had to punish the workers that performed below standard. The latter, it could be assumed, would disappear because of low pay. The promise Taylor held out to employers was that a process of self-selection of workers might be the result of the differential rate. Bad workers would shun the company paying a differential rate; good workers, on the contrary, would be attracted to it. The point for Taylor was not the pay as such but the pay as a result of adhering to the standards set by the planning department. The standards are the things that matter; they had to make sure that labor would be inserted in the total process of production in the most efficient manner. The differential rate was an outcome. It can hardly be considered a core element in the Taylor system and constitutes, in fact, a dated element if seen in the light of developments in the field of industrial relations and personnel management that were already well under way around the turn of the century (Nelson, 1980; Nelson, 1975; Brandes, 1970).

Taylor developed his system with an eye on the ASME engineers as well. The engineering profession itself, however, underwent drastic changes during the heydays of Taylor's activities, and it is only against the background of these changes that Taylor's achievements can be weighed. Some derived from the economic status of the engineer, others from the associated, but not identical, issue of "shop or school." All had a direct bearing on the conception of professionalism: as a mode of the production and distribution of knowledge and experience, as a mode of control on numbers and performance, as apprehension of the differences between mental and manual work, and as a claim on leadership.

The shop engineer, exemplarily represented in the ASME, took pride in the experience of apprenticeship. It was a peculiar apprenticeship, though, since it regularly had been preceded by an academic, classical education, including knowledge of at least one foreign language and, often, a visit to Europe. It was an accepted affair of the elite, such that, for instance, Taylor could accept a lowly apprenticeship in his home town without having to fear the disdain of the social circles he came from and wanted to belong to. This was, in fact, typical, and Philadelphia was a representative town for this type of education, inside and outside the walls of academe. Taylor himself deviated somewhat from the pattern; he did not finish his university education and later, already well established in the engineering community, took an outside course in school engineering. But where culture was at stake, Taylor was a vivid defender of the shop and the advantages of the practical education of apprenticeship. The shop culture was heavily bent toward invention and innovation. It stood for a scientific method but opposed the codification of its empirical and applied knowledge. The schools, it was feared, would both reduce and transform the knowledge thus gained to an abstract curriculum. The advance of mathematics and the plea for a minimum of mathematical knowledge as a criterion of admission to the schools were seen, and rejected, in this light. Also, the shop defenders resisted the introduction of the "elective system" in the institutions of higher learning, that is, the substitution of the old, broad, classical curricula by more specialized tracks (for Taylor's and the shop engineers' view on education, see Nelson, 1975: 186–187; and Calvert, 1967; on the introduction of the elective system, see Hall, 1984: part 3).

In part, these conflicts and oppositions reflected the strategies of the American northeastern elite in the face of changing circumstances. The post–Civil War economic expansion called for a growing supply of technically educated people in amounts that simply surpassed the capacity of the recruitment canals of the old shop engineers. Between 1880 and 1920 the number of engineers increased from 7,000 to 136,000 (Stark, 1980: 101). The large majority of them were products of the newer technical colleges and institutes. They were, in many ways, the opposite of the shop engineers or, rather, of its vocal elite, assembled in the ASME. The shop elite were socially and culturally homogeneous. Next to being engineers, they considered themselves "gentlemen." They did not eschew commerce but, rather, saw commercial competition as a healthy test for the demonstration of technical ability. Often, their interest in scientific management derived from their business experiences, which is, to no surprise, one reason for their vivid attention to the "labor problem." They resented the big corporation and, for much the same reasons, government intervention as well.

Their position on the "metric standard," to replace the English scale of measurement, is an illustration. The engineers recognized the advantages of the metric system, its simplicity, and thus its useability in the movement toward standardization. They also knew very well that the compulsory introduction of the metric system would create enormous losses for many producers, colleagues possibly, who had often during many years invested in equipment and materials constructed with the help of the English system. Their solution to the problem, expressed several times at meetings of the ASME, was to oppose compulsory regulation in favor of a policy that shifted the test to the market. If, the argument ran, the metric system was better, it should be able to prove itself by pushing the English system out of the market contest. But the market would have to be competitive, without monopolistic restrictions or artificial rules from the government. The shop, it turned out, could be a factory, but it could never be a trust or a holding company.

The ASME itself is the best example of the shop culture and its elite pretensions. Founded in 1880, its membership was heavily concentrated in the Northeast, and there was never any doubt about its permanent seat in New York or about the fact that the meetings of the society had to be held in the northeastern region. Its founders came from the ranks of the shop engineers, and the leadership of the society rested firmly with them. Many of them carried on the tradition of the engineer–entrepreneur in the interchangeable-parts industry:

The members of the elite who led the ASME worked in the industry-oriented machine shops, engine shops, pump and valve works, foundries, instrument and gauge plants. This is really quite a restricted segment of industry. It is small in dollar volume, numbers of employees, total capitalization, and other common measures of importance used by the economist.... Entry into the business requires only a moderate amount of capital...but requirements of know-how are very high, restricting entry to those individuals who possess technical skill, some capital, and a generous helping of business acumen. Thus the engineer–entrepreneur is almost a sine qua non of these industries. (Calvert, 1967: 229)

In the, roughly, first thirty years of the ASME, the school engineers were underrepresented in the society and, especially, in its leading positions, so much so that the ASME establishment at times expressed worries about the future if the numerically strong position of the school engineer remained ignored. All the same, these were minority rumblings, unable to become the official point of view of the society and balanced by exactly the opposite views (Calvert, 1967). The number of members did not at all keep pace with the explosion of the engineering profession as a whole. A little more than a hundred members were counted in 1880. In 1907 there were almost 3,000 members, more than half of them still of the businessman–engineer type (Calvert, 1967: 114–115).

On average, the ASME stayed aloof from taking political stands. The mechanical engineers regarded themselves as technical experts, not as politicians, and they kept their distance from the political marketplace, ideological skirmishes included. Their self-definition stressed technical expertise, and the assessment of quality through competition in the marketplace. For an increasing number of engineers, however, the marketplace was only a distant

reality. Theirs was a career in the large corporation, in an intricate division
of labor, and in a permanent status of employee dependency: "No longer the
independent small businessman who worked in and directly oversaw the
operations of his own machine shop, the industrial engineer became an
employee in a large capitalist firm" (Stark, 1980: 101). Their managerial
aspirations were far from nonexistent; indeed, Taylor's celebrated "Principles
of Scientific Management" of 1911 justified these aspirations. But the idea of
independence, of the engineer directing a shop, had vanished. Eventually,
this reality had to gain currency in the ASME, if only because the society was
more and more incapable of controlling both standards of performance in,
and the conditions of access to, the profession. The startling thing is that they
had no policy, other than that concerning their own. Even the codification
of standards of professional performance was long delayed, apparently because such codification inevitably would sound the death knell over the old
practices of personal acquaintance and social position as informal entry barriers. On this point, things started to change shortly before the First World
War; elsewhere, the balance was only tipped because of the war. By that time,
Taylor had already died.

The background of the school engineer was more middle class than that
of the shop engineer. In a sense, this was the outcome of sheer necessity.
The demand for engineering competencies simply outnumbered the supply
of the old shop engineers. This development was not typical for the mechanical engineer, for it could also be observed in the recruitment for the
electrical and chemical engineering positions. Yet at first sight, considering
the social background of these engineers, it is somewhat puzzling that their
professional associations succeeded in establishing workable relationships
with the civil engineers earlier than the ASME was able to do so.

Social background apart, the school engineer shared several experiences
and outlooks with the civil engineer. First, their certainty that independent
business would be beyond reach brought them closer to the civil engineer's
disdain of the marketplace than to the defender of the shop culture. Second,
the distance that the civil engineer maintained from manual work came as a
matter of course to the school engineers. They had had an education apart
from the shop and, thus, manual work, since they had been prepared for
staff positions, again removed from direct contact with manual workers. The
high, sometimes even sentimental and paternalistic, esteem in which manual
work was held by the shop elite was as alien to the education of the school
engineer as it was integral to the education of the shop engineer. Taylor, for
one, was deeply convinced that his apprenticeship had taught him not merely
the tricks of the trade and the feeling of the complexities and intricacies of
the job of the skilled workers but also their codes, their modes of associating
and solidarizing, and their convictions about what was a reasonable amount
of work for reasonable pay. However, he was not one of them and never
wanted to be. But a successful engineering task, and on this score Taylor was

in perfect agreement with the majority of the ASME members, required intimate firsthand knowledge about the work, the product, its method of production, and the workers. Compared to that, the schools by definition were impractical.

This difference between the shop and the school engineer again refers to their position in the process of production. The school engineer, as an employee, is typically a member of a larger organization. Tasks, responsibilities, and discretions will be more or less bureaucratically determined. The shop engineer, on the other hand, identifies with the owner–producer point of view, someone competent enough to judge most of the ins and outs of work and close enough to it to advise or lend a helping hand. It is, in short, the difference between the division of labor in the corporation and the shop. This difference can also be observed in the matter of leadership. The school engineer is a member of the staff, aspiring for managerial positions but far from certain of actually achieving managerial status. In the effort, the "scientific management" movement, codified in the "Principles," was applauded as an ally. The shop engineer assumed a position of leadership as something of a birthright. Here, the categories of master and servant were more than legal shibboleths. The style of leadership was more often than not authoritarian, tinged with a dose of paternalism. Industrial citizenship, the prospective fad of the corporations and symbolized by personnel departments and welfare capitalism, was an object of scorn.

The ultimate wisdom of Taylor, both in his system and in his scientific management ideology, was that the solution to the problem of production would also be the solution to many other problems, of class hatred, for instance, though not of class. Yet without the hatred, the problem of class would prove to be manageable. The solution of the problem of production was an expert responsibility; it would not come from the direct workers or from the financial interests. Invoking Lenin, whose insistence on "scientific socialism" bears a more than superficial resemblance to Taylor's "scientific management," one may venture the thesis that the consciousness of the possibility of the solution, and of the methods of achieving it, would have to be imputed from the outside vantage point of the professional.

But how far outside is "outside"? It seems as if this question somewhat perplexed Taylor and his followers. Taylor's consulting practice did indeed grant him a considerable degree of autonomy, and even then Taylor became progressively more convinced of the need for an almost absolutely free hand. The Taylor engineers, moreover, were only allowed their discretionary powers, because of the trust and the esteem Taylor had built up over the years. Their autonomy, thus, was not role specific but person bound. Besides, this form of professional autonomy could hardly be said to evoke a warm response from the swelling ranks of the employee–engineers. Their need for autonomy was not served by the ideal of the independent consultant but by the written codification of standards of competence, performance, and admission. Independence in their situation simply meant the creation of a community of interests, not as an alternative to the corporate order but as a mode of compromising between a bureaucratically subordinate position and a professionally autonomous one.

In the creation of an upwardly mobile professional identity, Taylor's scientific management was an asset to the school engineer. But the Taylor system presupposed, for its application in the form required by Taylor, a bureaucratically independent position, unattainable for the majority of engineers. That is the major reason that the Taylor system, if introduced at all, usually was molded and adapted so as not to upset the distribution of capabilities and managerial discretions. Emerson, and later Bedeaux, were much more keenly aware of this than the Taylorites, and many of their successes can better be attributed to this touch of "realism" than to their engineering efficacy (on Emerson, see Nelson, 1980; Calvert, 1967; on Bedeaux, see Littler, 1982).

The Taylorites and the school engineers tried to capitalize on the issue of maximizing output. This, if nothing else, would found their claim on managerial status. For a short time, not surpassing the limited days of the Progressive Era, this seemed a promising prospect. There was a goal: maximizing output. There was the enemy: sectional interests, stemming from labor, the financial world, and bossist politics. There was an urgent problem: the threatening disintegration of America, because of the growing amount of industrial strife since the late nineteenth century, the violence and hatred it provoked, coupled with the huge problems caused by the permanent infusion of new populations and cultures. But the momentum of the Progressive Era was short lived and, with it, the momentum of scientific management. Its goal continued for some time to command attention, although no longer unabated. Ford carried on the slogan of the maximum output; others introduced the diversification in and the stratification of markets, displacing therewith the claim to hegemony of the engineer. The problems of the Progressive Era also continued into the twenties and thirties, be it under drastically changed conditions of migration and, accordingly, labor supply. But the enemy, epitomized in images of predatory financial capitalists and trusts, was already on the wane in the heydays of Taylor. The identification of the corporation with the dominance of the financial interests was a partial truth at most, although Taylor, sharing the myopia of many Progressives, boasting of themselves as "trustbusters," took it for the whole truth. Already in Taylor's days, however, financial capitalism was being supplanted by managerial capitalism, and for this the simple opposition of production versus finance was totally inadequate (Chandler, 1977).

SUBCONTRACTING, HELPERS, AND INSIDE CONTRACTING

Flow production calls for considerable managerial expertise. It enhances managerial responsibilities to the same degree that it reduces managerial discretion. Decisions must be based on experimentally established standards. In Taylor's view, the responsibilities and expertise had to be joined in the pivotal position of the engineer. Interference by nonexperts, managers or workers, had to be avoided. The discretion of, for instance, the skilled workers had to be trimmed down to the precise requirements of the organization of production. The integrated nature of the production process practically dictated the necessity of coordination and exacting administration. Continuous-flow production seemed to be the natural terrain for the application of Taylorist methods.

If so, it was a Taylor system without Taylor. Although not completely absent in continuous-flow production, and certainly not unaware of its techniques and methods, Taylor, or his assistants, never gained a real foothold in this type of industry. Most of the industries Taylor advised were, technically as well as organizationally, of the heterogeneous variety. Here, managerial discretion was large, and so, in Taylor's eyes, was managerial incompetence. By implication, the existing management came under attack. Management, in many industries, was a very diffuse category, however. In smaller shops, no distinction could be drawn between the owner and the manager. The shops catered to a relatively well-known market. The clients of these shops were often people who knew the owner personally and who had built up a relationship of trust with the shop and the services it could render. This was, in fact, a rational situation. Products were complex, and improvements, most of the time, were made not on demand but on the initiative of the producer (Rosenberg, 1972). The fast-growing demand for precision instruments and interchangeable parts in the later part of the nineteenth century introduced another kind of manager. Markets, if only because of their size and geographical spread, became progressively depersonalized. The emergence of subsidiaries, often preceded by distribution and service agencies, are a response to an impersonal market; they do not retard the deployment of the large anonymous market but are, rather, one of its products.

The new market situation put a premium on size. Shops grew; also, shops and factories were bought by commercial and financial interests. Often, they were consolidated in larger entities. This, in itself, created considerable organizational complexity. The organizational problem was amplified by the ignorance of the managers in these enterprises about matters of production. Taylor, in his engineering years and during his consultancy period, got acquainted with a sizeable number of precisely such enterprises. Their managers often lacked the technical expertise and the organizational capacity to run the operations effectively, let alone to integrate the operations into a streamlined overall plan of production. Several forms of labor recruitment were employed, all of them examples of the haphazard control of management over the processes of production. The most renown forms of labor recruitment have been subcontracting, the helper system, and inside contracting.

Contractors were a common phenomenon in late nineteenth-century industry. They took care of one or several parts of the process of production. In fact, they were independent businessmen, except that their products were not marketed under their own name. They negotiated about price and quantity with the principal. In the hiring of personnel, the purchase of materials and tools, the methods employed, the wages paid, and sometimes the location of work, they were independent. Finally, they were not themselves employees of a principal.

Inside contracting is similar, although the differences are significant. Here also, the contractor negotiates with the employer about price and quantity. But the principal is an employer, and the contractor is an employee. One immediate consequence is that the risk of the contractor is enhanced, since the employer retains the right of changing the required quantity during the period of agreement. The length of the working day is established by the employer, who also may veto the eventual union affiliation of the contractor's labor force. Materials were ordered on account of the employer, who also owned the tools and machines (Clawson, 1980: 71–73). But in the initiative of ordering materials and in the method of using machinery, the employer followed the contractor. Also, the contractor hired, and fired, his own men and paid their wages.

One remarkable thing about the phenomenon of inside contracting is the timing. The system was prominent in the last quarter of the nineteenth century. This was the period of the establishment of the large company, and it is in these that the inside contractor found employment for his services. It is, in Dan Clawson's words (1980), a form of prebureaucratic management. Inside contractors put some tens of hundreds of men to work, which is formidable, in view of the fact that the average shop or factory employed twenty workers in this period (Rosenblum, 1973: 69). The earnings of inside contractors could be high and regularly were higher than those of the managerial staff, who were formally their superiors.

The inside contractors built their powerful position on their knowledge of production. More often than not, they were former craftsmen who no longer used their expertise in direct production but rather in management. Their stronghold, however, was not merely in growing companies but in companies that both grew and were technologically complex. The typical examples are the machine tool industry, the industry of precision instruments, and, in general, industries connected to the complex of interchangeable parts (Clawson, 1980: 77, 83). There is, since many of these industries also had a northeastern base, some overlap between exactly the industries where inside contracting was prominent and the industries that around the turn of the century invited Taylor to streamline the process of production. The further development of the applicability of the interchangeable part in American industry, and through it of mechanization and standardization, was facilitated by the internal contracting system, although this same development undermined the contractors' managerial position. This is not to state that the system was technically or economically inefficient. It was not. Its deficiencies were above all of an organizational nature. The inside contractor was, by his very existence, a threat to company hierarchy. His income, although not fixed, could be higher than that of other managers, even of those higher in rank. Lines of authority were cut off at the places in the company where an inside contractor reigned. The expertise of the inside contractor might credit him with a higher actual than formal status, whereas the reverse could hold for the other parts of management.

Most problematic was the issue of continuity. The inside contractor represented the presence of the market, and thus insecurity, within the organization. Prices and quantities were results of negotiations and could not unilaterally be set with an eye on optimum administrative and technical rationality. The check on materials and tools permitted some insight into the actual workings of inside contracting. Naturally, this was a limited insight only, since management was unable to judge critically the exact performance of the contractor and his men. The Taylor engineers, however, did possess a competent judgment. The complaints Taylor and his engineers directed at, for instance, the management of the Tabor company, or of Remington's or Singer's, were double edged. It concerned both the powerful position of the production managers, inside contractors included, and the ignorance of top management. One of their achievements, however, has been to undercut the organizational role of the inside contractor, therewith enabling for the first time in the companies concerned the planning of the process of production, together with the organizational integration of production in the company activity as a whole.

The third form of indirect labor recruitment is the so-called helper system. It could be found in the textile, glass, pottery, and iron industries in the Northeast. There, factory production was more advanced than in the machine tool industry. Skilled craftsmen were ordered to hire a few helpers who assisted them in procuring the necessary materials and tools, in cleaning up, in some maintenance work, in putting tools back in their place, and so on. These helpers were paid by the skilled workers. Labor costs could be reduced if the skilled would only do skilled work and the unskilled the routine menial jobs. The curious thing was the managerial responsibility the skilled were supposed to shoulder. They were, on a small scale, labor contractors. The responsibility was not their initiative. In fact, they often preferred the employer to take on the hiring, paying, and firing of helpers or even the dissolution of the helper system as such. The skilled feared the helpers as potential competitors, who would learn many tricks of their trade by mere observation and, eventually, imitation. If so, they would lose their check on the number of workers and, since the helpers might accept work at lower rates, suffer a loss of income. Besides, the skilled workers were well aware that their managerial tasks were the product of the ignorance of management about the process of production. If the helpers had to be paid out of their wages, this indicated that management as yet possessed no other ways of influencing their, and their helpers', productivity. Predictably, then, skilled workers did not see themselves as junior managers but as workers. Their autonomy was not based on a formal managerial position but on their knowledge of production. They planned and controlled not merely the work of their helpers but their own work as well (Nelson, 1975: 40; Stark, 1980: 100; Clawson, 1980: 94–96).

The helper system was a threat to company hierarchy, although less so than inside contracting. The weak chain in the structure of command in this instance was the foreman, whose formal superiority over the skilled workers often found no practical recognition. The skilled workers claimed their own autonomy and resented interference with their methods of work and standards of performance. The foreman, often a former craftsman, was informed on both methods and standards. But as long as both planning and execution of the work were controlled by the skilled workers themselves, the position of the foreman was shaky. He risked an all-out fight with the skilled workers, who guarded nothing so jealously as the secrets of their trade, while his support was no more than an, in view of his low managerial status, incalculable support from an incompetent higher management. The fact that his income often was lower than that of the skilled worker underscored his uncertain position. Here, again, it is the engineer who may tip the balance. Once management has adequate knowledge on issues of production and skill, it can set its own standards and demand that they be followed. This will not end the functions of the helpers, but it will finish off the helper system.

The Taylor engineers confronted all three forms of indirect labor recruitment. From their point of view all three were inefficient, since they were rooted in a form of managerial discretion that was just another name for incompetence in matters of production. From the point of view of the owners of these shops and factories, indirect labor recruitment spelled the disadvantages of unpredictable market disturbances, a danger pressing both in times of high demand, when output must be guaranteed, and in times of slack, when cutting costs became imperative. In the abstract therefore, engineers and owners shared the identical problem. As the engineers were soon to find, however, slack periods proved more amenable to the reception of their ideas than periods of peaking demand. This points to the perennial conflict of interests and the modes of their accommodation. In periods of high demand, a company seldom will take the risk of provoking a walkout, since that might prove more expensive than a policy of giving in. In slack periods, a walkout may be a welcome event for an employer, and thus a more provocative attitude, not just on wages but also on methods and standards of work, pays. Taylor, in the period of his own consulting practice, repeatedly ran into difficulties once the economic tide became favorable. His days of victory, for instance at Bethlehem Steel, were when the company was in economic trouble; he had to leave when the market for Bethlehem turned expansionary.

There was a second reason why slack periods were good periods for the consulting engineers, because these were the same periods in which managers came under fire. A new management could be more competent in matters of production. More important, however, is the fact that a new management had a free hand in the redistribution of power. The balance of interests, characteristic of any going concern, is disturbed if the top layers playing the interest game are replaced. Replacement sometimes was the most simple and most effective precondition for reorganization, and it was this card that the Taylor engineer wanted to play (Nelson, 1975: 75).

PIECE-RATES AND BONUS-SYSTEMS

One clear effect of mechanization and standardization is the change brought about in pay systems and wage structures. The steel industry, the earliest example of successful mechanization, was the first to recognize the insufficiency of tying wages to productivity. Mechanization had ended the days in which the individual worker was able to influence his own output. This was reflected in the shrinking wage differentials between skilled and unskilled labor, as it was in the advance of the semiskilled. It was also reflected in the determination of the wage level. This used to be fixed by establishing a relation between tonnage and wages. With mechanization under way, however, tonnage was dropped as an indicator and was replaced by the "related factors of trade conditions and labor supply" (Brody, 1960: 41). Even when piecework was maintained, it was a matter of form only. It no longer influenced labor costs and output. The base rates were to be pegged to the common labor rate, not to tonnage. Piece-rates and bonuses were not dropped completely. They were kept on as incentives and played a role in the emerging internal labor market in the steel industry after the turn of the century (Brody, 1960; Stone, 1974; Elbaum, 1984: 83–89). The days when "trade and labor market conditions" alone reigned were short lived. Once the period of intense competition in the steel industry was over, symbolized in the J. Pierpont Morgan-led merger that united Carnegie and a few other leading steel companies in the new U.S. Steel, the wildest fluctuations in wages, prices, and employment were leveled off. The old piecework system, nonetheless, was not reinstated. Wages and employment became the object of corporate policy, expressed in the creation of training facilities and career lines.

The lead of the steel industry in technology, organization, and the adaptation of skills set an example for many other industries. It was important in the education of Taylor. His first job was with a steel company, and one of his formative consultancy activities took place at Bethlehem Steel. Taylor's occupation with Bethlehem Steel started in 1898, almost ten years after his job at the Midvale steel company. It coincides with the steel industry's grand

transformation, between 1890 and 1910, especially in the plants controlled
by Carnegie. Taylor was never hired by Carnegie or, for that matter, by U.S.
Steel. It was, therefore, all the more remarkable that the changes effected by
Carnegie after 1890 so much resembled the Taylor system of his Bethlehem
days. Carnegie rationalized inventories, administration, cost analysis, and so
on. Costs were the focus and thus efficiency. Exact data were imperative;
production managers collected detailed monthly data on operations, inputs,
and outputs; they compared results and strove after improvements. Standards
were set each year, and each year they were higher. A competitive management system, allowing fast internal career possibilities from the ranks of
production, was installed. Here, expertise in matters of production and its
organization went hand in hand with managerial status—at least until the
coming of the U.S. Steel corporation, led by Morgan and his candidate Judge
Elbert H. Gary.

In the Carnegie plants all elements of the process of production were
integrated and, when possible, standardized. This involved heavy mechanization not only of the stages and departments of production but also of their
connections. As occurred somewhat later in the automobile industry, the
influence of technology affected skills not by making them obsolete but by
undercutting their organizational centrality. Discrete phases in the process
of production progressively disappeared and were succeeded by an uninterrupted, continuous production flow. Technologically, discrete phases
could and had to be identified; organizationally, the plants were reorganized
into one integrated productive mechanism. By 1900 the major problems were
mastered: the handling of materials, integration of production stages, and
continuous rolling of steel (Brody, 1960: 9).

In his proposals for a new organizational setup for the design and control
of the process of production, Taylor was ahead of his times. Assessing his
wage proposals is a more ambivalent affair, however. There is a certain
disjunction between Taylor's attempt to standardize the labor process and
his individualistic approach to labor relations. The former Taylor developed
into organic directions; the latter was still considered in terms of heterogeneous manufacture. His scorn of "welfare capitalism," as one attempt to
acknowledge the different type of labor relations required by organic methods of production, is well known and illustrative of his own limited point of
view on wages and incentives. Indeed, the "differential piece-rate" advocated
by Taylor suggested obedience to the standards of performance and productivity. But precisely that nexus was cut through not only in the mechanized
steel industry but in principle in every industry organized along Taylorist
lines.

The steel industry again set an example. Internally, the steel industry
erected the type of job ladders, with limited ports of entry, that became
known in time as internal labor markets. The job ladders had an individual-
izing effect, since a rise along them, although conditioned by training and

sometimes even certified courses, depended on competition between workers for scarce advancement opportunities (see Brody, 1960; Stone, 1974; Elbaum, 1984). But in their rewards and career promises, they did not so much connect output to income as income and advancement to effort and loyalty.

On this score, Taylor and his engineers were traditional. They attacked the old premium and bonus systems, however, because they rewarded efforts and outputs, without critically questioning the two sides of this equation. The differential piece-rate was designed to command obedience to the standards set by the planning department, reflecting the most efficient organization of production, and to reward the "one best way" of going about one's task. Insofar as Taylor recognized something like an internal labor market at all, it was tied up with individualized work of great variety and with methods in which recurring changes could be anticipated (Taylor, 1903: 142). The new and growing reality of work strictly tied to the dictates of machines or continuous processes has no systematic place in Taylorism.

The differential rate nevertheless produced noteworthy side effects. The standard is one of them. It emphasized the duty and task of managers to regard the process of production as a problem, the solution to which was one of their major assignments. Leaving all the rigamarole about the scientificity of standards for what it is, the standard signaled the end of the days of a management ignorant on matters of production. Standards were not given, nor were they the average of what observation in the workplace produced. Standards had to be set, and this had to be done in a way that would open them to experiment and measurement. They called for exact registration of the effort and results of labor. This, in itself, was a huge step to be taken, since it entailed no more or less than an investigation into forms of indirect labor recruitment, which, by definition, largely escaped outside scrutiny. Yet the needs of registration and investigation were indissolubly linked with the introduction of premium and bonus systems and with all forms of the piece-rate. Sometimes management would be satisfied with a weak form of registration, like the recording of average hours and output only. Most employers, however, were interested in the possibilities of cutting costs, in the effect of changing rates on output, or both. The purely empirical registration of a status quo in these situations would not suffice. A more active approach was needed.

Taylor's differential piece-rate was such an approach. In Taylor's public statements, as in those of his adversaries, the differential rate was put forward as one of the major elements of the system. In retrospect, this is almost ironic. The overhaul of the method of wage determination in the steel industry, in its relation to output and the organization of production, had been far more dramatic than anything Taylor had ever proposed. The Homestead strike of 1892 had practically killed the skilled steelworkers' union and, with it, its grasp on the relations in production, wage determination included. In fact, the Homestead strike had been provoked by the Carnegie company with the sole objective of liquidating the union (Brody, 1960; Rayback, 1959). The strategy worked. The "moral code" of workers' conduct in the shop had been broken, as had the union's "legislation" on job access, boundaries, competencies, and remuneration (Montgomery, 1980: 11ff.).

Taylor set out for the same attack on codes and legislation, but whereas the steel industry succeeded, Taylor did not. One reason is that forms of indirect labor recruitment in the late nineteenth-century steel industry were not very prominent and, in fact, were on the decline. The helper system did exist, be it in a diluted form. Many of the helpers were actually hired directly and paid by the company (Stone, 1960: 63; Elbaum, 1984), being a measure of management control of the technology and organization of the production of steel and steel products. Taylor, on the other hand, was hired by companies who lacked such control. Unions were prevalent in industries using the helper system (such as textiles, glass, pottery, and iron; Nelson, 1975: 40). More than pointing to workers' strength, the unions filled the vacuum created by managerial ineptitude. The internal contractor symbolized a further weakness of management. Since management was the critical variable in the top-down approach of the Taylor system, it may be inferred that the strategic flaw in the practice of the system concerned the relation of management and engineer rather than the relation between management and the worker.

The planning department was to assume all managerial responsibilities for the process and the organization of production. It was a key factor in the reform of management. About the foreman, Taylor was very explicit. But on the relation of the engineer and higher management, Taylor's remarks not only are very few but elusive as well (Taylor, 1903: 135–136). Critical in his view was the position of the foreman. Formally, the foreman's position in the hierarchy of management was that of subordinate or "junior" member. In the day-to-day operations, however, his position often was strategic, since he was responsible for methods and timing of production, for setting rates and quality standards, and for hiring, firing, and discipline.

This position came under fire from three sides in the late nineteenth century (Montgomery, 1980: 32–33; Nelson, 1975: 35ff.). First was the rise of mass production techniques, such as in the steel industry and in meatpacking. There the foreman held out for some time in hiring and firing, especially in unskilled labor. As soon as the costs of recruitment, in connection with labor turnover, became an object of managerial concern, however, the days of the foreman's discretion in this field, too, were numbered. The second attack on his position of power was the consequence of indirect labor recruitment, be this of the inside-contracting or helper variety. The third attack may be associated with the advance of the engineer and, thus, of Taylor as one outspoken protagonist. First, Taylor removed the control of the foreman over production and costs. Then, the discretion over rates, and thus the foreman's influence as a trainer, had to be transferred to the planning department. Finally, the projected institution of functional foremanship and its integration in the planning department would eliminate the traditional foreman altogether (Nelson, 1975: 35ff.).

The weakness of the planning department and functional foremanship is not that it complicates the constraint of the unity of command. More important is the fact that the functional differentiation it calls for vastly overrates the hand of the engineer. The assumption of the Taylor system is the centrality of the organization of production. Managerial responsibility and engineering expertise in Taylor's view are but two sides of the same thing (Taylor, 1903: 63, 66–68). The relative autonomy of problems of business administration, and of social and human engineering, is nonetheless at least as much a characteristic of modern management as is the relative autonomy of the organization of production. All require specialized expertise, and the weight they must carry in organizations is by definition one of the major managerial problems. Business administration was hardly existing as a managerial specialization during Taylor's lifetime. Nor was social engineering, although in the engineering educational programs the social sciences were replacing the older classical emphases, Taylor's disapproval notwithstanding. Social engineering is at once close to and immeasurably distanced from the Taylor system. It is close to the Taylor system because it is closely linked to the social organization of the shop. It is distanced from his system because its point of departure is the explicit recognition that the social relations of work are not completely determined by the organization of production. Hardly a prominent development, it was not completely lacking in the first two decades of this century, especially in those companies experimenting with privately sponsored forms of social insurance (Nelson, 1969; Lubove, 1968). But human engineering, in the shape of industrial relations and personnel management, definitely was on the move in Taylor's days (for the educational aspects, see Noble, 1977: 263ff.; for the practical introduction of these themes in American industry, see Brandes, 1970; Jacoby, 1985; Brody, 1960).

Nor was this an isolated development. The dual tendency in American industry around the turn of the century, connecting violence and repression of working-class culture and tradition with a series of positive interventions in life-styles and living conditions, could be observed in urban reform movements as well. To some extent, most of welfare capitalism is a replica of the larger movement toward the reform of urban politics and the creation of acceptable conditions in the city in diverse areas such as playgrounds, parks, housing, sewage systems, urban transit, and schools, along with the attack on the saloon and the brothel, in close company with the attack on the political boss system (Boyer, 1978). Taylor was not estranged from this movement, but his involvement betrayed the limits of his productivist ideology. Taylor could be found on the first board of directors of the National Society for the Promotion of Industrial Education (NSPIE) of 1907 but in the same period scorned the attempts at modernizing higher education (Noble, 1977: 308; Hall, 1984). Both, however, belonged to the outlook of modern management, and Taylor's halfway allegiance to it is one more testimony to his position as a typical figure of transition.

TAYLORISM AND THE UNION

Introductory Notes

The American Federation of Labor, founded in 1886, differed substantially from its main predecessor, the Knights of Labor (Grob, 1961: 138–162). First, its member unions organized predominantly the skilled workers. Industrial unions like the United Mine Workers of America were also affiliated with the AFL, but their voice was never strong enough to silence the majority influence of the craft-bound unions. The Knights, on the other hand, had attracted a growing number of unskilled and semiskilled, whose power in the early eighties of the previous century was expanding. Second, the AFL was more decentralized organizationally than the Knights had been. Indeed, one of the weaknesses of the Knights was that its centralized organization was unfit to cope with the growing strike and union demands of its new members of the eighties. In contrast, the facilities and powers of the AFL, compared to its constituent member unions, were very limited. In part, this may have reflected the different stand on political action of the two labor organizations. The AFL kept its distance from politics and intervened only if and when the labor conditions of the working population were at stake. Its avowed rejection of any larger goal of transforming society was both aimed at the heritage of the Knights of Labor, as at the socialists within and without its own ranks. The refusal of the AFL of allowing any ends but those related to the employment interests of its members made for an organization that, when compared to the Knights, had lost all resemblance to a political party. The smallness of the central agencies of the federation, its severely limited funds, the absence of a central strike fund, and the heavy reliance on professionalism in union negotiations with employers point to the decentralized nature of the AFL and to the importance attached to collective bargaining within the respective union jurisdictions (Brody, 1968: 288–303; Pelling, 1960: 83ff.).

Third, the AFL was an organization of the wage dependent, whereas the Knights of Labor had welcomed small farmers, merchants, and shopowners as well. The Knights fought for a new society, based on the principles of producers' cooperatives, embedded in the social and competitive relations of small-scale production and exchange. Their foe was monopoly, symbolized by the trusts and Wall Street. Union activities in a strict sense were subordinated to this wider goal, adding another organizational strain on the flexibility of the Knights, especially after the massive influx of unskilled and semiskilled labor, new immigrants and western proletarianized small merchants and farmers, in its ranks. The AFL, in contrast, took wage dependency as a matter of fact and as something permanent. The AFL unions were not out to fight against monopoly so much as to fight for themselves.

The acceptance of the employment relationship by the AFL testifies, according to Selig Perlman, to a fundamental shift in perspective that differentiates the AFL from earlier organizations such as the Knights and from later contenders such as the Industrial Workers of the World of 1905. As Perlman said: "Unionism . . . first became a stabilized movement in America only when the abundance consciousness of the pioneer days had been replaced in the mind of labor by a scarcity consciousness—the consciousness of job scarcity" (1928: 310). As Perlman showed, however, it is not just perceiving scarcity that is peculiar to American labor but also the relationship between scarcity and abundance. The dominance of the scarcity consciousness has to be articulated against the backdrop of abundance. Indeed, the oft-quoted reliance of the AFL on "voluntarism" makes sense only against this background.

Businessmen are characterized by the consciousness of abundance or the consciousness of "unlimited opportunity." In general, workers are defined by its opposite, a consciousness of scarcity of opportunity:

Starting with this consciousness of scarcity, the "manualist" groups have been led to practising solidarity, to an insistence upon an "ownership" by the group as a whole of the totality of the economic opportunity extant, to a "rationing" by the group of such opportunity among the individuals constituting it, to a control by the group over its members in relation to the conditions upon which they as individuals are permitted to occupy a portion of that opportunity—in brief, to a "communism of opportunity." (Perlman, 1928: 309)

This general insight must in the American case be qualified on several accounts. One is the enormous strength of private property in America. Whereas in England in the nineteenth century the classical doctrine of private property had already been diluted through the denial of the essential ideological nexus between effort and property rights (Neumann, 1936), in the United States pre-emption was still a common affair (McConnell, 1966). The end of pre-emption and the close of the frontier both date from the turn of the century; they are two sides of the same coin. Since any trade union is an infringement on the rights of an employer's private property, the degree to which this institution is entrenched in the public will be an important variable. In the United States the entrenchment has gone very deep indeed. During the major part of the nineteenth century the institution of private property spread from its eastern base all over the continent, documented and symbolized, in terms that could be directly taken from Locke, by "laboring pioneers, creating property for themselves as they went along and holding it in small parcels. This was the way not only of agriculture but also of the mechanical trades and of the larger scale industries" (Perlman, 1928: 312). The early labor unions and parties were motivated not by the wish to deny private property but by the claim that American abundance had to be distributed more equitably, in view of the dangers presented by large industry and the financial and monopolistic forms of property it engendered. Property was to be an opportunity for all; therefore the monopolization of its conditions by financial interests, by absentee ownership, and by regulation of markets through monopolistic devices had to be fought.

The AFL dropped the antimonopoly edge from its arsenal, just like it refrained from endorsing the "greenback" and "free silver" movements, the typical expressions of the cause against the alleged powers of Wall Street. But the AFL confessed its continuity with the earlier movements by clinging tenaciously to the institution of private property, in particular the property inhering in one's own labor power and the conditions under which this could be alienated. This had to create an irreducible zone of conflict with the property rights of the employer. The conditions of hiring and using labor created an area of conflicting property rights that, unless the workers organized, would lead to the disappearance of the free worker and, by the same token, to the disappearance of private property as a realm of open opportunity. In the AFL view the trade union posed no threat to private property; rather, property in one's labor power demanded an organization of labor to neutralize the power advantage of the employer relative to the employee.

Second, the recognition of an unresolvable conflict area between capital and labor, founded in their mutually exclusive property rights, was limited to the economic field. The AFL never accepted the logic according to which the cleavages in the economic field were repeated and echoed in the political sphere. The economy was not the *source* of politics, in whatever sense we use that ambiguous word. The lack of politically organized "class consciousness" of the American working class and trade union movement is not a denial of the reality of class. The limitation of the conflict to the economic field, or the attempt to prevent its spilling over into politics, explains both the radicalism of many of the actions of the AFL—since they were power conflicts, rather than conflicts over legitimate authority—and its "economism." It also explains much of the bitterness of employers' resistance, since in their perspective the struggle hinged not on power but, in mirror image, on the legitimate authority associated with the exercise of their property rights.

In retrospect these perspectives show inconsistencies. The AFL's insistence on the economic field, the legal recognition of trade unions included, was correct in that the polarization of private property along the employment axis does call for the trade union and collective bargaining as complementary and satellite institutions of private property in the means of production (Neumann, 1936; Selznick, 1980: 66). But the practice of the AFL relative to government intervention did not reflect the by now common distinction in

American law between labor law (dealing with trade unions and collective bargaining) and legislation on the employment relation (dealing with equal opportunity, worker's compensation, minimum wages and hours, unemployment compensation, and so forth) (Selznick, 1980: 121). Their opposition to the political determination of the latter realm of employment laws was ill grounded and came forth from their identification of labor law and the employment relation and the reduction of the latter to the former. In this, the AFL demonstrated a shortsightedness exhaustively paralleled by the American employers, who advocated a concept of corporate-sponsored "welfare capitalism," inclusive of unemployment compensation, old-age pensions, medical facilities, and, on the other end of the line, grievance procedures and "company unions" (Jacoby, 1985; Brandes, 1970). Voluntarism proved a common practice of the AFL, employers, and, as we shall show below, the Taylor engineers. Moreover, the idea of property and property rights in one's own labor power was bolstered by the political status of the American worker, especially the ballot (Brown, 1986: 206ff.). This feature, unique to the American situation, contributes to the focus on economic forms of cleavage, to the neglect of political forms. As Perlman reminded us, the economic line "becomes blurred by the constant process of 'osmosis' between one economic class and another, by fluctuations in relative bargaining power of employer and employee with changes in the business cycle, and by other changing conditions" (Perlman, 1928: 313).

Next to private property and the problems of class, there was a third factor accounting for the American road to trade unionism: the impact of immigration. The "job consciousness," that is, the right to one's job, characterizing the union movement was constantly overhauled by the inflow of new workers, who, by their very presence in the labor market, were a threat to existing titles and prerogatives. It is true that the slow and highly uneven development in the twentieth century to a more industrial unionism in the United States has shifted from an emphasis on job rights to an emphasis on employment rights, but this is not fundamental. The actual issue for union organization, whether on a job or an employment base, is the precondition of a somehow "settled" (Perlman, 1928; Thernstrom, 1968) working population. Some continuity in presence is essential for the very possibility of organizing. The reliance on attractively salaried union professionals, however, did counteract the organizationally disruptive tendencies of a population constantly on the move, but the force of the professional option should not be overestimated (Brody, 1968). The immigrants, even apart from their country of origin and their skills, were the daily reminders of the difficulties of organization and of the efforts needed to sustain the perennially unstable cohesiveness of the existing unions. In this respect the American unions were no exception to the practices of organization in other countries. Yet the sheer magnitude of immigration in the United States did provoke union responses unknown, or unseen, in other countries. The defensive weapon of the "charter" (granting a union the exclusive right to organize a specific field or trade, regardless of the existing state of organization in the field or trade), combined with the all-out fight against "dual unionism" wherever it threatened to appear, may be directly attributed to the protection of unions—especially when they were weak or even nonexistent in the given area and thus vulnerable to immigrant and employer initiative.

The Union and Scientific Management

At the time the Taylor system reached its completion, the AFL grew rapidly. In the period between 1897 and 1904 three noticeable developments may be observed. The first two are the ones just mentioned: the completion of the Taylor system and the growing strength of the AFL. The third is the rapidly increasing size of the average enterprise, brought about in this period mainly by mergers and acquisitions (Edwards, 1979: 218–219; Griffin, Wallace, and Rubin, 1986: 149).

Total membership of unions in the period mentioned above quadrupled, from about half a million to 2 million. The AFL fared even better, with a growth of 560 percent (Griffin, Wallace, and Rubin, 1986). Union membership as a percentage of all nonagricultural employees rose from 3.5 in 1897 to 12.3 in 1904 (Troy, 1965: 2, table 2), a ratio to be surpassed only at the close of the First World War. The picture for business, however, was more mixed, since the growth in average enterprise size was also the result of an unprecedented high rate of business failure (Griffin, Wallace, and Rubin, 1986). To survive, efficiency and costs were imperative. When, after 1904, in conjunction with an economic downturn, the rate of growth of the unions slowed, this in no way alleviated the constraint on business efficiency.

Apart from their record in steel, the unions were relatively successful in mining (both in coal and ore), transport (train, transit, and especially water transport), construction, carpentry, government works, and the metal trades. In the newer science-based industries such as electrical equipment and appliances, chemicals, oil, and rubber, they were weak, as they were in the newer mass production industries (Rayback, 1959: 207–226). On the whole, however, key sectors in the American economy definitely had to reckon with the influence of the unions. In practice, this meant that the "legislation" of the unions—specifying the description of jobs, job access, job competencies, and standard rates of pay—and the "moral code"—specifying the behavioral relations in the shops themselves, including effort norms, acceptable forms of inspection and supervision, and an emphasis on group rather than individual performance—were formidable obstacles in the attempts of employers to rationalize their shops. Facing the transformation of local competition in nationwide competition and fearing the threat of being taken over, employers had no alternative but to focus on costs and thus on the social and technical relations in production.

The institution symbolizing the effective power of the unions was the closed shop. Within an organization this meant that for a given range of jobs the employer confronted a completely organized labor force. In approaching the labor market the organization had to deal with the union, acting as a broker in labor. The union effectively checked both the amount and the quality of the available labor force, thus combining the functions of an employment agency and of inclusive collective bargaining. The recruitment discretion of the employer was therewith severely curtailed. The craft unions, moreover, by definition organized workers whose occupational interests depended on a trade as a whole but not on any one particular employer or even one industry. Threats to the union's legislation and its moral codes were countered with solidarity strikes and boycotts (Montgomery, 1980).

The union's position was far from secure, though. It was weakened by its own exclusive strategies, by the grand employer's initiative of the "Open Shop" campaign, by the courts, and by Taylorist or Taylorist-associated reorganizations of production.

Exclusiveness

The rise of the factory originally was accompanied by the rise of the helper system. In companies using the helper system, unionization was usually strong. Skilled workers in these factories had a craft orientation: They planned and executed their work and that of their helpers, and they had achieved their status as a result of apprenticeships according to union prescription. They had to admit the presence of helpers but feared the possibility of being outflanked by them. Both company training and the willy-nilly on-the-job-training that they couldn't prevent the helpers from acquiring were real dangers. But the very fact that the helpers were perceived as a danger is proof of the crisis of the apprenticeship mode of training workers. Indeed, the period around the turn of the century presents evidence of the decline of apprenticeship: Both the advance forward to a position of independence and the influx of new trainees coming from the shops and educated in them were blocked. Yet the closed shop practice was critically dependent on an apprenticeship system, controlled directly or indirectly by the union. The campaign for the "open shop" by the National Association of Manufacturers (NAM) was, consequently, accompanied by the assault of the same organization on the apprenticeship system by means of employer-controlled vocational education in the form of the trade school (Fisher, 1967: 122). To counteract the NAM attack, the AFL would have had to open its doors to the new group of the semiskilled. The federation as such might have been willing to act accordingly (on the position of Gompers, see Pelling, 1960; Grob, 1961), but the controlling position of the national unions forbade any such action. In fact, when the shattered steelworkers' union at last gave in to the exigency of recruiting the semiskilled—under pressure, to be sure, from AFL headquarters—it was not just too late; it also could not help reminding the mainly foreign-born semiskilled of the advantages to be expected from keeping their relatives and compatriots in the country of origin (Brody, 1960).

The "Open Shop" and the National Association of Manufacturers

American employers have always been highly organized. Most of these organizations, as elsewhere, were directed at improving the situation of the trades involved, without any specific aim toward labor. At the end of the nineteenth century, accompanying the dual growth of collective bargaining and AFL unions, many erstwhile informal and local organizations started to formalize along nationally defined trade lines, topped since 1895 by a national trade organization, the National Association of Manufacturers. These new organizations were directed at, and more often than not against, labor and collective bargaining. In fact, there is a direct nexus between industries in which unions were growing and in which new employer organizations emerged (Derber, 1984: 79–80, 194–105; Griffin, Wallace, and Rubin, 1986: 155). Like the AFL, as distinct from its member unions, the NAM itself did not conclude contracts. Both central agencies collected and distributed information; played on public relations; lobbied; took part in relevant initiatives such as reforms in education, the tariff, and factory organization; initiated, sponsored, and financed organizing drives; and the like. The main difference on this formal plane seems to be that the financial situation of the NAM was rosy compared to that of the AFL with its limited funds (Griffin, Wallace, and Rubin, 1986: 163).

In 1903, with unionization still advancing and with growing economic problems for especially the smaller and medium-sized, as well as unionized, companies (they were the core of the NAM's membership; Derber, 1984; Jacoby, 1985; Weinstein, 1968; Griffin, Wallace, and Rubin, 1986), the NAM launched its "open shop" campaign. At stake were both the existence of collective bargaining and the existence of the unions. The expedient was the attack on the closed shop, branded an un-American institution, since it was assumed to hamper freedom of contract and to be a conspiracy in restraint of trade. Remarkable, indeed, are the legal metaphors the NAM exploited in its defense of a total employer's prerogative in the shop. Obviously, the correct device against the unlawful and un-American actions of the unions was the "yellow dog contract." This contract was not just individualized, and thus the opposite of collective bargaining; it also invited the worker voluntarily to renounce any inclination to join the union.

This, then, was a declaration of war. The yellow dog contract was not an invention of the NAM; indeed, the existence of these and related contracts had made the practice of the closed shop a bare necessity for any union to survive. The NAM vigorously promoted the use of this type of contract. But it did more. It supported employers—financially, legally, and politically— who in following the open shop drive were confronted with union-led strikes, walkouts, and boycotts. It emphasized and lobbied for the necessity of keeping the stream of immigrants going. It pushed industrial education. It disseminated information and advice on factory reorganization. It started or supported organizing drives to enlarge the strength and the scope of the open shop issue. It besieged trade journals and the wider public opinion with its conviction that more than mere monetary interests were at stake. In effect, it was successful. After 1904 the absolute number of union members stagnated for more than a decade, and the proportion of unionized workers in nonagricultural employment actually declined (Troy, 1965: 2). But the NAM was not solely responsible for the halt in union expansion. Associated member groups, in the metal trades especially, were active also on their own. Nonaligned employers evidently fought unions as well, and the recession after 1904 may have contributed to the union difficulties. But the impact of the NAM was considerable. One estimate (Griffin, Wallace, and Rubin, 1986: 163) summarizes the evidence: "This 'suppression' of unionization, it should be remembered, is independent of the labor movement's own 'inertia' and of growth or declines induced by industrial and firm size changes, economic prosperity, movements of the business cycle, political process . . . , and collective action, in the form of strikes, of the working class itself."

The Courts

The open shop campaign of the NAM is one excellent illustration of the importance to be attached to employer's and managerial ideologies (Bendix, 1956; Griffin, Wallace, and Rubin, 1986; Goldman and Van Houten, 1979). The open shop campaign was an ideological campaign, an attempt to stretch the line between inclusion and exclusion, acceptance and rejection, in favor of the employers. "Law" was American, not privilege; freedom of contract and unmitigated trade were American, not compulsory union membership and monopoly. In devising its codes and shibboleths, the NAM struck gold. The Sherman antitrust act had already codified the anxieties about monopolies and restraint of trade. The change in the origins of immigration to a Mediterranean base and Eastern Europe put a premium on being more American than the flag. Finally, the wave of violence that swept American labor relations around the turn of the century posed a threat to the very possibility of an orderly society—the pleonasm in the latter expression was no longer a matter of course, or so it seemed.

The best mark of ideology in the United States is the court. This, much more so than in politics or positive law, was nowhere more evident than in the application of the antitrust and conspiracy laws against organized labor. The courts owe this important position to three related circumstances. The first is the Constitution of the country, which, for all practical purposes, is more a series of declarations of intent and goodwill than it is applicable law. What the Constitution is worth depends on its interpretation by the courts and ultimately by the Supreme Court. Second, the American political system is designed to "check and balance" the dangers of too radical a change effected from one majority to the next but also to check the grip of whichever political majority is on the judiciary. The courts, thus, enjoy a considerable amount of independence from the political balance of forces. Third, all positive laws may be put to the test of being in accord with the Constitution, a task relegated to the courts (Gumperz, 1932; Neumann, 1936; Potter, 1955).

The courts got saddled with the problem of determining what kind of a contract the labor contract really was. Crucial was the issue of authority. The problem is admirably expressed by Philip Selznick (1980: 135): "Ideally, even under contract doctrine, the employer might be granted the right to make rules, but he would not have the unrestricted right to decide whether the rules he has made are consistent with the contract." Even if it might be assumed, that is, that an employee respects and voluntarily accepts management's prerogative as to the social and technical organization of production, the ensuing authority would still be conditional upon the freedom of interpretation by both parties to the contract. Such a literal reading of the purposive employment contract, in fact, came very close to the opinion of the unions. They did not question, at least not formally, managerial prerogative. But they did demand a voice in the interpretation of the employee's side of the contract, including work rules and their eventual changes. On the other hand, such a reading of the employment contract was practically equivalent to inviting a permanent crisis of authority in the shops (Fox, 1974).

The issue came to a head in the period of ascendancy of the AFL around the turn of the century and the counterattack launched by the NAM in its open shop campaign. For the AFL it was not a legitimate matter of law. The freedom of contract included collective bargaining and the right of employee representation and organization. For the NAM it was a matter of law: in its view the closed shop and even collective bargaining were infringements on property rights and hindered the full deployment of the freedom of contract. In its attack on the AFL unions, it did not at any time seek the destruction of the unions through the courts—this treatment was reserved mainly for the International Workers of the World. Instead, it focused on the issue of restraint of trade, by either invoking state laws to that effect or the federal Sherman antitrust act (and later also the Clayton Act). The charge was simply that unions by holding on to the closed shop, or by organizing to obtain the closed shop, invariably used means like strikes and boycotts that represented a restraint of trade and were, thus, unlawful. The common practice was to ask a court for an injunction. This saved the time-consuming route of a trial with an always uncertain jury, while the order of a judge, even if the order was challenged by the union in a further trial, carried full weight until its eventual overruling. Nothing, indeed, is more detrimental to collective action than the incapacity to choose one's own means and, particularly, timing.

Both the appeal on the clause of the restraint of trade and the means of the injunction worked well for the employers (Griffin, Wallace, and Rubin, 1986:

160–161). The effects on the unions were crippling; the solidarity strike, very successful during the nineties, and the boycott were weapons foregone (Montgomery, 1980). The use of the injunction undermined the possibility of mobilizing people at the right time. But the upholding by the courts of the yellow dog contract as legitimate was most revealing, since here the courts had to speak out on the nature of the labor contract itself. In the majority of cases, the courts vindicated the reality of what Selznick called the "prerogative contract" (Selznick, 1980: 135), an interpretation of the labor contract that dominated the legal scene already at the end of the nineteenth century. In this respect, the AFL was not in touch with the times, for by the end of the nineteenth century "the employment contract had become a very special sort of contract—in large part a legal device for guaranteeing to management the unilateral power to make rules and exercise discretion" (Selznick, 1980: 135). The employment contract, although nominally a contract of the purpose variety, was assumed to contain the old contractual element of the statuses of the master and servant relationship, with the notable exception of the possibility of termination at will. Legally, the AFL was in a no-man's-land, and the NAM had inherited the world.

Taylorism

Taylor was not a friend of the unions nor of the NAM. From their side, the coolness and even aversion was reciprocated. Although the NAM did stimulate factory reorganization and diffusion of systematic managerial practices, the Taylor approach was not embraced. Reflecting the actual situation in many smaller shops, David Parry, the NAM president during the open shop campaign, evaluated the Taylor system as too strict, such as that it would kill the element of innovation and leniency, deemed to be essential for the effective running of a shop. He warned of the danger of "the drying up of knowledge and ability through system" (Haber, 1964: 71). Presumably, this is shorthand for the simple fact that the Taylor reforms presupposed a sizeable enterprise, for small shops were, in terms of size, unable to profit from the elaborate division of labor, such as functional foremanship, that the Taylor system necessitated. Their use of systematic management was limited to administration, routing of the work flow, and the fight against unions, perceived to be the precondition for extended control of the shop. Precisely on this last point Taylor and the NAM parted company (Haber, 1964: 70). If anything, in the fierce competitive struggle of the early twentieth century, the traditional authority of the foreman was enhanced, rather than fragmented. Hiring, firing, discipline, and rate setting were his provinces, so much so that many companies were hardly aware of the number of people they actually employed, their rate of turnover, or the degree of favoritism and nepotism that the discretion of the foremen solicited. On their part, the foremen possessed hardly any means but the speedup to satisfy the demands for higher output at reduced cost (Jacoby, 1985: 16–23, 40–49; Nelson, 1975).

The rate-setting power of the foremen was progressively more geared to forms of incentive pay, coupled with piecework. Under the impact of cost considerations, however, the rates were cut almost as often as the incentive began to pay off for the workers under its regime. Yet, incentive pay, the administration it engendered, the timing of work, and the effort it called for were integral aspects of systematic management, whether of the Taylor variety or not. Also, the very system of incentive pay was a break with the standard group rates that the unions stood for. As such, it was an attack on the union's moral code for the shop.

Small wonder, then, that the differences between the pure Taylor system, with its factual and often diluted applications, and other forms of systematic management were hardly perceptible for the workers immediately concerned. Taylor himself contributed to the confusion by pressing his differential rate in isolation from the rest of his system. His activities at Bethlehem Steel, but at other places as well, are an example. There the differential rate was introduced for the "shoveling" workers, generally unskilled ones, with an Eastern European background. The rest of his system was applied elsewhere at Bethlehem, creating at least the impression that the much publicized differential rate was an autonomous element of the system and could in itself be used as a method of cutting costs (Nelson, 1980: 91ff.). The association of Taylor with the speedup did not come out of the blue, then. Surely, Taylor's rates were standard, and the incentives promised even higher pay for the workers. Taylor opposed rate cutting, except for those workers performing below standard. The workers themselves had absolutely no guarantee, however, that the rates, along the movements of the business cycle, would be upheld, and often they weren't. Besides, the harsh punishment for below-standard performance weeded out many older workers, again hardly contributing to an acceptable relationship between effort and remuneration.

The AFL opposed the Taylor system from the start. Member unions warned of the "Taylor shops" and, when they still held the position of employment brokers, refrained from sending unionized workers to these shops. Elsewhere, the targets were the rates and the time studies (Nadworny, 1955: ch. 2; Rose, 1975: ch. 4). The grand attack by the Federation on the Taylor system came in 1911, spurred by Gompers' reading of the "Principles" and fueled by the events at Watertown Arsenal and the famous *Eastern Rate* case of 1910–1911. In 1915 the Hoxie report provided further ammunition to buttress the negative judgment of the AFL.

In the first decade of this century the U.S. Navy became one of Taylor's clients. Some of the navy's docks, shipyards, and stores were unionized, so some circumvention was deemed appropriate. In 1909 Barth, one of Taylor's disciples from the beginning and, in outlook, his closest associate, started working on the Watertown Arsenal with time studies. In August 1911 the workers protested the use of a stopwatch, qualifying it as "humiliating" and "un-American." A walkout was the result (Nadworny, 1955; Clawson, 1980).

Next, a congressional committee of investigation was installed. All parties to the conflict were heard, Taylor included. The committee could not decide on clear policy prescriptions. In fact, it was in a predicament. Politically, the influence of the AFL was not to be underestimated. Also, Taylor's attack on managerial attitudes had not impressed the committee. On the other hand, the advantages of standardization of tools, parts, routing, feeding, and pace of machinery were unmistakable (Nadworny, 1955: 64). But politics decided against Taylor. In 1912 a new secretary in the Department of War, F. D. Roosevelt, declared himself unimpressed by scientific management, after which the experiment was continued in a very reduced form. The conflict flared up again in 1914. A new report, this time by the department itself, was prepared, ultimately leading in 1915, just two and a half weeks before Taylor's death, to the exclusion of all work for army and navy that was monitored by the managerial expedient of the "stopwatch/time-measuring device" (Nadworny, 1955: 80ff.). In 1916 the interdiction was extended to all assignments financed by the federal government, a measure kept intact until 1949 (Noble, 1977: 271).

The AFL sailed stormier water with the *Eastern Rate* case. This was a trial before the Interstate Commerce Committee concerning the complaints of farming and industrial interests about the increasing rates of a railway company. The increase was, among other things, the consequence of higher wages that the company had agreed upon with the union. The industrial interests hired the famous lawyer Louis Brandeis to defend their case. Brandeis was successful: The rates were scaled down to their previous level. It was scientific management that did the trick. Brandeis attacked the railroad for its incompetent management and claimed that costs could be cut substantially, without lowering wages or profits and without the necessity of higher freight rates. In conjunction with some Taylor engineers Brandeis decided to use the name "scientific management" as the general denominator of his approach (Haber, 1964: 55). But he did add one important element to it, which was not approved by Taylor. According to Brandeis, scientific management and collective bargaining could go together, a stand far beyond Taylor's opinion, in which collective bargaining was rejected. In fact, the only function Taylor entrusted to the unions was as part of an unspecified grievance procedure (Bendix, 1956: 369).

The issue was whether the unions should be involved in the setting of the rates and, thus, the timing of work and effort. Brandeis did not approach the matter as a political economist; his attitude toward labor was more similar to that of the social worker (Haber, 1964: 77). In that, he was not alone. Some of the Taylor engineers, notably Cooke and Valentine, were of like opinion. But Taylor himself was adamant, and so was the AFL. Brandeis' position put them in an ugly spot. Brandeis, "the people's lawyer," was sympathetic to labor, and the enormous publicity that surrounded the *Eastern Rate* case, itself an expression of the "efficiency craze" that swept the United States during the period, popularized both scientific management and its compatibility with labor (Nadworny, 1955; Haber, 1964; Clawson, 1980).

In his plea for worker–management cooperation under the banner of scientific management, Brandeis foreshadowed events to come. At the time, neither Taylor nor the AFL was ready for it. But the emphasis on cooperation struck one very sensitive chord in the Taylor system. The pretention that rates were set scientifically was weakly founded, a fact that Taylor sometimes admitted, but more as a consequence of imperfections than of principle. Yet his position was severely undermined by the presentation of the Hoxie report of 1915, published shortly after Taylor's death. This report, again the result of federal initiative and sponsoring and named after the president of the investigating committee, summed up the gaps between the pure system and its practical state.

The most striking feature of the survey was the early discovery that there was nowhere any uniformity in the application of scientific management, including the order of installation, the manner in which the techniques were used, and the completeness of the systems. There existed little parallel between the writings of the industrial engineers and the use of their methods in the factory.... The report revealed that a great many discrepancies existed in the use of functional foremanship, "scientific selection of the worker," discipline and other facets of the program. But the most glaring variations and deficiencies were found in the application of time study and task-setting, the keystones of Taylor's system. (Nadworny, 1955: 91)

The glaring shortcomings and their designation as "keystones" fit neatly in the AFL kit. The AFL had been careful to evade infringements on managerial prerogatives. But exactly the points it had singled out as the heart of the Taylor system and at which it wanted to strike, rates and time studies, now had been coined as the weakest links in the Taylorist chain. It looked as if it was harvest time for the AFL. But the war, and its preparations, changed everything and everybody.

World War I and After

After Taylor's death the revisionist element among the Taylor engineers became stronger. Consensus was stressed, meaning the possibility of fruitful cooperation between efficiency engineers and organized labor (Nadworny, 1955: 101ff.; Stark, 1980: 106). This was not meant as an attack on professionalism. With Brandeis, people like Morris L. Cooke and Robert G. Valentine were convinced of professionalism and its blessings. Theirs, however, was a concept of professionalism that allowed for a distinction between the technical and the social organization of the workshop on the one hand and between the relative autonomy of production and that of recruitment, selection, and career opportunities on the other hand. In due time, the Taylor society moved away from the purely engineering method to the method of the personnel manager (Jacoby, 1985).

Since Taylor never presented a "psychology" of the worker but only a method of the "one best way" of getting things done, the emphasis on newer professions and their "methods" struck at the ideological core of the engineering profession. America's preparation for and its entrance into the First World War in 1917 gave a boost to the new professionals of personnel work and to forms of cooperation between the Taylor engineers and the AFL unions. Personnel professionals, engineers, and unions were assembled in the National War Labor Board. The war effort systemized the movement toward a standardization of skills to an unprecedented degree. These were the first grand years of the "grading" and "testing" of people, recruits, and personnel alike. The effort to standardize the labor process further, and thus to contribute to the larger output the war necessitated, constituted a second branch of government activity (Noble, 1977). A third branch consisted of the employment relation: recognition of the right to join unions, collective bargaining, installation of grievance procedures, enforcement of industrywide standards for wages and working conditions, and creation of personnel departments for the control and administration of hiring, firing, and discipline (Jacoby, 1985: 137–147).

During the twenties, the personnel movement continued, although much of the terrain it had conquered at the expense of the foreman proved a very temporary affair, due to wartime exigencies and labor shortages more than to converts in the ranks of management and employers. The creed of professionalism suffered, expressed especially in the statements of the new American Management Association, the minority opinion of people like Cooke notwithstanding. Despite the drawback, especially in regard to the autonomy of the personnel department relative to the foreman's discretionary powers, personnel work was there to stay (Slichter, 1929; Jacoby, 1985: ch. 6). The unions, also, soon lost the gains made during the war, a result of both the employer's initiative of the "American Plan" of the twenties and of the combined forces of the governmental retreat from the employment relation and the renewed hostility of the courts.

The major continuity of the war developments into the twenties was the sustenance and even extension of the relationship between the AFL and the Taylor engineers. The concept of efficiency times consensus, prepared by Brandeis and the revisionist Taylor engineers, was now embraced by both groups (Haber, 1964: 149ff.). The AFL was out to prove its loyalty to "efficiency," the engineer to "consensus." The cooperation materialized at the Baltimore & Ohio Railroad (B&O), in the clothing industry, at the Naumkeag textile mill, and in the northeastern printing industry (Nadworny, 1955: 123ff.). The model established seemed simple enough: rates and timing were joint products of engineers and unions; strife was to be resolved through grievance machinery. On their side, unions like the Amalgamated Clothing Workers of

America and the International Printing Pressmen erected their own bureaus for cost-reduction studies and engineering problems. Even the International Association of Machinists applauded the B&O arrangement, on the proviso that the name "scientific management" was not mentioned (Nadworny, 1955: 125). The AFL itself finally hired a former Taylor engineer as its management consultant (Nadworny, 1955: 138).

The AFL action did not get them very far. The Taylor engineers lost their hold on industry. The AFL was unable, and sometimes unwilling, to adapt its strategies to a more industrial recruitment base and thus stayed outside the growth industries like automobiles, electrical appliances, rubber, oil, steel, and steel alloys. The Taylor society itself developed into a forum for the discussion of industrial democracy, worker–management cooperation, prevention of unemployment through corporate planning of seasonal production, and the like. What kept it together was the bedrock of professionalism, couched in the old conviction of voluntarism: the belief that private and informed action could have prevented much that had gone wrong in American industry and in society at large. One example of the tenacity of voluntarism was the issue of the prevention of unemployment. In a typical figure of speech, the American translation of seasonal unemployment became "structural unemployment." Cyclical unemployment was recognized, but it, unlike the seasonal type, was left out of the plans to combat unemployment.

Many industries, the automobile industry for one, were seasonally very irregular, so the ideas about work sharing, production for stock, or a greater economy in the use of fixed capacity did not fall on barren soil. But it had to be a paying proposition, such that when the twenties turned deflationary and stocks were not so much an asset as a liability, the "prevention of unemployment" was accordingly dismissed (Jacoby, 1985: 202). These, and related, developments soon put the employment stabilization movement off its track. The conviction, nonetheless, that unemployment could be fought by proper use of private means and intelligence was unshaken. In this, corporations, the Taylor society, and the AFL were of one opinion. The AFL feared corporate welfare plans, since they threatened to jeopardize their own resources of assistance and thus mobilization. But it resented as much and for much the same reason, government intervention in the field of assistance, unemployment compensation included. That the shifting and unstable balance of exit and voice indeed had changed, and therewith the relations between economics and voluntarism on one side and politics and regulation on the other side, was beyond the comprehension of these actors and actor groups. It would take the Great Depression to get the message across.

All of this still does not explain the ease with which the AFL adopted the cause of the Taylor engineers during and after the war. Why, as was apparently the case, was there no option but scientific management? The answer, in retrospect, is not that hard to find. At the end of the nineteenth century the AFL could no longer pretend that it played an important role in the training and education of the majority of the skilled. The craft status of the AFL unions was prey to a process of erosion that had started long before the AFL itself had been formed. A craft, in the end, is more than the knowledge and the control of labor processes. It is above all the check on the access to such knowledge and control. A craft, not possessing its own canals or institutions, criteria, and certification of training, is a contradiction in terms. An occupation, calling for skilled knowledge under the control of the public or the employer, is no longer a craft. It is a "skilled occupation." In the disappearance of time-worn forms of apprenticeship, then, we may seek the answer to the question of the swing the AFL made during and after the First World War.

4

STANDARDIZATION II: TRAINING AND EDUCATION

If one were to classify Taylor in the index of occupations, three possibilities stand out. He was an engineer and a management consultant, but in his own view he was above all an industrial educator. He insisted on the use of "object lessons"—as opposed to independent educational and training facilities in the shop—and his functional foremen were above all "teachers." Moreover, he was adamant on the issue of training and developing the workers up to the limits of their physical and intellectual capacities (Taylor, 1903, 1911). At the same time, his vision was limited. He had a distinct social division of labor in mind, with the new immigrants (his "Hungarians") at the bottom. Also, his use of written and detailed instruction cards and the one entry the workers had to make on these cards show that his view of the American worker, though common, was no longer representative. For the new immigrant, his education had nothing to offer. Yet the presence of the new immigrant was one important item on the agenda of educational reform projects of late nineteenth- and twentieth-century America.

It is very difficult to generalize about American education as a whole. Federal regulations are rare, indirect, or motivated by objectives (equal opportunity for one) other than strictly educational ones (Mosher, 1982). The Constitution does not mention education as a federal obligation, and the Tenth Amendment reserves all fields not expressly designated for the federal government for the states. Until recently, however, the states, especially those in the northeastern part of the country, have been only too glad to delegate authority to the cities and their governments (Kirst and Wirt, 1982). This makes for a patchwork of educational provisions concerning curricula, financial and taxing regulations, certifications, school types, and so on. The differences pertain not merely to the distinction between North and South

(Judd, 1934) but also to many distinctions within these areas. For practical reasons we limit our discussion to the northeastern and north central areas.

As a point of departure for our discussion we choose the so-called Gary schools, the educational experiment started in the early twentieth century in Gary, Indiana. Gary was a boom town. It had been named after the Indiana-born U.S. Steel president, Judge Gary, who in his own way, from farm boy to one of the mightiest men of the country, personified the great American dream. The town was founded by U.S. Steel in 1906 as the site necessitated by the new plant of the company. Yet it grew largely on its own. For a few hundred skilled workers and officials, the company built houses; for the far more numerous semiskilled and unskilled workers, no provisions had been made. For a time, the city must have resembled an adequate stage for a John Wayne movie: "a wild and woolly frontier town" (Levine and Levine, 1970: xxvii). But it grew: already in 1909 it counted 12,000 inhabitants and had shaken off its roughest past. In 1914 more than 30,000 people inhabited Gary, and it was to continue growing, if only against the background of the 140,000 employment capacity of the steel plants in its vicinity. The foreign population, crowded together in the southern part of the city, comprised more than thirty nationalities in the early years and accounted for roughly half of the total population (Bourne, 1916: 3–5, 7).

Planning, organizing, and running a school under such circumstances in an extraordinary venture. Yet Gary was by no means exceptional. Many northeastern and midwestern cities faced comparable difficulties and uncertainties, associated with large and relatively unpredictable new enrollments and a vexing variety in background, cultures, and languages of the students. It may be added that U.S. Steel had no special urge to finance and influence the schools; in this respect Gary was no company town. The organization of the schools became the task of another Indiana farm boy: William Wirt. He promised the city administration to produce more classes at lower cost, to renew the curriculum, and to transform the school into a major community institution. In practice there was an effective use of school facilities (buildings, libraries, classrooms, etc.) by the students and the community at large; integration of classical, vocational, and recreational activities; a longer school day and school period (ten months, five days a week, eight hours a day); coeducation; and the opening up of the school for evening and summer classes. Wirt lived up to his promises, so much so that philosopher–pedagogue John Dewey became one of the advocates of the Gary schools, along with many other progressives (Bourne, 1916: 144). Very soon, larger and smaller cities, from Chicago to Winnetka, Illinois, adopted parts or the whole of the Gary system (Bourne, 1916: lix–lx). New York, on the eve of America's entry into the First World War, announced plans to introduce it as well.

The Wirt ideal was the "complete" school, encompassing all classes from kindergarten through high school. Already by 1915 three-quarters of the schoolchildren of Gary were in a complete school (Bourne, 1916: 18). Practically from scratch, the Gary experiment had proven that it was possible to create a going school organization in a few years, an organization able to accommodate, at the end of 1914, some 5,000 students. Why was it so attractive? How did it manage to keep the truancy figures, even granted the fact that U.S. Steel refused to employ anyone under sixteen years of age, so low (Bourne, 1916: 156)?

There may have been economic reasons for the attractiveness of the Gary schools. Due to the efficient use of buildings and other facilities, the number of pupils per square foot—the result of an ingenious rotation scheme—was large, and so the costs per pupil compared favorably to those in other cities. Also, the system was flexible. By stretching the school day and year and by elaborating the rotation orders, the number of pupils it accommodated could be increased without calling immediately for new buildings and facilities. But this is not all. What made the Gary schools a winner in the eyes of progressives like Bourne and Dewey was the new curriculum and educational practices these schools embodied.

The enthusiasm of people such as Dewey and Bourne for the Gary schools rested on two considerations. One was that these schools promised adequate compensation for the losses in education that the decay of apprenticeship had brought about. The effects of learning by doing, the intermingling of education and practice, had been assets of the apprenticeship system that the Gary schools were to recoup. The practical methods employed in the Gary schools had been designed to avoid the dangers of rote learning and the isolated treatment of the three Rs. Also, the curriculum provided for much more than mere reading, writing, and arithmetic. The connection with practice was established, already at the level of the common school, by means of a junior "helper system," while high school students functioned as assistants and integrated many vocational elements in their regular studies. The tasks performed in the classes concerned, for instance, plumbing and other maintenance and repair jobs. Instructed by a skilled tradesman, the job created opportunities for writing (e.g., the names of the materials used), administration (e.g., registration of stocks, time), natural sciences (e.g., teachings on gravitation, friction), and so on. The same system functioned in the subjects of home economics. For the students the setup promised the visibility and usefulness of their activities; for the teachers the system promised attentive students and, in view of the wide latitude the system allowed to student initiative, only a minimal disciplinary effort.

A second consideration was the socializing effect and intent of the Gary schools. The school competed with the parents and "the street" in capturing the time, imagination, and environment of the child. It would set the example in cooperation, social relations, civic behavior, and order. The family, especially the poorer family of foreign origin, could no longer be entrusted with the socialization of its children. Poverty, working parents, crowded and low-quality housing, and the separation of work and living had created a situation in which many parents were unable to prepare their children for the job demands, civic standards, propriety, and discipline needed in industrial and urban society. In fact, many school reformers were convinced that the alternative was not between the family and the school but between the street and the school. There, the choice, they assumed, was not hard, especially when, as in the Gary schools, the school had become a community on its own.

The Gary schools were innovative. Education was departmentalized, such that the pupils moved from classroom to classroom and from instructor to instructor, creating optimal opportunities for the use of school facilities and instructors' expertise. Depending on the tasks of a class, subjects could and would be coordinated (e.g., trade education, English, and natural science). Desks, tables, and chairs could be moved about, so that the spatial organization of the class might be adapted to the task at hand (even in the thirties in many schools desks and so on were still fixtures; see Zilversmit, 1976). Collective meetings were scheduled once a day. Each class had its own mentor, guaranteeing that departmentalization would not develop into a loss of group cohesion. Mentors also were to keep in touch with the parents of the pupils. Small wonder, then, that professional pedagogues found much to their liking in these schools.

The professional applause was not unanimous. Professionalism in education was far from a united movement. Although the integration of vocational subjects in the curriculum stood in high professional esteem, the administrative difficulties the Gary schools demonstrated were seen as a serious drawback of the system. Yet control and administration were at least as pressing professional concerns as the contents and construction of curricula. The praise of the pedagogues was accompanied by the criticism of reform-minded administrators. In a 1918 report on the Gary schools by the New York-based and Rockefeller-funded General Education Board (Flexner and Bachman, 1918) many points of critique are enumerated, with the administrative deficiencies as their common denominator. The Gary schools needed more, and not less as was the case, record keeping as to the precise effects of its innovations. Too often the substandard pupil could go about unnoticed, because the data on exact performance were lacking. Pupils, by devising their own tracking emphases within the curriculum, could practically avoid subjects they felt no inclination toward. The junior helper system and the method of assistants mixed classes and grades, without administering the consequences of these methods. What the Gary schools lacked, apparently, was a professional, administrative apparatus. The criticism was timely, but it is interesting to see it pointed at the Gary schools, for the boards of these schools were far from the ward-controlled bodies that were the usual targets of administrative critique. Be that as it may, the interests of the administrators and those of the pedagogues were diverging. The latter wanted a curriculum inviting the use of all abilities and aptitudes of the child; the former wanted a curriculum easing the transition from school to the world of the occupation. Whereas the pedagogues stimulated individual leeway, the administrators stressed comparability of results and, thus, degrees of uniformity (Tyack, 1974: 196–197).

The reasons the parents in Gary left no record of protest, while in New York parents successfully fought against the introduction of the Gary experiment, must be seen in this same context. The grading and tracking fad of the administrative reformers had not gained the upper hand in Gary, but it was already in force in New York. Introduction of the Gary type of education in New York would simply have meant the furthering of special tracks for vocationally classified students—especially the children of the new immigrants. "Garyizing" was accordingly resented, for it was perceived as an open attempt to block the chances of social and occupational mobility of immigrant children. Riots occurred in New York in late 1917. A journalist wrote: "One mother cried out from the platform against the Gary system, shouting: 'We want our kinder to learn mit der book, der paper und der pensil . . . and not mit der sewing and der shop' " (quoted in Levine and Levine, 1970: xlii; on the protest against Gary schools, see also Callahan, 1962). Faithfully, the journalist also put another complaint on record: "Dey are unser kinder, not theirs" (Levine and Levine, 1970: xlii).

The New York parents identified two vital points: the ease with which the Gary system could be subordinated to the demands of preparing for a wide array of strictly manual occupations and the danger the schools constituted for the authority of the family. Modernization of education seemed hardly more to them than the adaptation of the schools to a changed labor market; Americanization was a threat to the unity of the family, including its educational role and the rank of education in the family's scale of values (Tyack, 1974: 248–255). The fight over the curriculum in New York became fused with the issue of control and the influence of bossist politics. The Democratic party in New York, controlled by Tammany Hall bosses, carried the elections for a new mayor in 1917. One of its planks was explicitly directed against the Gary schools. Predictably, the new mayor prevented any action along "Garyizing" lines. The New York parents had won the battle.

They lost the war, however. In the same year, 1917, Congress passed the Smith–Hughes Act, granting federal money for state and city initiatives in the field of vocational education. By that time all of the major industrial states already had invested in vocational education. Gary had been no exception; on the whole, the fight against the Gary system amounted to no more than occupying a small island, leaving the mainland intact. New York suffered, from the point of view of the administrators, a temporary setback. The movement toward expert control, grading, tracking, and testing, in combination with the adaptation of the schools to vocationalism, continued unabated. The boost the First World War and its aftermath gave to the administrators more than offset the very minor defeat in the case of "Garyizing" the New York schools. The professionalization and bureaucratization of control were successful (Tyack, 1972, 1974; Bowles and Gintis, 1976).

Ward control of schools was progressively diminished; school boards became smaller, and the presence of manual workers on the boards was virtually nullified. This situation enabled the administrators all the required opportunities for classification. The introduction of group tests, meant to screen aptitudes and competencies of pupils, led swiftly to the establishment of standards and the grouping of pupils as below, on, or above standard. Only for the above-standard pupils did the high school remain the preparatory school it had once been, as it did for the roughly 10 percent of the pupils in private high schools (Holton, 1982: 1687–1688). For the remainder of the pupils high school functioned as a terminal school or even as a waiting room, preceding manual and lower clerical employment. The testing practice opened the avenue of separating and grouping the pupils thus identified and of advising parents about vocational opportunities and appropriate learning tracks for their children.

Despite these developments, the comprehensive high school as such was under no attack; the once-popular ideas of creating independent vocational schools, apart from the high school, did not materialize other than as places for the dropouts and misfits of the regular high school. The debate about vocationalism in the United States and the associated development toward tracking and grouping of distinct sets of pupils reflect the rise of the high school as a mass institution (Jacoby, 1985: 70; Tyack, 1974: 180). They do not, however, testify to the victory of vocational over general education. In that sense, the apprenticeship system had no heirs.

BREAKDOWN OF THE APPRENTICESHIP SYSTEM

The breakdown of the apprenticeship system was accompanied by the rise of the problem of child labor (Douglas, 1921: 55ff.). In a craft setting the work of children and apprenticeship are synonymous; as soon as child labor is perceived as a "problem," a public issue, one may infer that the position of power of the crafts has eroded and that the education of the children will become a disputed matter. In early nineteenth-century America the first signs of child labor, new educational initiatives, and craft reactions became visible in those states where industrial methods of production were advancing. The textile industry took the lead in the widespread employment of children. Provisions for the education of children came about in the same context of industrialization and urbanization, although the early extension of education in rural areas remains an important development in its own right. For the very young children, the day school was erected, filling the gap of the cultural training the children no longer received from the employer. Sunday schools show a comparable pattern: the growth of Sunday schools correlates strongly with the spread of industrialism; these schools, catering like the day schools mainly to the children of the poor, teach the children the basics of the three Rs, as well as the virtues of obedience, self-discipline, and propriety (Douglas, 1921: 56; Boyer, 1978: 34ff.), the same virtues, expressed with the same motives, that the reform educators and administrators stressed in the period around the turn of the century.

Around 1850 in the centers of the textile industry (in Massachusetts, Connecticut, and Rhode Island) almost half of the work force consisted of children under sixteen years of age. In part, no doubt, this is one consequence of the difficulties employers encountered in recruiting unskilled labor. Yet more and more the presence of totally uneducated youth was seen as an abuse. Education ranks high in the United States; its importance was uncontested once the right of suffrage had been granted to the major portions of the white male population (Rubinson, 1986: 536). Class antagonisms were to erupt from time to time over the control of the schools but not, however, over the school itself. Estimates are that, if one corrects the figures for the black population in the United States (who often were excluded by law from education; Sowell, 1978: 16–19), already by the 1830s the American was on average the most educated person in the world (Rosenberg, 1972: 35). Public funding for public schools dates from the first half of the nineteenth century. In view of expanding industry and expanding urbanism, education was put forward as one instrument to forestall their centrifugal tendencies.

Americanization, in the early nineteenth century, clad in the codes of the rural life-style and mores, gave the first impulse to the propagation and consolidation of public education. Its timing depended on the first manifestations of modern industry, its motives, and its force derived from worries about the moral fiber of a fast-changing society. Culturally, many schools impressed on their pupils the norms of hierarchy and deference that nineteenth-century Americans associated with wage labor (Rodgers, 1978). But the aims of the schools were much broader than the still limited industrial field of employment. The growth of the cities and the moral dangers they presented, the imminent danger of Catholic hegemony in the cities due to the Irish and German predominance in immigration, the threat of disorder the city poor evoked, and the unchecked movement to the West contributed to the view that education was vital in preserving the order of the country. Vocationally, on the other hand, the schools had very little to offer: rote learning was the standard, and the world of educational contents differed sharply from the everyday world of home and occupation.

During the eighties of the previous century the vocational irrelevance of the schools became a public issue in its own right. America was on its way to becoming the first among the industrialized nations. Wage labor slowly was recognized as the main station of the large majority of the population. Social mobility, accordingly, had to be promoted within the confines of a wage-laboring status, not as an escape from such status. The schools, moreover, were well on their way to becoming the foremost socializing institutions for children, since, along with the advent of wage labor and the separation of work and home, the socializing competence and opportunities of the family were diminishing. The relation of the school to the labor market, no longer disputed as the main link between the worker—both present and future— and the occupations, was ripe for scrutiny, change, and adaptation.

The schools were taken to task for their apparent incapacity to train the young for useful employment or even to capture their imagination. The plea for more actualized and realistic education was widespread. Even those revolting against the spread of industrialism deplored the distance of the schools from the world of work. Initiatives with industrial arts education (Lux, 1982; Cremin, 1961; Rodgers, 1978: 76ff.) led to the establishment of a series of private and public manual training schools, next to the introduction of arts and crafts in high schools and elementary schools. By 1890 manual training could be found in thirty-six cities, including the largest in the country, in fifteen states (Cremin, 1961: 32–33). Although heavily promoted and often sponsored by businessmen, its results were meager.

Criticism soon abounded. Employers had little use for trainees in the older crafts, for they were often the very crafts that still controlled employment by union regulations on apprenticeship. Also, industrial arts tended to strengthen the unity of conception and execution in its programs (Jacoby, 1985: 67), bolstering the idea of independence rather than preparing for wage dependency. The students, moreover, seemed unimpressed by the assumed dignifying qualities of manual work; their interests were more in the realm of clerical and technical occupations, the professions and supervising work included (Cremin, 1961: 32–33). If vocational education was to stand a chance it would have to shed the worn-out pretense of culture and become instead a straightforward preparation for industrial employment opportunities. Schools to that effect existed, one example being the New York Trades School of 1881. There the object was more tuned to the demands of modern industrial employment and consisted of "a combination of technical and trade instruction specifically designed to produce qualified journeymen" (Cremin, 1961: 35). In time, some of the manual training schools dropped their cultural ambitions and adopted the pure and simple trade orientation. Yet the struggle between practical expediency and cultural obligation lingered on as one divisive issue within the vocationalist reform movement.

The problem of vocational education came to a head in the second half of the nineties. The economic tide picked up; industry grew at a very fast rate and with it the demand for labor. The unions profited from the situation: it was, in fact, the last time they gained in the field of apprenticeship regulation. For many trades—like textile, leather, clothing, wood, iron and steel, office and sewing machines, tobacco, and rubber—nonetheless, apprenticeships were nonexistent or simply extinct (Nelson, 1975: 96; Douglas, 1921: 114ff.). In newer industries, like the automobile sector, apprenticeships were also relatively unimportant. Many of these industries thrived and were in the vanguard in the use of industrial methods of production. The demand for skilled labor grew accordingly. Leaving the mushrooming white-collar jobs and their training requirements apart, one may think, on the plane of skilled work, of a new demand for tool-and-die makers, repair and maintenance personnel, some machine feeders, quality controllers, and so on. On the plane of semiskilled work the obvious reference is to the machine tender, member of a fast-growing occupational group, found in an ever-widening circle of industries. The manual training and trade schools were as yet unable to satisfy the demands of industry for skilled and semiskilled workers. Indeed, lack of clarity about the level of skill they were preparing for, skilled workers or "journeymen," was common. New initiatives were imperative. The larger corporations started their own schools for training the skilled worker. In steel, electrical appliances, and oil, for instance, private companies established corporate schools. The National Association of Manufacturers (NAM), well aware that company schools were simply beyond the reach of many of the smaller companies, pushed the trade school, also mainly catering to skilled occupations. In part, the limitation to the skilled was an answer to the islands of control and the claim as such on the skilled worker of the AFL unions. It was also the consequence of employment practices of the companies involved.

The economic risks of private company or trade schools are high. Unless the training is completely company idiosyncratic, the danger is real that the fruits of the training investment will be harvested elsewhere. The same holds for trade education; there, the problem is that many trade skills cut across the lines of the industries sponsoring and controlling the trade schools. The decisive question thus is how specific the specific training that companies supply can be. It is well known that companies do not want to invest in general occupational training. They would provide it only "if they did not have to pay any of the cost" (Becker, 1964: 188). Now, most training that firms provide is neither completely general nor completely idiosyncratic but somewhere in between. This type of training Becker called "specific": "Training that increases productivity more in firms providing it will be called specific training" (Becker, 1964: 195). Such training entails incurring costs before it engenders higher returns in the shape of income out of enhanced productivity. Who is to pay for the cost, and who is to share in the returns?

There is no general answer to these questions, because everything depends "on the likelihood of labor turnover" (Becker, 1964: 198). With high turnover rates neither employer nor employee will be interested in shouldering the burden of costs, since the time of reaping the results of higher productivity may never come. With low turnover rates some mutual sharing of costs and revenues between employers and employees becomes the most feasible solution. Specific training, the type the corporation and trade schools set out to offer for the prospective skilled worker, would be a paying proposition only insofar as the companies concerned were able to stabilize and predict their employment needs. Yet on the whole, these companies proved incapable of doing so. Even apart from the habituated mode of employers' thinking about labor power as just another commodity, their lack of grip on the market, the influence of the economic cycle, and the swiftly changing technology and methods of production contributed to a continuing unpredictability of employment and, thus, to a swaying curve of labor turnover. The planning of employment, indeed, became a widely discussed topic in the early decades of the twentieth century, but its practical upshot was slight, the short period of the American participation in the First World War excepted.

This situation underscores the fact that privately financed and run educational trade facilities were more an answer to an emergency than a structural solution to the problem of vocationally relevant schools. Labor turnover, moreover, was not the only problem in devising vocationally effective learning tracks. The discussion on labor turnover and its effect on the viability of specific training presupposes that it is economically possible to isolate the costs of training and the resulting changes in productivity. But in many cases of on-the-job-training, costs and results cannot be isolated at all (Eckaus, 1963). First, much training is part of one or several jobs and their respective productivities and cannot be transferred to specialized training institutions. The possibility of measuring costs, independent of productivity, is thereby short-circuited. But not only are costs difficult to measure; productivity behaves likewise. The major sociological flaw in the specific training argument presented above is the suggestion that productivity is measurable per individual employee. But industrial methods of production and organization often exclude such measurement. The tendency of mechanized industry and organic methods of organization is to shift the measurement of productivity from the individual to the organizational unit. What we are discussing, in the end, is not an occupational series of labor markets but the emergence, and in fact the very likelihood, of the internal labor market (Marsden, 1986, ch. 7).

The main consequence of the shift to a more collective unit of productivity measurement is that training requirements and skill come to inhere in the job rather than in the employee. The employer, thus, does not really have the choice between training and not training, since it is the job that defines the training, not the other way around; the real choice is in the recruitment and ultimate selection of those that will be trained and those that won't be. Here, but for very different reasons, turnover and its predictability turn up anew as decisive. The main, negative, indicator for the predictability of turnover for several decades has been the country of origin and, thus, the possibility of remigration. Also, the trainability of prospective employees, prepared by publicly funded education and measured by the number of years in school and the type of education received, was bound to become a matter of some substance.

For good reasons, then, the debate on vocationally relevant but publicly funded education was not silenced by the emergence of the private corporation and trade schools. Rather, this debate became ever more intense in the period immediately before and after the turn of the century (Tyack, 1974: 189). In 1907 the many city and state initiatives in the propagation of vocational education came together in the foundation of the National Society for the Promotion of Industrial Education (NSPIE). The main objective was to involve the federal government, next to states and cities, in the campaign for vocational education and in its costs. Both the NAM, the large corporations, and the professional interest groups—educators, welfare workers, and engineers—were represented in its board of directors. The AFL was invited to join in the initiative, and, with some delay, the federation accepted.

The NSPIE proved a very effective lobby. Although its final goal was a federal law and federal funding, it prepared the terrain by pushing state laws. Already by 1910, twenty-nine states had passed laws favoring and financing vocational education. More instructive, possibly, is the fact that when Congress in 1914 nominated the Commission on National Aid to Vocational Education, the majority of its members came from NSPIE (Cremin, 1961: 54–55). The commission worked fast; in the same year it published its findings and recommendations. They included the financing of the educational staff required for vocational (trade, industrial, and agricultural) subjects, assistance in their training, public (but not ward) control of the administration of fundings, and financial state involvement next to the federal commitment. A final recommendation concerned the stipulation that the monies were to go to below-college educational activities.

The federal Smith–Hughes Act of 1917 followed these recommendations almost to the letter. Despite this victory, the impact of the act was limited. The federal Bureau of Education hardly had the organizational and bureaucratic power to push the issue of vocationalism vigorously (Rubinson, 1986: 542). Also, the wish for a stratified system of education, differentiating technical and vocational education from high school education (after the much admired German example), was not honored. Vocational education was integrated into the comprehensive high school, more often than not on a voluntary basis (Taylor, 1982: 2002; Holton, 1982: 1692) and recruiting a limited number of students, seldom surpassing 10 percent of the total (Tyack, 1974: 190). A few hundred independent vocational and technical schools do exist; these schools, located in the larger cities, enroll predominantly those students that dropped out of the regular system (Holton, 1982: 1688). On average, the evaluation of students specializing in vocational subjects is low (Taylor, 1982: 2008; Tyack, 1974: 190). If there was a victory for the vocationalist lobby, then, it was a Pyrrhic one. One of the major stakes, the stratification of the educational system, had been lost. Instead of segregated tracks, additions to existing ones remained the pattern, leaving the popular recruitment base of the high school intact and strengthening the pressures for a longer curriculum. The "ratchet" effect, producing a longer and longer school career, defeated the issue of vocationalism.

Apart from the intrinsic difficulties that beset vocational education, the vocational model the society wanted to promulgate was from the beginning somewhat outdated. In spite of the claims to relevance and actuality, vocationalism did not recognize the changed nature of the factual labor demands of industry. For one thing, the sharp differentiation in skill requirements—separating, for instance, highly trained drafters from machine tenders—was not echoed in the vocational programs. The programs all had a distinct bias toward the promotion of skill and dexterity rather than, for instance, physical endurance. Second, as Paul Douglas observed at an early date (1921: 123ff.), the education the large majority of workers needed had become at once broader and narrower—narrower in that training in specific processes did not require large amounts of time or intricate facilities. Many jobs could be learned in a few days or weeks, and the shop was often a more effective place of instruction than the school. On the other hand, the education had to be broader: "in that it should include more training in industrial life, in hygiene, civics, and so forth" (Douglas, 1921: 123ff.).

The flaws of the vocational initiative were, apparently, twofold. Propelled by the shortage of skilled labor, brought about by the breakdown of the apprenticeship system and by the sheer growth and mechanization of American industry, the vocational reform movement failed to take notice of the industrial labor force below the skilled level. Yet as the steel experience had demonstrated, the quantitative development of the skill groups showed a more than proportionate rise in the share of the semiskilled and a relative decline in the share of the skilled and unskilled. A standardization of skills was one necessity of the times, but the actual vocational projects were far too limited in outlook to achieve the standardization of qualifications. In the end, the comprehensive high school, by embodying the value of trainability as such, performed better. Also, the industrial interests in the NSPIE overplayed their hand. The grip of industry on public education was there, but it did not displace the fundamental goal of Americanization, the training in "industrial life, hygiene, civics, and so forth." This aspect of education was largely beyond the perspective of the society; its representative members, like Taylor, tended to equate education and production (Collins, 1979: 113). The more important tasks, however, were in the realm of integrating millions of immigrants and their children not just in American factories but above all in the shaky order of American life. Apprenticeships socialized the young and educated for a vocation in one and the same movement. This unity could not be recaptured through vocational education. The victory of the comprehensive high school over the differentiated vocational school testified to the predominance of the socializing function of the schools, as did the transformation of the high school into junior and senior departments (King, 1972; Holton, 1982). The same predominance was echoed in the low status of the vocational subjects—and their students—in the overall curriculum of the high school.

THE AFL

The sudden upsurge in youth labor in the nineteenth century worried the established crafts. The early unions were not in the last instance a response to the introduction of factory methods of production and the competition from youth labor. One attempt the unions made to forestall the threat of their low-cost and malleable competitors was to renew the regulations of the apprenticeship system (Douglas, 1921: 62ff.). Both by law and on their own, the unions tried to curb the decay of apprenticeship. In some trades, such as metal and printing, the unions held out for some time. On the whole, however, they did not cover much ground. The number of apprenticeships declined in relative numbers in the second half of the nineteenth century. In 1860 there was a ratio of one apprentice to thirty-three workers; in 1880 the ratio was one to eighty-seven; in 1890, one to sixty-two; in 1900, one to eighty-eight; and in 1910, one to ninety-eight (Douglas, 1921: 74).

On public elementary education and later on the public high school, the position of the unions generally has been in the affirmative. Sometimes there were qualms about the implied tax burden of public education, but the preference for public over private schools was never in danger (Rubinson, 1986). Vocational education posed a more puzzling problem. The preference for publicly funded and controlled education again was strong (Cremin, 1961: 40–41), but the real problem was the transplantation of the codes of apprenticeship to the new vocational endeavor. When the NAM in 1903 started its antiunion campaign, emphasizing both the open shop and the case of vocational education, it found the AFL empty handed. The federation simply had no point of view to defend on vocationalism. In 1907, when the NSPIE started, the situation was no different. The invitation to join in the activities of the NSPIE did lead, however, to the formation of an educational committee that, with several delays, published its findings in 1910. It was a remarkable report. It contained the explicit condemnation of the old-time apprenticeship as wasteful, inefficient, and exploitative (Cremin, 1961: 40–41). The report, adopted by the federation in 1911, supported vocational education as a publicly controlled addition to general education. Separate trade schools were advocated but with the proviso that half of the education in these schools had to be general. The insistence on learning the "whole" trade, including civic and social skills, was maintained in the report, as was the refusal of education geared to the preparation for fragmented labor (Douglas, 1921: 320–321). Possibly in an attempt to separate the skilled worker from his lower level colleagues, the report stressed the usefulness of vocational guidance and thus, albeit only implicit, some form of tracking. The report made the AFL more than ripe for cooperation with the society. Predictably, the acceptation of the 1914 NSPIE report created no big problem for the AFL; nor did the Smith–Hughes Act. In fact, the main troubles confronting the AFL in this period, concerning vocational education, stemmed from the adamant and fluctuating position of the NAM. The NSPIE stepped in to resolve the antagonism of the two organizations and proved its worth by securing the support of both the AFL and the NAM for the federal act of 1917.

The rapprochement of the AFL and the Taylor engineers, thus, was no isolated affair. It was accompanied by a less publicized but at least as drastic change in the field of vocational education. The recognition in 1910 that the old apprenticeship system was dead was more than recognition of a fact. It meant that the AFL no longer sought to revive union regulation of contents, duration, and control of training for skills. In its proposals it was not always clear which roles the unions, the employers, and the "public" were to play, but the fact that vocational education was pushed as an affair of these groups remains significant all the same. By rejecting education preparing for fragmented work, however, the AFL once again denied the reality of unskilled and semiskilled work. In that respect it shared the shortsightedness of the large majority of the vocational plans for reforming education. The decisive fact is that the dearth of skilled labor, owing its very existence to the new realities of unskilled and semiskilled work, found a better expression in the new status of the high school as a terminal station than in all of the vocational options combined.

5

A MARKET FOR MIGRANTS

There is a curious and often elusive interplay between the ascendancy of the professional and the presence of the 'new' immigrant. The new immigrant, around the turn of the century, overshadowed both the attack on the spoils system and bossist politics and the rise of professionalism in education and elsewhere. The new immigrant, to be sure, is not a person or a member of a group. Above all, the new immigrant is the product of the social and political response to the numerical rise of the wage-dependent population, together with its recomposition, highlighting the advance of the semiskilled and the new realities of unskilled work. Italians, Hungarians, and so forth were not the original identities of the immigrants around the turn of the century. They were administrative designations, applied to immigrants on entering the country. Also, they were used as labels that employers—and unions—attached to groups of workers as expressions of crudely defined working habits, mobility behavior, ability to endure harsh working conditions, and potential skill or the lack of it. Generally, the new immigrants were perceived as a danger to the established order of society. Generally, again, the educational reforms were directed at their children, whereas the political reforms, the change of school boards included, were directed at the adult new immigrants (Tyack, 1974). Educational politics, the growing amount of regulations concerning the right to vote of the late nineteenth and early twentieth centuries (Piven and Cloward 1988), and the civil service reforms of the same period—that is, the attacks on the spoils system and bossist politics—were variations on the theme of the new immigrant. Even the beginning growth of administratively independent suburbs, undermining the fiscal base of cities and thus the sheer possibility of rewarding spoils, may be seen in the same light (Gordon, 1978; Ashton, 1978: 69; Markusen, 1978: 101).

There were undoubtedly real distinctions between the immigrants from North and West Europe and those from South, East, and Central Europe. But they were hardly along the polarized lines of old and new. The distinctions, in fact, were not due to cultures, religions, nationalities, or even skills so much as to the development of the labor market and the employment relationship: the emergence of a dual and internally stratified labor market (Markusen, 1978). The dualization was portrayed in polarities like skilled/ unskilled, native/foreign, and Protestant/Catholic. Employers and unions, in their attempts to control education, echoed these polarities, although the unions played less on the Catholic theme—the Germans, many of them Catholics, dominated some skilled trades and their unions. Yet the major development was the rise of the semiskilled, and precisely their presence was glossed over in the crude distinctions of the era. This was not a specifically American bias; in the United Kingdom in the late nineteenth century, the presence of the semiskilled was obscured as well by the ruling bifurcation in skilled and unskilled or artisans and laborers (Hobsbawm, 1964: 182–183). Specific to the United States was the fact that the old polarity, although hardly reflecting the reality of the machine era, was hardened and overlaid by nativist antagonism.

The semiskilled, more often than not, were former unskilled workers, and the swelling of their numbers required that the ranks of the unskilled were constantly replenished. Also, the phenomenally high rates of turnover of the unskilled and semiskilled made it all but imperative that the stream of immigration keep flowing. On this point, the unions and the employers followed sharply diverging policies. The unions favored immigration restriction; the employers, on average, did not (Hutchinson, 1981: 492–504). Underlying it all was the fact that the need for unskilled workers declined relatively, though definitely not in absolute numbers, after the turn of the century, whereas the need for semiskilled workers grew, absolutely and proportionally.

On two accounts it proved difficult to freeze the new immigrant permanently into unskilled stations, although the very designation "new" was a major step in that direction. The new immigrants were politically not without power. Literacy tests; the shift of the task of voter registration from the city administration to the prospective voter; the sharpened administration of the residency requirements of voting, combined with the assumption of this task by the city administration instead of the city bosses; gerrymandering; and the slow but secure dismantling of the spoils system indeed did reduce workers' turnout of the vote, particularly of the more recent immigrants (Piven and Cloward, 1988). But the process took time, and its results were never completely secure. Moreover, it had unintended consequences: the Republicans lost their grip on the industrial city to the advantage of the Democratic party, the embodiment of spoils and bossist politics, epitomized in Tammany Hall. Also, it weakened the ethnic base of politics and, therewith, the malleability of the occupational structure along strictly ethnic lines. The latter development was bolstered also by the simple fact of length of residence: The longer one was in America, the larger the chances that for political purposes ethnic loyalties and strongholds would weaken (Dahl, 1961: 32–51). The victory of the New Deal coalition would be one effect; the rise of the CIO and industrial unionism, another.

Second, the new immigrants soon were, when compared to their presence in the total working population, almost three times overrepresented not just among the unskilled but among the semiskilled as well (Kolko, 1976: 74; Montgomery, 1980: 35; Nelson, 1975: 80; Rosenblum, 1973: 77). This simple fact explains the upsurge of interest in the problem of labor turnover. Unskilled work and high labor turnover are generally seen as related. Generally, the marginal position of the unskilled is reinforced by the recruitment policies of the employer and thus tends to become a self-fulfilling prophecy. Semiskilled work, on the other hand, is the type of work calling for low labor turnover, for its skills are specific for the process of production at hand and its position in the process of production is crucial to the guarantee of precision, reliability, and continuity. No one perceived this better than Henry Ford's lieutenant, James Couzens, who, in devising the $5-a-day project in conjunction with the introduction of the final assembly line, restricted the bonus to working males with dependent families or, at least, dependent wives (Sward, 1948: 47ff.). The intention was clear: Ford had recognized the strategic organizational importance of the semiskilled and had tried to combine this with the available labor supply of new immigrants by influencing their discretionary mobility. The demand for a "family man" correctly dismissed the issue of skill; at the same time it drove a crude wedge into the middle of the new immigrant population, differentiating those who were intent on staying (indicated by the family man with dependent wife and children) from the immigrants bent on remigrating to the country of origin or at least possessing the option of doing so (indicated by the absence of a dependent family). The former were candidates for the Ford bonus plan; the latter were excluded from it.

The assumption, apparently, was that only the family man would try to get a job at the Ford plants, not by subjecting himself to a (actually nonexistent) sophisticated recruitment technique but by a process of self-selection, checked by the investigations of the Ford Sociological Department. But although Ford's plans were the most publicized, they were by no means unique in the field. The attempts at employment stabilization through rewarding length of tenure (as an access to pensions, for instance) were haphazard, grossly incomplete, and selective; also, they were mainly directed at the skilled workers, to the neglect of the semiskilled, and they were out to influence worker behavior more than company performance, for example, by rewarding loyalty to the company instead of emphasizing the stabilization of production or the use of capacity and work force. On the other hand, they were signals that corporate America was beginning to recognize the fact that the employment relationship of the semiskilled posed radically new problems.

IMMIGRANTS: OLD AND NEW

The proportion of native workers in industrial enterprises was remarkably low in late nineteenth-century America. Second-generation immigrants, the sons of Germans and the Irish especially, were far more prominent in the ranks of industrial labor, skilled labor included, than were Americans born from Americans. This corroborates the Habakkuk thesis on the presumable preponderance of unskilled labor in the movement into agriculture in the first half of the century—underscoring its inelastic supply— whereas after the Civil War the skilled workers took the lead, reflecting their escape from the advance of industrialization as well as the by-then higher costs of establishing oneself as an independent farmer (Habakkuk, 1962: 130). Also, it emphasizes the fact, relating in particular to first-generation German immigrants after the forties of the previous century, that the first generation of skilled immigrants tended to stick to trades that were already on the decline, both in the country of origin (this had in fact been one motive in their decision to cross the ocean) and in the United States. These trades, when protected by localized markets and imperfect transportation, held out for some time in the new environment but on average could not promise a viable future for the children of these first-generation immigrants (Griffen, 1977: 195ff.; Laurie, Hershberg, and Alter, 1977: 141ff.; Gutman and Berlin, 1987: 386ff.). Some of the trades were mechanized swiftly: Shoemaking was an example. More generally though, many of these trades were consumer oriented, and with few exceptions the first great wave of industrialization in America concerned the producer goods rather than the articles of final consumption. Philadelphia, Taylor's home town, was a good illustration. Between 1850 and 1880 the economic weight of the city shifted to the producer goods. The shift was accompanied by the rise of wage employment in the economic activities concerned, mirroring the growing use of steam power, the spreading of mechanization, and, by consequence, the increasing capital costs. The financial entry barrier into the industry grew, nullifying for most workers the prospect of economic independence in these trades. In contrast, the amount of required capital hardly changed between 1850 and 1880 in consumer industries (Laurie, Hershberg, and Alter 1977: 129ff.). Both the number and the average size of the iron and steel industry and the machine tool industry rose considerably in the period considered. The increasing number of consumer industries, however, more often than not betrayed the retreat into smaller and smaller companies. Baking, shoes, and, to a smaller extent, clothing, furniture, and meat were examples (Laurie, Hershberg, and Alter; 1977: 131, table 19). In the latter industries, also, we notice the polarization of activity into sweat-shops at the one extreme and the beginning of mechanized factory production at the other extreme.

Employment conditions may be divided in like manner. The workers in the consumer industries on average worked longer hours and for less pay. Also, especially in the smaller companies in the consumer industries, employment was very fluctuating, and this exerted a negative influence on yearly income (Laurie, Hershberg, and Alter, 1977: 131–134). Finally, in this period, just before the deployment of systematic forms of management and the emergence of the Taylor system, the skill requirements in the producer goods industries were maintained or even heightened, and the consumer goods industries, whether mechanizing or not, introduced ever more one-sided forms of a division of labor and, thus, relied on routine qualifications (Laurie, Hershberg, and Alter, 1977: 134–136). The preference of second-generation Germans and Irish for employment in the mushrooming producer industries—at any rate before the advent of mass production and organic methods of production—therefore comes as no surprise.

In the eighties things started to move fast. Industrial productivity, industrial output, and especially productivity per worker accelerated considerably compared to that in the earlier decade (Clough, 1953: 24; North, 1966: 28ff.; Huberman, 1947: 207ff.). Again, during the eighties the emphasis in the sources of immigration started to shift in the direction of East, South, and Central Europe. Also, the size of the stream of immigrants grew. During the eighties the total number immigrating was almost twice as high as during the seventies. Fifteen percent came from Russia, Austria–Hungary, and Italy. It was the start of a gigantic migration stream. One decade later one-third of the total number of immigrants came from these countries, and in the first decade of this century, the decade that recorded the largest influx of immigrants in the history of the United States, this proportion had risen to two out of every three (see Table 5.1).

The large majority of the labor force populating the expanding industry was new. The relative absence of native workers in the industries is remarkable. Computing the data from the 1880 census, one finds that on a national scale native white Americans, representing three-quarters of the total population, accounted for less than one-quarter of the total population, accounted for less than one-quarter of the industrial working class (Gutman and Berlin, 1987: 382ff.). The large majority of the working class at the time was formed by new immigrants, the children of first-generation old immigrants and blacks. They were, compared to their share in the total population, strongly over-represented in the industrial working class. The old working class was, then, not old; there simply was no "old" working class. This fact is of the utmost importance in understanding the labor history of the American working class.

The sharp break in the ideology and practices of working-class organizations, symbolized by the gap between the "republican" ideals of the Knights

Table 5.1
Decennial Immigration to the United States, 1880–1919

	1880-1889	1890-1899	1900-1909	1910-1919
Total, millions	5.2	3.7	8.2	6.3
Percentage of total from				
Ireland	12.8	11.0	4.2	2.6
Germany	27.5	15.7	4.0	2.7
United Kingdom	15.5	8.9	5.7	5.8
Scandinavia	12.7	10.5	5.9	3.8
Canada	9.4	0.1	1.5	11.2
Russia	3.5	12.2	18.3	17.4
Austria-Hungary	6.0	14.5	24.4	18.2
Italy	5.1	16.3	23.5	19.4

Source: A. Kessler-Harris and V. Yans-McLaughlin, "European Immigrant Groups," in Essays and Data on American Ethnic Groups, ed. T. Sowell (N.p., 1978), p. 108, table 1.

and the pragmatism of the AFL, represents more than differing assessments of the times. Involved is, in a very literal sense, a change of actors along with a change of theater. In short, the AFL was not an organization of the old worker but, rather, of his children (Gutman, 1987: 339; Gutman and Berlin, 1987). The eighties did not spell the disappearance of the crafts. They had in fact already been abandoned by the second generation of the old stock. But the threat to the recently established position of the skilled wage worker— typified by the sons of the first-generation Germans and, to a lesser degree, of the Irish, for instance—was only too real, a threat indicated by the introduction of systematic management practices or, more generally, the rise of the organic type of production organization. The rise of organic manufacture was made possible by the new immigrant; his presence was identical with the weakening of the resistance against changes in the methods of production (Rosenblum, 1973: 129ff.). The most tangible effect of the change in the sources of immigration was "not on the manufacturer's choice of technique but on his ability to give effect to his choice" (Habakkuk, 1962: 131; Rosenblum, 1973: 76). No organization understood it better than the newly formed AFL.

The reality of the frontier and the making of an American nation had coincided, fusing the ideas of the possibility of economic exit and the character of American citizenship (Aglietta, 1979: 74). But since the eighties the dream of economic independence was over. The AFL itself was one expression of the acknowledgment of the end of the frontier. Yet insofar as the distinction between "old" and "new" immigration made any sense at all, it was with reference to the "frontier." "Old" was the "republican" dream of economic independence, a dream that still motivated the many artisans arriving in American all through the nineteenth century from the North and the West of Europe. The American promise for them was the escape from a permanent status as wage laborer. "New" were their children, in particular the children of those immigrants arriving after mid-century. "New" were also the many immigrants who had arrived since the eighties, if only because the generalized possibility of viable and economically independent exits within the American economy and its territory had all but vanished. The old immigration from Europe, with the partial exception of the Irish, had been motivated by the commercialization of European agriculture and the consequences of the in-dustrial revolution (Pollard, 1981: 148–153). To a large extent, it was an attempt to escape the European threat to economic independence. The new immigration, using the word *new* in its conventional interpretation, came from countries experiencing, in the late nineteenth century, the spread of commercialized agriculture but without an accompanying upsurge in indus-trialism (Pollard, 1981: 192–207; Rosenblum, 1973: 48ff.). Again, the pattern of migration was—at least initially—predicated on the escape from economic dependence. This time, however, independence was to be achieved in the country of origin, rather than in the United States.

In this interpretation, a real distinction is made between "old" and "new." The difference relates not to motives, skills, cultures, or races but to the situation in the home countries. *Old immigration* comes from countries that offer no real options in the achievement of economic independence; *new immigration* originates in countries that do. It would lead us to suspect a remarkable consistency in the view of wage labor in America as no more than a temporary station in one's life, as an investment for one's independent future. Old immigrants, facing the opportunities of the frontier, were to be settlers; new immigrants, out to resettle in the home country, were to become more like birds of passage. Was this, then, a major difference: resident birds or birds of passage?

In an inverted sense, this difference between "old" and "new" did indeed strike a chord in the public response to immigration and its changes around the turn of the century. Old and sedentary habits were identified, as were new habits and habits keyed to a temporary job and sojourn. In itself, the distinction is harmless and may serve to identify changing emphases in the complex specter of reasons for migration. The use to which it was put, however, was not so innocuous. The distinction got overlaid with nativist characterizations, and "new" was taken to mean both the unwillingness and the incapacity to assimilate in the life, culture, and institutions of America. The unwillingness was measured by the rates of return of the new immigrants, by their age and sex composition, and by the applications for naturalization. The incapacity was measured by a confused hodge-podge of racial and cultural characterizations.

"Old" and "new" do not relate to the date of arrival. The peak of Nordic immigration, the Norwegians included, to the United States, for instance, occurred in the eighties and later decades (Norman, 1979: 51, table 1; Kessler-Harris and Yans-McLaughlin, 1978). Yet these immigrants were designated as "old." The Italians, on the other hand, independent of date of arrival or original location in the North of South of Italy, were definitely "new." The temporal dimension, implied in the designations of "old" and "new," was but a thinly veiled disguise for a much more vehement racial classification.

Two important reports, the first published in 1910 (the Dillingham report), the second in 1923 (the Laughlin report), are sad witnesses to scientific abuse, instrumental to the derogation of the new immigrant. The Dillingham report was the outgrowth of an attempt to introduce the literacy test for immigrants. The ruling assumption was that the new immigrants were far more illiterate than the average native American and, also, that they would show a poor educational record. This, in the end, was the basis for the idea of a literacy test to promote selective curtailment of immigration. The findings, however, were unsettling. A 1909 investigation, conducted independently of the committee's research, had indicated that illiteracy was more widespread among native children than among the children of the new immigrants. The same investigation, in parentheses, proved that girls performed better than boys in the schools (Tyack, 1974: 200–201). The committee's experts came to the staggering conclusion that length of residence was a far better indicator of the ability to speak English than country of origin. They also found that the performance of new immigrant children in schools was comparable to that of the children of native parentage and of old immigrant stock. The differences in performance within any group, on the other hand, were large, suggesting that "the quality of the schools and the social environment were more significant variables than parentage" (Handlin, 1957: 98). None of this, however, influenced the committee's conclusions. They simply stated that the "high rate of illiteracy" among the new immigrants was caused by "inherent racial tendencies." If the phenomenon does not exist, the committee must have thought, all the more reason to stick to the ultimate cause: race. Nor was the committee alone in the idea. Apart from the wide publicity the Dillingham report received, it did also influence the 1917 decision of the Congress—passed over a veto of President Wilson—to introduce the literacy test in immigration. One wonders whether the committee was really surprised when the application of the literacy test revealed that it did not discriminate between immigrants of old and new stock (Gordon, 1964: 102).

The failure of the literacy test to produce the desired results in curbing the new immigration gave a new impetus to initiatives to reach the goal by other means. Again, just before the temporary expedient of the 1921 immigration restriction law, an inquiry was set up to undergird the inferiority of the new immigrant. This time the demand was more explicit. Harry Laughlin was requested to study the relationship between biology, immigration, and social degeneracy (Handlin, 1957: 104ff.). So he did. Again, the methods used were grossly inadequate, the categories prejudiced, the indicators suggestive, and the data base highly suspect. But even granted these distortions, the results did not fit the assumptions. The combined index of social adequacy (consolidating the findings on feeblemindedness, insanity, crime, epilepsy, tuberculosis, and dependency) proved nothing. The Swiss, to be sure, were adequate, but so were the people from Austria–Hungary and Rumania, more so in fact than the Germans, the English, and the Scandinavians (Handlin, 1957: 107–109). All the same, Laughlin concluded that "making all logical allowances for environmental conditions, which may be unfavorable to the immigrant, the recent immigrants as a whole, present a higher percentage of inborn socially inadequate qualities than do the older stocks" (quoted in Handlin, 1957: 105).

The 1924 Immigration Act faithfully echoed these biases. A national quota system was to guide admission to the United States. Section 11a of the act dictated that the national quotas were to be 2 percent of the 1890 population of a given nationality group in the United States. This clause contained the verdict: the greater migration from East, Central, and South Europe came after 1890. Beginning in 1927, the act prescribed, the maximum number of new arrivals had to be limited to 150,000 a year. The allotment to each immigration country was to follow a simple ratio that favored the old-stock countries and would continue to do so by the very application of the act. It read: "the annual quota of each nationality shall bear the same ratio to said maximum total number of immigrants as the number of inhabitants of the United States having that national origin shall bear to the whole number of inhabitants" (quoted in Hutchinson, 1981: 192, 194).

Was there no research, then, supporting the nativist theses on the incapacity of the new immigrants to assimilate or, in general, on their social inferiority? Naturalization seemed to offer a clue. If the hypothesis on the temporary nature of the new immigration was correct, the inference should follow that immigrants of the old stock would naturalize faster and more fully than the new immigrants. The expectation, again, was not borne out by the facts. Controlled for length of residence, there was even a small negative bias toward the old-stock immigrant (Kolko, 1976: 71), especially of British and British-Canadian origin, who proved reluctant to adopt the American nationality (Handlin, 1957: 163). Length of residence was indeed a very critical variable. Research conducted on new immigrants too often drew conclusions unrelated to recency of arrival. Instead, the findings were attributed to national origins and the like. The disintegration of the new immigrant family—a popular theme of the times—was thus transformed from an indication about the ordeal that immigrant families encountered upon arrival into an incapacity to assimilate successfully into American life. Yet research conducted on the topic of the new immigrant family one generation or more later came to opposite conclusions. The Polish family, for example, once depicted as collapsed under the strain of the new American environment, proved its resilience to bad times during the Great Depression. What seemed a lost institution in 1918—

the time W. J. Thomas and T. Znaniecki finished their famous research on the Polish migrants to America—had been reestablished as a vigorous support for economic, social, and cultural survival one or two decades later. What held for the family held for the community (Golab, 1977).

In clinging to family and community, the new immigrants behaved like the old, albeit that their cultural assimilation in the United States was achieved at a faster rate (Gordon, 1964: 105ff.). This, then, suggested that family and community were not the brakes on assimilation that they were supposed to be but, on the contrary, media that helped accomplish successful integration into American society (Golab, 1977: 27). It was no more than a partial integration, though. Whereas cultural assimilation succeeded, structural assimilation did not occur (Gordon, 1964: 70ff., 110ff.). *Cultural assimilation*, or *acculturation*, is defined as the change of culture patterns to those of the host society (e.g., learning the language, visiting the schools, respecting the ruling codes); *structural assimilation* is defined as the large-scale entrance into cliques, clubs, and institutions of the host society, on the level of primary face-to-face groups (Gordon, 1964: 71). America, as Gordon has said, is not so much the country of cultural as it is of structural pluralism (Gordon, 1964: 159). The world of employment was no exception.

CHAIN MIGRATION

By the time the great wave of new immigration was over—with the coming of World War I—America had become an urban nation. Upon their arrival, the need to find a job and a place to live were the most pressing and immediate concerns for the immigrants. There were no employment agencies; rent control and housing regulations were weak or unenforced. The only support one could fall back on was the network of kinship, village, or regional ties of those that came earlier. These networks—sustained internationally by mail and by messages and information from returned migrants and locally by joining the existing community in its pattern of voluntary organizations, of housing and employment, and to an extent by following the political ward boss and the employment "padrone"—were of critical importance. The success of a boss in organizing an ethnic ward was contingent on the claims of the ward on political spoils—and thus on their own representatives. The "padrone," an employment broker and not necessarily distinct from the political system, lost grip once the community started disseminating its own information on jobs and job opportunities. It was the community and its institutions that linked the successive waves of migrants. Its necessity showed up during the hard times of the first few days or weeks and during spells of unemployment, when return migration was one option, migration to another part of the United States a second, and mutual solidarity within the community a third.

Return migration was high and followed the economic cycle. Bad economic weather was translated into heightened departure. Because of it, unemployment estimates were deflated, and the early discussion on unemployment insurance lost some of its edge. If unemployment could be exported, as it was, why the need for public insurance against it? In fact, as long as immigration was not restricted, and the pool of labor kept growing, unemployment was though to present no pressing problem. On the other hand, immigration restriction would lead not just to less new labor but also to the virtual disappearance of return migration and therewith to unemployment as a source of potential class conflict (Rosenblum, 1973: 125, 161). The estimates were that between 30 and 40 percent of the new immigrants returned. The precise figures are hard to establish; some of the returnees might go back to the United States again, entry and exit registration were not perfect, and the identification of the country of origin was often haphazard. All the same, the return percentage was high, higher than that of immigrants of the old stock. The general trend was that the later the period of migrating to the United States, the higher the percentage of return migration (Rosenblum, 1973: 46).

The responsiveness of the new immigrants to economic influences contributed to their negative image. Their behavior added fuel to the suspicion that the new immigration was a mere temporary affair. Also, return migration was taken as a sure sign that the new immigrant would decline any invitation to Americanize, unless one forced him to. The danger of facile generalization looms large, however. First, it is highly questionable to equate return migration and refusal to assimilate. Second, it is erroneous to put all of the new and the old immigration into two separate categories. The Jews and the Armenians, for example, came to America for political reasons, fleeing persecution in their places of origin. They were hardly keen on returning, unless the political situation would change dramatically. Migrants, on the other hand, who considered politics as secondary and the economics of their situation as the prime objective, had more options. The Italians, among the new immigrants, had very high return percentages (Sowell, 1983: 71ff.). But so had British and German skilled workers, especially since international transport had become easier by means of the large-scale use of steamships (Sowell, 1983: 154). Is it the influence of transportation more than the wish or inclination to assimilate, that explains return migration percentages?

The data to differentiate between back-and-forth international migration, and a temporary sojourn in the strict meaning of the word, are not available. On the other hand, the link established between return migration and unwillingness to assimilate (Sowell, 1983: 155) is highly improper. It was believed that the demographic composition of the new immigrants was biased to a disproportionate share of young and unmarried males—again, if the Italian rather than the Jew was taken as the typical new immigrant. But even granted the stereotype, what did it mean? Nineteenth-century English immigration was typified as well by a first arrival of the men and a later arrival of the women and children (Coleman, 1974). The black migration to the North in this century was heavily dominated by young males (Sowell, 1983: 153). To explain these patterns, one needs comparisons of conditions of departure and, especially, of arrival. The reference to assimilation can be missed.

The relaxation of the transportation constraint lowered the cost, the time, and the danger of international migration (Coleman, 1974; Handlin, 1952: 48–54). Independent of the question of attitudes toward America and the country of origin, then, migrating back and forth became more feasible than before. The fact that young men in particular came first may be explained in the same manner. Easier transportation made it possible to explore the costs and conditions of a future American life and only then to act on them. Instead of being an expression of aloofness from American life, return migration and a predominance of young males may simply have indicated the wish to prepare thoroughly the final decision to build a future in America. The emphasis is on "may," but the generally acknowledged readiness of the new immigrant in joining voluntary organizations and the sheer number of those organizations (Handlin, 1952: 170ff.; Barton, 1978: 150–175) supports this "may" more than the reverse inference of nonassimilation.

But how does one account for the difference in magnitude of return migration between old and new immigrants around the turn of the century? In the period 1908–1910 the return migration for the new immigrants was, according to the Immigration Commission's tabulations, 37 percent; for the old it was in the same period a mere 13 percent (Rosenblum, 1973: 125). Often, it is precisely data like these that led, and lead, observers to stick to the notion of the transient nature of new immigration. It may be true, as for instance with immigrants from the South of Italy, that their long tradition of small, private plots of land, a tradition interrupted by the Great Depression of 1873–1895, had kept the idea of economic independence in the place of origin alive. Mutual benefit and credit societies of Italians financed not just immigration but agricultural undertakings in the region of origin as well. Many of these societies were renewed in the United States, and some continuity of objective is plausible (Barton, 1978: 155–156). But this was hardly the overall picture. Where the possession of land had been more communal than private, there were no expectations of private landholding, and the vision of return—if at all—would be prompted by other things. Moreover, many migrants did not come from a peasant background, and even if they had one, their voyage to America had been preceded by the experience of seasonal migration in the countries of Europe. Italians and Poles, for instance, had a history not just of agricultural seasonal labor but also of work in the mining industries of France and Germany (for France, see Cordeiro, 1983; on the Polish in German mining, see Moore, 1978; Roth, 1977). Small traders, artisans, and shopkeepers were just as uprooted as the peasants from the agricultural hinterland. The decay of peasant society included the drying up of their markets, locally bound, depending on shrinking local purchasing power, and under fire from imported products. The latter also destroyed the many remnants of household industry (Barton, 1978).

Earlier migration experience, the crossing of artisans and merchants, and the events of household industry create a different image of the new immigrant than in the classic picture (Handlin, 1952). The classic view portrays a traditional "peasant," who is innocent of monetary and commercial habits and unused to modern contractual relations and who compares the highly diversified, impersonal, and abstract social relations in America with the total, personal, and concrete relations back home. Rather, a more Durkheimian (Durkheim, 1893) path is observable, in which the breakdown of the traditional division of labor leads to a realignment of, not to the disappearance of, solidarity. It is this solidarity—no longer mechanical, not yet organic in Durkheim's terms—that enables the entry into and sometimes the very creation of a new division of labor.

The sequence of events immediately before and immediately after the crossing to America confirms the importance of "solidarity." The breaking up of traditional modes of subsistence led, in the countries of South, East, and Central Europe, to many initiatives in devising new schemes to cope with economic hardship and its various sources. The loss of private and communal landholdings may have acted as the prime mover in introducing habits of migration. Clearly, these habits were at odds with pre-existing kinship networks, traditional forms of hierarchy and deference, and the functions these fulfilled in the total fabric of the community. The typical responses were twofold (Barton, 1978: 154ff.). First, the kinship networks were redefined, for instance, through foster parentage or donations, such that mutual assistance was kept alive. Kinship, then, proved to be a flexible medium, capable of adapting to new circumstances. (The same flexibility of kinship—even to the extent of severing the relation between blood relationship and kinship—was one answer slaves had to the rude destruction of families in the South [Gutman, 1987]). Second, these new extended families created a growing number of voluntary associations, catering to specific needs like education, occupational interests, illness, political aims, and death. These associations were both segmented, strengthening the renewed kinship network and excluding others, and specialized, underscoring the degree of fragmentation the erstwhile more unified communities had undergone. To be sure, many of these associations failed, one reason being the emigration of its members. The fact, that they were erected, however, was of primary importance.

The credit associations and insurance institutions for funerals and illness, set up in the old country, were renewed in the United States. Did this structure of mutualities determine the flocking together of the new immigrants in urban villages and in similar lines of employment, instead of the other way around? Also, did the new immigrants in this action unknowingly follow the pattern laid down by Germans, Scandinavians, and other immigrants of the old stock?

Scandinavians concentrated in a few areas in the Midwest (Akerman, Kronborg, and Nilsson, 1979; Norman, 1979). Germans were more spread out over the country but as a rule stuck together in small towns or in readily identifiable sections of a city. They possessed their own clubs, churches, sometimes schools, and mutualities. The German organizations suffered a severe blow because of World War I and never really recovered from it (Luebke, 1978). Until those days, however, there was a strong German community in the United States, counting, on a national scale, some 7 million German Americans, the largest single nationality group in the United States.

Organizing along language, kinship, regional, or even village lines was a habit established in the United States long before the arrival of the new immigrant. In this respect, the immigrants were not new but merely later arrivals. These views are speculation, however, stressing the continuities and not merely the differences between old- and new-stock immigration. The history of immigration to the United States is marred by many preconceptions of the difference in motivating forces on the decision and the character of the new compared to the old immigrant. The capacity to assimilate and its history of racial stereotyping are hardly taken seriously any longer. But the willingness to assimilate still looms large in many contemporary assessments of the new immigrant. The emphasis seems, even given the scanty evidence, misguided. A reasonable case can be made for the thesis that the high return migration of the new immigrant reflects a comparatively difficult structure of opportunities, rather than an instrumental attitude or, even, the constraints of the propelling factor: the situation in the region of origin. Cultural assimilation, again, was not a true problem, and chain migration did not stand in its way. Structural assimilation, on the other hand, is a different affair. For structural assimilation to occur, direct contacts between people in primary groups is a precondition (Parenti, 1969). Here, the world of work is one key element.

NEW IMMIGRANTS AND JOBS

The new immigrants were a very mobile population. Next to return migration, movements to other regions and cities occurred frequently. These movements, according to the usual logic, must have strained the efforts at organizing. But even if they did, it did not discourage the appearance of new organizations, continuing what the previous ones had started. The networks the immigrants established connected the home country and the places of arrival; they also connected the immigrant communities within the United States. This setup made for readily identifiable job slots in which the different immigrants' communities fit. But when applying for a job, it was not the group that applied, although this, too, was not an unknown phenomenon. The padrone, regularly supplemented by a series of American labor agents, often worked on a group basis. Padroni "negotiated deals with employers, sent the workers off to their destinations, and collected and distributed the men's salaries after deducting their service fees" (Dinnerstein, Nichols, and Reimers, 1979: 145). Obviously, the transaction costs of the padrone were reduced if the negotiating concerned as many workers as feasible. This could include the use of a group as a strike-breaking entity (Dinnerstein, Nichols, and Reimers, 1979: 145, 151). After the turn of the century, however, employers started to rely on the new immigrants' own organizations and ties (Jacoby, 1985: 19). As long as the responsiveness of the immigrant to the economic cycle could be taken for granted, this was a feasible policy. It did necessitate, though, a massive amount of immigration, since mobility and qualifications required varied inversely during the heyday of the new immigration (Jacoby, 1985: 36). A decline in immigration, as during World War I and after, was bound to create trouble—unless new labor reserves could be brought into play.

The high mobility rates (100 percent per year was not considered very high) were predicated upon a type of technology that embodied skills to the utmost extent possible in the machinery and its organization rather than demanding qualifications in the men (Montgomery, 1980: 34; Gordon, Edwards, and Reich 1982: 37). The reverse of this situation is, however, interesting on its own merits, for the resulting jobs were adapted to the men, rather than the other way around (Slichter, 1929: 184). In the middle of an abundant supply of unskilled labor, one usually finds labor scarcity. In fact, in view of the high turnover rates, the threat of scarcity amidst plenty was ever present. Nothing optimistic is implied in jobs that are adapted to men. It did not endanger the drive system or the practically untrammeled powers of the foremen, but it did signal, first, that selection and recruitment based on labor qualifications was de-emphasized to give way to hiring procedures on the basis of crude behavioral indicators and prejudices. Second, adapting the job to the man meant that training for and on the job were excluded. Unskilled work, then, was work performed by people whose labor qualifications were of no interest.

The actual qualifications of the new immigrants are difficult to ascertain, in spite of the fact that government statistics tell a clear story. European immigrants reporting employment in the period between 1899 and 1910 show marked occupational differences according to national origins. The English and Germans, for instance, score high on skilled occupations; the new immigrants, on the whole, do not. They represent most of the workers in the category of "laborers, including farm laborers" (Kessler-Harris and Yans-McLaughlin, 1978: 117, table 2). But are these classifications useful indications of skill, or do they measure the degree of industrialization and its effect on the occupational division of labor? A farm laborer may have had some previous experience with economic independence and thus have acquired the skills of foresight and planning associated with being one's own master. Experience with rudimentary accounting and commercial skills may have been far more widespread than the occupational classification suggested. The same is true with mechanical skills in repair and maintenance. Many of these skills were depending on a mastery of the written language. It has been suggested that this factor, working at least initially to the disadvantage of the new immigrants, determined their exclusion from a skilled occupation in America and that the factor of skill itself played a less important part (Rosenblum, 1973: 85). Also, the peak in the shortage of skilled labor coincided with the diminished immigration due to World War I, again implying that the skills of the new immigrants were more important than was officially registered (Slichter, 1929: 184). Insofar as literacy and attitudes toward education are fair indicators of skill, the record of the new immigrant appears in an even more favorable light (Tyack, 1974: 200, 214–215).

Many a new immigrant had a background in mining. Around 1910 more than 50 percent of the mineworkers were foreign born. Of the semiskilled in industry, they accounted, in 1910, for four out of ten. Among the unskilled in industry, they numbered forty-five out of a hundred (Rosenblum, 1973: 77, table 3–11). The industrial workers, moreover, were predominantly employed in the larger, fast-growing industries. The oil industry, chemicals, and rubber increased their employment between 1870 and 1910 nineteenfold. Two-thirds of their employees were foreign born (Montgomery, 1980: 35; Nelson, 1975: 80, table 5). These same industries, soon joined by the automobile sector, showed rapidly rising rates of capital input and productivity per manhour, underscoring the economies of scale (Ross, 1968: 34–36). In meatpacking, documented in Sinclair's classic *The Jungle*, and in the iron and steel industry (Brody, 1960: 96ff.) the situation was not much different (Jacoby, 1985: 32). There was, in short, a heavy concentration of new immigrants in unskilled, and to a somewhat lesser degree in semiskilled, jobs.

Unskilled and semiskilled did not prevent segmentation of the work force. Indeed, to a considerable extent the irrelevance of labor qualifications was the precondition for ethnically guided splits motivated by inklings about work habits, discipline, and the like. The Germans and Irish were considered adept as skilled workers; Poles and Hungarians were deemed fit for heavy, hot, and dirty work; the Jews were supposed to excel in dexterity; and the Slovaks were said to be mainly stupid, the Rumanians dishonest, and the Italians too "susceptible to the opposite sex" (Jacoby, 1985: 17; Brody, 1960: 120). Foremen, or their employers, sometimes called in the help of group leaders of new immigrant communities and, once a community had been formed, church officials, but this left the stereotyping unchanged. For employers, the decisive consideration was the assumed transient nature of the new immigration (Brody, 1960: 109). New arrivals, whatever their motives to immigrate may have been, consequently received the most unskilled and menial jobs. With longer residence, however, promotion into semiskilled work was a real possibility (Brody, 1960: 107–108). This did not imply the supersession of the segmented world of work, since here, too, the stereotyping influenced the rating of the group before it touched upon its individual members. The sieve of ethnic prejudice divided old and new; more devastating, perhaps, was the divisive effect it exerted on the shape of segmentation within the flow of the new immigration.

This is not the whole picture. Sometimes groups were deliberately mixed, the objective being the prevention of strikes or unionization (Jacoby, 1985: 149). In other firms, the groups, possibly with the same objective, were kept separate. In all cases, however, the firm acted on a self-fulfilling prophecy. Since the immigrant worker was not inclined to stay, he could be treated as a malleable, interchangeable part. If he moved on, after having received enough of the treatment, this could be taken as proof of his transiency. New arrivals were in steady supply. If he stayed on, this was a fair enough indication that his work habits had been adapted to the rhythm of industrial America; thus an opening to semiskilled work could be contemplated. The mechanism illustrates the critical importance of unskilled labor, with respect to its size and replenishment and to its status as a clearinghouse for the eventual advancement to semiskilled labor.

NEW IMMIGRANTS AND UNIONS

The working conditions of the new immigrants were often abysmal. Newly arrived steelworkers, in the period between 1907 and 1913, stood a chance of one out of four of being in an industrial accident (Gutman, 1977: 30). Wages were low and employment irregular; when families had come, women and men both had to work to survive. Household industries therefore often cropped up next to districts of large-scale industry (Golab, 1977). Hours were long and so was the workweek. Six or even seven days of at least twelve hours a day were usual. Periods of frenetic activity were followed by periods of forced idleness. Unemployment insurance, workman's compensation, sickness benefits, and so on were absent practically everywhere. Where, then, was the effort to unionize?

We must, in answering this question, distinguish between the union as an institution and the functions a union may perform for its members and for the community at large. The new immigrants formed no unions. One reason may have been that many of its functions—insurance; mutual assistance in case of accidents, sickness, and death; cultural presence, newspapers and periodicals included; educational activities; information on employment facilities—were already catered to by a host of specialized or informal associations of the immigrants' own making. Forming a union would have involved the risk of dismantling these associations, with which they had acquired some experience. More important, however, was the simple fact that the possibility of a successful union depended on the power to check the number of potential job competitors. This entailed, as the case might be, enlarging or curtailing the amount of new immigration. In both hypothetical cases, this implied effective influence on policy formation at the federal level since immigration policy had, starting in 1875 and ending in 1882, become a responsibility of the federal government (Hutchinson, 1981: 66, 75, 83). Such influence was out of the question. The political leverage of the new immigrants touched on city and, to a smaller degree, state affairs; it rarely extended beyond them. Their own organizations, moreover, were somewhat adequate to deal with nearby problems and people, but with distance came the waning of the influence of the immigrant association. Stretching the organizational capacity beyond the boundaries of cities and states took time, but in time it happened, explaining in part why union organization for the new immigrants, as for the old, was largely a second-generation phenomenon.

Third, what little control there was on employment opportunities and international migration was regionally and linguistically circumscribed. The recruitment practices of foremen and employers in this instance worked to the same effect as the international exchange of information between places of arrival and region of origin (Nelson, 1975: 79–80). This limited control did not call for a union. In fact, what could a union have done beyond what the wide array of voluntary immigrant associations already took care of? It would certainly have provoked an adverse response from employers, and the strength of this consideration, fed by the constant influx of new workers from a variety of national origins, may indeed have contributed to the comparatively late unionization of unskilled and semiskilled workers in the United States, relative to, for instance, the United Kingdom (Holt, 1985: 191–192).

The new immigrants were organized but not in unions. There is, in other words, a long labor history in the United States that does not coincide with the history of trade unions and of political parties but which is labor history all the same (Tronti, 1972: 53; Poulantzas, 1977: 122). What of the existing unions? When the great wave of new immigration began, the steel union had already been defeated in the 1892 Homestead strike. Unofficially, then, the epoch of the open shop drives had started. The United Mine Workers, one of the few AFL-affiliated industrial unions, organized the new immigrants in its ranks, and here the new immigrants accepted the invitation without qualms. The Brewery Workers and the International Ladies' Garment Workers also were industrial unions associated with the AFL, organizing among the new immigrants (Pelling, 1960: 119ff.; Montgomery, 1980: 41ff.). The more industrial the organization, the more the union recruited, and recruited successfully, among the new immigrants. But the majority of the AFL unions was not so organized, and they determined the overall policy of the AFL regarding the new immigrants and their eligibility for union membership. On the whole, this policy was full of disdain and hostility. The unions of skilled workers were in favor of a ban on immigration, and when this could not be effected until after World War I, they used their organizations to erect formidable barriers to prevent the new immigrant from joining the union and from forming any other union organization. The "charter" of a union, in the end, may have served more as a discouragement to the representation of the new immigrant than as a mode of recruiting new members.

The sad results of this policy are well known. Those industries showing a high concentration of new immigrants remained largely unorganized until the thirties. They were also the industries in which employment grew the fastest, in which mass production methods were the most widespread, and which commanded an ever-growing proportion of total industrial capital outlay and output (Tawney, 1979: 5, 101–102, table 3, 103, table 4). R. H. Tawney commented: "The most striking feature of American industrial development for more than twenty years before the split [i.e., the 1935 emergence of the CIO] in the trade union movement was the rapid expansion of the metal and machine-making industries. The most striking feature of the American trade unionism of that period was the weakness of the hold which it had on those industries" (1979: 25). The steel industry and the automobile industry thus remained unorganized. Indeed, the major 1919 attempt to organize the steel industry was carried predominantly by the new immigrants, whereas organized labor "failed the steelworkers" (Brody, 1960: 257), one important motive being the self-erected wedge between native and immigrant steelworkers (Brody, 1960: 258–262). In the automobile industry it was the attempt of the Industrial Workers of the World (IWW) to organize the workers that influenced Ford's timing of the introduction of $5 a day. The AFL, on the other hand, was hardly a factor the Ford Company had to reckon with (Bock, 1976: 62–65; Meyer, 1977; 110–116; Sward, 1948: 50–51; Foner, 1965: 383–390).

The Industrial Workers of the World, founded in 1905, was the most important union federation that explicitly welcomed the new immigrants (a comprehensive statement on the IWW is in Foner, 1965). The IWW vehemently opposed the AFL, promoted dual unionism, and expressed its contempt for the crafts and their organizations. It was the AFL's antithesis. The first sentence of the preamble to its constitution could not be more clear: "The working class and the employing class have nothing in common." (quoted in Pelling, 1960: 111). Theirs was an uncompromising syndicalism, directed against the wage system as such and all of its manifestations, such as collective bargaining, union labels, and written contracts (Montgomery, 1980: 92). Its first few years were ridden with internal strife, leading eventually in 1908 to a split within its ranks (Foner, 1965: ch. 1). From then on, next to the original IWW, with headquarters in Chicago, the Detroit IWW, led by Daniel De Leon and his Socialist Labor party, was formed (on De Leon, see Cot, 1980; Stevenson, 1980). The two organizations remained contenders, sometimes even producing mutual paralysis in conducting a strike action (Ebner, 1985: 254ff.). After 1908, the Chicago IWW directed its attention to "the workers whom the AFL would not and did not reach—the migratory workers of the West and the unskilled industrial workers of the East—the most poorly paid and ill-treated" (Foner, 1965: 123). Despite the effort, the IWW did not grow into the mass organization of the new immigrants. This, no doubt, was partly due to the persecution that the IWW since its inception had to endure from employers, the police, the courts, the National Guard, and vigilantes (on the importance of violence in this respect, see Gutman, 1977: 31: Piven and Cloward, 1979: 102ff.; Bock, 1976; Foner, 1965; Graham and Gurr, 1969; 281ff.). But internal dissensions and external violence do not tell the whole story.

The course of two major strike actions in the East, in Lawrence, Massachusetts (1912), and Paterson, New Jersey (1913), will shed more light on the relationship between the IWW and new immigrants (for a detailed overview, see Foner, 1965: 306–372; see also Guerin, 1977: 55ff.; Meltzer, 1967: 170–190; Thompson and Murfin, 1976: 53–63). In Lawrence, as a consequence of a 1912 Massachusetts state law, the maximum number of working hours per week for women and persons under 18 years of age was reduced from 56 to 54. The textile employers of Lawrence responded with an equivalent reduction of wages and decided that the hours and the wages of the men, not referred to in the state law, were to be diminished to the fifty-four-hour standard as well (Foner, 1965: 315 n). The workers accepted the challenge. First, a group of Polish women quit their jobs; soon, Italian workers followed, and before long 25,000 Lawrence workers, speaking all in all forty-five languages, were on strike (Bock, 1976: 52–53). Despite scabbing, arrests, and violence, the strikers had their way. Wages were brought back to their previous level; strikers were reinstated at their previous jobs. The victory was in no small measure due to the IWW, which sent some of its best and most renown organizers to Lawrence, among them "Big Bill" Haywood. They took care, once the strike had begun, of internal discipline, publicity, timing, the supply of food, and even the safety of the children—the latter by means of the famous "exodus" of children to sympathizing working-class families in nearby towns and cities. In fact, the whole arsenal of tactics the IWW had employed a few years earlier at the lost steel strikes of McKees Rocks, near Pittsburgh, was put to a new test at Lawrence. It worked, much to the chagrin of the employers who were only too aware of the IWW influence.

The 1913 strike at Paterson was lost. Paterson, New Jersey, had a long tradition in the manufacture of silk products. The mills, however, had become obsolete by 1913, and its owners—some of whom had opened new plants in Scranton and Allentown, Pennsylvania, with newer equipment and cheap labor, mainly consisting of the wives and daughters of the workers in the mines—confronted the workers with a choice between the closing of the Paterson plants or a reduction of wages, combined with a speedup. The workers, predictably, wanted neither, and the strike was a fact. As in Lawrence, the strike was massive, involving a large majority (25,000) of the Paterson silk workers. The IWW rushed in to support the strike, this time, however, to no avail. The IWW and the strikers "could not win in the old silk center against modern technology in other towns, with the better looms owned by the same large interests" (Thompson and Murfin, 1976: 61).

After Paterson, the role of the IWW in the East became insignificant. Activities in the rubber and automobile industry were, on average, short lived and did not lead to noticeable membership increases. In fact, after the Lawrence gains had been lost, membership of the Chicago IWW as a whole remained relatively stagnant at an oscillating level around 15,000 (Thompson and Murfin, 1976: 79). The task of the IWW had been too gigantic. Any organization would feel the pressure in the face of such a dramatic rise in membership in so short a time, especially with new members coming from such diverse backgrounds. The decision of the IWW to subdivide its new membership into eighteen language groups was a practical one. It demonstrated both the impact of the organization in overcoming the differences between these groups and the impossibility of discarding these differences. Also, the IWW had not stressed its ideology so much as bread and butter issues and human dignity, beautifully expressed in the rallying cry of the Lawrence strike: "We want bread, and roses too" (Rosenblum, 1973: 165; Meltzer, 1967).

Its ideology, nevertheless, did not fail to materialize. No collective bargaining occurred, nor was it set in motion. That bargaining and the implied mutual adjustments and adaptations could be one major objective of organization and that a contract in the first place meant the struggle to get it (Tronti, 1972) went against the grain of the Wobblies. They, at least officially, declined all action along that path. The idea of the Wobblies was different: "rather than laying down a list of grievances to be dealt with at the bargaining table, they onesidedly fixed wages and working hours, wrote them down on a piece of paper at the factory gates, and left it to the bosses to come down and take note in order to respect it, thereby executing workers' orders" (Bologna, 1976: 87; Bock, 1976: 93ff.). In practice, as might be expected, the principle was not applied literally. The IWW organizers sometimes proposed workers' committees to deal, in negotiating with the employer, with all possible grievances (Bock, 1976: 73). These were not to be IWW committees, though, but committees selected by the workers themselves. Despite these pragmatic solutions, and possibly even because of them, the position of the IWW on collective bargaining and regular negotiating procedures remained unclear. For all workers, on the other hand, who expected to progress from work designated as unskilled to semiskilled positions, this was exactly the crucial question.

Skill was treated by the IWW as a hoax. It was identified with the narrow status politics of the AFL, driving an artificial wedge in between the ranks of wage labor (Montgomery, 1980: 109). The gap with skilled labor, insofar as represented by the AFL, seemed unbridgeable. More important in the present context, however, is the utter absence of opinions and practices of the IWW relative to the distinctions between the unskilled and semiskilled workers.

Tolerance for discipline and obedience would be demanded from both industrial groups, presumably more so than initial qualification. But it is misleading to look upon these "social" skills and competencies as abstract and self-contained entities. Industry does not consist of assembly lines alone, and even the work on an assembly line can be done with more or less accuracy. Yet the degree of accuracy is more than a function of reliable performance or strict obedience to the rules. Involved as well is some work-related capacity to evaluate the margins of the labor process, to anticipate and prevent, to correct mechanical flaws, to assist colleagues on the line, and thus to disobey the strict order (Wood, 1985: 84–90; Burawoy, 1979).

One of the vital distinctions between unskilled and semiskilled work is precisely the degree to which work-related qualifications can be enhanced and used to the advantage or detriment of the continuity of the labor process. As a general rule, unskilled work in this sense is only indirectly strategic for the continuity of the labor process. Semiskilled is crucial, and the qualifications thus formed may transform a job into part of a career. An internal labor market and semiskilled work, therefore, are feasible. The definition, control, hierarchy, and maintenance of semiskilled work is a major task of employee representation. An internal labor market and unskilled work, to the contrary, are almost a contradiction in terms. The work of the semiskilled allows for differentiation, for different "stations" the worker may travel along. The work of the unskilled does not allow for such stations. Indeed, one important union task concerns precisely the struggle for access of unskilled workers to semiskilled work. Here, the IWW missed the point. The new immigrant didn't.

MOBILITY, TURNOVER, AND IMMIGRATION

In the period 1900–1909 two-thirds of the total number of immigrants came from Russia, Austria–Hungary, and Italy, the typical countries of the new immigration. In that decade more than 8 million people immigrated to the United States, three times as many as in the peak decades of the pre–1880 period. In the second decade of this century two things happened. Due to the war, the total number of immigrants declined sharply to somewhat over 6 million. Second, the source of immigration began to shift anew. The share of the countries of the new immigration declined to approximately half of the total, whereas immigration from Canada increased substantially to cover about 10 percent of the total. The immigration-restriction legislation of the twenties was to reaffirm these tendencies. Total immigration was reduced, and since the Americas were exempted from the legislation, immigration from Canada and Mexico assumed a prominent position in the overall picture (see Table 5.1; Jacoby, 1985: 134, 170–171).

The First World War marked the end of the exodus from Europe to America. Labor turnover grew into an important problem, once international mobility had become thwarted because of the war. For the same reason, the labor market temporarily became a seller's market. The problem of a high turnover of labor could not now be met by a renewed inflow of new immigration. The habitual crude recruitment methods, which had been tolerable during the days of high immigration, augmented the magnitude of the problem. Labor turnover of 100 percent or more per year, so common in the decades before the war, threatened to create acute shortages of labor. The shift to new recruitment areas was one response, as was the tapping of the black labor reservoir of the South through internal migration and the large-scale employment of women (Jacoby, 1985: 133–134). But the tight labor market remained, since demand for labor was high and the army conscription reduced, along with the towering turnover rates and soaring absenteeism (Jacoby, 1985: 135), the available supply. Since many of the new recruits were given unskilled work only, the highest quit rates occurred among them (Jacoby, 1985: 117, 136). By implication, the usual and crude device of selecting for semiskilled positions—length of stay—failed as well.

Even without the war, turnover would have developed into a major problem. The war quickened the pace of the introduction of new employment practices; it did not determine them. Nor was the discouragement of the new practices in the aftermath of the war the sign that the employment relationship was back in its prewar fold. The war and its aftermath did prove that the terrain of the employment relationship was a battleground between workers and their unions, personnel professionals, foremen, the employers, and the government. The withdrawal of the government from the field after the war, the favorable labor market for the employers, and the weakening of the unions brought back to the foremen much of what wartime exigencies had handed over to the new personnel professionals. Wartime personnel innovations were scaled down during the twenties, but they were not abandoned. Personnel departments, influencing hiring and firing and conducting job analyses, were there to stay, especially in the larger industries (Baron, Dobbin, and Jennings, 1986: 357; Jacoby, 1985: 173, table 6.5).

Organizational reasons must be mentioned for the function of personnel departments. The economies of scale that large production promised could be exploited only through influencing throughput. The cost advantage of the large enterprise "cannot be fully realized unless a constant flow of materials through the plant or factory is maintained to assure effective capacity utilization" (Chandler, 1985: 405). Scale may be technological; its economies "measured by throughput, are organizational. Such economies depend on knowledge, skills, and teamwork—on the human organization essential to exploit the potential of technological processes" (Chandler, 1985: 405). In mass-production industries, this meant a renewed emphasis on the precision of standardized parts and processes and a heightening of the efficiency of machines and tools. The swift spread of electricity meant both a greater reliability of measurement and an enlargement of the items that could successfully be measured. Electricity was used by 30 percent of industry in 1914 and by 70 percent in 1929. The electrical motor replaced the steam engine; between 1914 and 1927, 44 percent of the stock of steam engines was sent to the scrap heap (Leuchtenburg, 1958: 179ff.; Huberman, 1947: 211).

Electricity from the generator as a source of power was cheaper than steam from the boiler. The same held for the machinery driven by electricity; it raised output and was a less expensive outlay (Gillman, 1965: 189, 1957: 91ff.). Finally, the output of electricity-fed instruments began to catch up with the output of machines. The output and sale of measuring instruments especially thrived, enabling the automatic control of temperature, pressure, and amounts of raw materials, parts, and whole products, separating the flawless from the faulty products along the way. The use of electrical measuring instruments promoted greater speed of the machinery without greater wear and tear and with earlier detection of mechanical faults and breakdowns (Gillman, 1957: 93–94). Enhanced economy in the use of a whole series of raw materials completed the picture (Gillman, 1957: 94–95).

The effects on the labor market were impressive. Manufacturing establishments employed as many men in 1929 as they did in 1919 (Leuchtenburg, 1958; Jacoby, 1985: 169, table 6.3). The fact that unemployment figures on the whole did not differ very much from those in the previous decade was not due to industry but to clerical, commercial, and service employment. Industrial productivity per hour increased in the same period five times as much as it had in the previous decade (Gillman, 1957: 96), and technological unemployment became the topic of the day. If, then, the rationalization drive and the associated changes in personnel relations of the twenties was a mere response to the labor shortages of the war years, something of an overkill may be observed. But the rationalization of production involved much more. The technological changes and innovations of the twenties responded to the organizational demands of mass production. Among them the complex problem of internal transportation loomed large.

The assembly line was the most visible contribution to the solution of the problem. Its spread coincided with the spread of electricity. Technologically, the assembly line was not a new invention. But its widespread use as the very embodiment of the logic of mass-production organization was. It tended to freeze the workers on their spot while moving the product, the materials, and the tools. It gave a new impetus to the large-scale use of job analysis, time and motion studies, and, in the end, the development of collective bargaining to compensate for the broken link between output and individual exertion (Aglietta, 1979: 118ff.; Gordon, Edwards, and Reich, 1982: 170ff.). Above all, while it reduced every job to insignificance, it made the continuity of the process contingent upon the reliability and predictability of the performance of all. Cooperation, once the province of the work team, here was built into the architecture of the labor process as a whole (Popitz et al., 1964). In the same movement, product markets, markets of raw materials and energy, and labor markets are transformed from data into strategic variables. Vertical integration may even be necessitated by the strategy of controlling sources of raw materials and energy. The expansion of Ford in the early decades of the company is an example. For reasons of market strategy, at times supported by vertical integration, product diversification became a dominant strategy in the twenties. In the well-known case of General Motors this even led to the partial replacement of the functional organization by a divisional—product rather than function-defined—structure of organization. Also, the renewed wave of mergers and consolidations in the late twenties form part of the strategy of firms to obtain a better grip on their market environments (Aglietta, 1979: 255). But the major conditioning influence was simply growth. Machine bureaucracies do not just promote growth; they also are depending on the continuation of growth (Piore and Sabel, 1984; Chandler, 1962: 13–16, 1977: 484–490).

Growth, however, was a target more easily formulated than attained. The period 1900–1915 showed many economic fluctuations, often, especially after 1907, violent ones. The period of the twenties, despite its favorable overall trend, was again unstable (Baran and Sweezy, 1966: 222ff.). The recession of 1921, for example, was one of the sharpest until the coming of the Great Depression at the end of the decade. It added to the necessity of organizational muscle and the incompleteness of its results. The fact that the economic growth of the twenties was propelled mainly by the automobile industry—which was, with the steel industry, the symbol of irregular employment—may serve to place the objective of stable and predictable growth in its proper perspective. Market regulation in an oligopolistic vein, more supported than constrained by the antitrust laws (Chandler, 1977: 375–376), was instrumental in stabilizing the share of larger and smaller companies; output and sales as a whole, on the other hand, turned out to be far less manageable. Product diversification was one important instrument in streamlining capacity utilization and in reducing balance delay time occasioned by problems of proportionality (Chandler, 1977: 489; Aglietta, 1979: 119–120). This policy instrument, however, could be useful only if the condition of continued and unabated growth in the interest of full-capacity utilization was met. It was not.

The return of the buyer's market in industrial employment during the twenties did not lead to an equivalent return of the foremen's prerogatives in hiring and firing. Every one in three industries with more than 250 employees had by 1927 a personnel department. Centralized employment, that is, the loss of the foreman's role in hiring and firing, had become the habit in just over 40 percent of these larger industries, whereas the loss of decisionary power of the foreman in promotion and transfer of employees had been introduced in 20 percent of the firms (Baron, Dobbin, and Jennings, 1986, table 1, pp. 351–354; Jacoby, 1985: 173, table 6.5, and 191, table 6.7). Also, there was, despite the large supply of labor, a noticeable decrease in rates of turnover. From the point of view of labor, a decline of turnover in a buyer's market is easy to understand. To all appearances, a sizeable amount of industries met them halfway by simply not resorting to the old customs in hiring and firing and by an, on average, much more prudent policy on layoffs (Slichter, 1929: 196, 202). New hirings thus fell relatively, depressing the turnover rates. Accordingly, these rates fell by more than half during the twenties (Jacoby, 1985: 171–172; Slichter, 1929: 208). Finally, the drop in immigration due to the 1921 temporary restriction act and the 1924 National Origins Act was offset partly by the disappearance of return migration, partly by immigration from Canada and Mexico, and partly by the enormous increase of internal black migration.

Blacks became the new unskilled workers, be it in an industrial situation quite unlike that of the new immigrants. The labor market they found was not expanding but, especially for unskilled work, was contracting. Also, the rising proportion of semiskilled work in the mass production industries was the privilege mainly of the new immigrant. Unskilled work as a temporary station was a foregone conclusion for the black worker. The black urban population outside the South increased by 70 percent during the twenties, finding employment as unskilled workers predominantly in the industries with the most irregular employment patterns: steel and automobiles (Piore, 1979: 41, 158; Jacoby, 1985; Wilson, 1978: 70ff.; Katznelson, 1976: 31–33).

The most remarkable feature of the twenties in the field of the employment relationship was the curbing of power of the foreman. The interest of the larger firm in low turnover led to better administration of personnel affairs and to a centralization of personnel decisions, at first mainly relating to hiring and firing but soon extended to promotion and transfer and time and motion studies along with job analysis. Indeed, in the thirties, the latter would become one of the major tasks of the personnel departments (Baron, Dobbin, and Jennings, 1986; Jacoby, 1985). But only some 20 percent of the industrial labor force was touched by these developments during the twenties, and the majority of the effort was directed at the skilled workers.

The semiskilled should not be left out of the picture, though. The personnel movement was concentrated in the larger industrial firms and not in the craft-related and smaller ones. These were the same firms that employed a large proportion of semiskilled work, performed in very large numbers by the erstwhile new immigrants. It should be remembered that the occupational division between skilled and semiskilled work, both accounting for somewhat over 10 percent of the total labor force in the early twentieth century (Braverman, 1974: 426ff.), was skewed to the predominance of the semiskilled in larger industries, especially of the mass-production variety. This was, in itself, conclusive evidence that the spread of personnel departments and centralized employment influenced the position of at least a part of the semiskilled new immigrants. So did the experiences of Americanization and "welfare capitalism," well before the rise of the CIO and the recognition it achieved of the industrial status of the former new immigrant.

AMERICANIZATION

The peak of this century's Americanization campaign coincided with World War I and its aftermath, but the campaign itself was of much earlier vintage. Suppression of and disdain for habits and traditions of the Old World was already a trait of the "Know-Nothing" party of the 1840s and 1850s, the response to Irish Catholic immigration. Public education was propagated as one means of socializing the immigrant to the Protestant example. A temperance movement flourished for some time around mid-century. Also, restriction of immigration was proposed. Many of these movements returned in some form with the coming of the new immigration. An Anti-Saloon League was founded in 1895, an Immigration Restriction League in 1894. Public education once more was in the vanguard of educating the new immigrant to an American format. Programs of the Democratic, Republican, and Progressive parties never tired of emphasizing the necessity of a ban on Asian immigration and of a selective policy on the new immigration countries (Hutchinson, 1981: 621ff.).

What distinguished the Americanization endeavor from the earlier nativist response? One important interpretation of Americanization, in fact, stresses the continuity of nativism, connecting it with the rural response to the growth of the cities (Hofstadter, 1955). The adoption of the Eighteenth Amendment in 1919 (barring the manufacture, sale, and importation of intoxicating liquor) and the immigration restriction acts of 1917, 1921, and 1924 were the last victory of the country over the city. The withdrawal of the Eighteenth Amendment under the first Roosevelt administration, on the other hand, signaled the political upper hand of the city, supported and symbolized by the former new immigrants and their children (Lubell, 1951: 50–54; Bernstein, 1960: 509).

This is a strong argument, if seen against the background of the city's minority position in America's population up to 1920 and the political majority position of rurally dominated states in Congress. But it is also grossly simplifying. The Immigration Restriction League was a product of Boston, and its most vocal spokesman in Congress was for several decades Senator Henry Cabot Lodge, representing Massachusetts (Feldstein and Costello, 1974: 171ff.; Hutchinson, 1981). Their plea for immigration restriction rested more on the support and sympathy it set out to evoke in labor circles than on rural America (Hutchinson, 1981: 493; Boyer, 1978: 213). The Anti-Saloon League succeeded in promoting the passage of legislation in thirty-one states, before the Eighteenth Amendment was enacted. One-third of these states were industrial (Boyer, 1978: 211–213). In fighting alcoholism and vice in general, New York and Chicago were in the forefront (Boyer, 1978: 191–195). They, to be sure, were the cities with the largest numbers and the highest ratios of new immigrants. But they definitely were not rural. If anything, they were the cities in which the Progressive movement flourished, and as good a case can be made for the intimate relationship between Americanization and progressivism as for Americanization and the rural response to the city.

The city, industrialization, and immigration had been recognized as one of a kind from the days of the Irish immigration to the period of the new immigration. With the acceptance of industrialization came—however slowly—the acceptance of the city, and in consequence the reform impulses toward the immigrant changed as well. Nineteenth-century reform movements had fused bigotry, repressive proposals, and attempts to curb immigration. Reform and repression, immigration restriction, and xenophobia fed on each other and, in fact, should be considered a whole. The twentieth-century Americanization movement formed no exception to this American rule. Here, too, repression went along with positive reforms, and immigration restriction was defended with an eye on the purity of the race as well as with educational and socializing promises.

Municipal reformers were successful in relating political corruption in the cities, crime, poverty, and the presence of the new immigrant. This formed the web of this century's Americanization, at least insofar as it had an identity belonging to, and yet distinct from, earlier manifestations of nativism. The political rights of the new immigrants, being granted the vote before official citizenship had been attained (filing the intention of naturalization and a residence clause of, on average, one year would do the job) meshed with both the all-American political institution of the spoils system and its concomitant weak bureaucracy and with that second American feature, the decentralization of the political system, its explicit fragmentation of power, and, again, the little leeway this afforded to bureaucracy. These conditions conflicted with the demands of modern industry and modern politics. But as long as they reigned, the political bosses were its centripetal forces. They kept the system together, preventing too great a dispersal of power and creating a form of "controlled decentralization" (Merton, 1967: 127ff.; Allswang, 1979: 137).

Instead of endangering the American political institutions the new immigrants' political presence exacerbated and for many came to symbolize the problems generated by the spoils system and decentralization. Their willingness to Americanize was not measured by their political prudence during the war or their initiatives in visiting and creating night schools or in sending their children to school (Feldstein and Costello, 1974: 383ff.). Rather, the measure was control of the schools by experts, the destruction of ward control, and the explicit rejection of ties with the country of origin. Said Woodrow Wilson in 1915: "America does not consist of groups. A man who thinks of himself as belonging to a particular national group in America has not yet become an American" (quoted in Gordon, 1964: 101). "Immigrant origin" and "un-American" had become interchangeable, with the blessing of the same president who contributed substantially to the professionalization and bureaucratization of the American political system and who somewhat later decided to make the world "safe for democracy."

To sum up, Americanization in this century consisted of two parts. One was the effort of reforming politics, an effort that partly coincided with the advance of the new immigration and found a convenient and, socially, widely approved symbol in it. The second was the fear of uncontrollable internal dissension engendered by the First World War and the regrettable but predictable response of repression and "pressure-cooking" assimilation (Gordon, 1964: 99). Labor problems figured in both parts. English classes proved an expedient many employers felt necessary. Working habits and cultural traditions, such as religious holidays or time taken off for funerals or weddings, could come into conflict with the demands of industry. The First World War strengthened the attack on habits and traditions. Supply of labor had become a critical variable, and one way to enhance it, next to the focus on mobility, was to reduce absenteeism, at least that part of it that was attributed to preindustrial custom and tradition. It resulted in a new upsurge of welfare capitalism and ended during the twenties in the "American plan." It worked, albeit in spite of rather than thanks to the Americanization campaign. The new immigrants did not contest Americanization. That assumption was false. American culture—whatever it was—was never endangered by the new immigrants. Nor were its political institutions. Before immigrating, the new immigrants had already chosen America; they had not been driven to it: "most migrants to industrial America...were not uprooted but ambitious, self-uprooted emigrants, drawn not from the most impoverished regions of Europe but from those in the throes of economic change" (Rodgers, 1978: 171). Their cultural forms, and thus their modes of solidarity, were geared to change and its acceptance. Acculturation under the label of Americanization was an objective far off the mark.

THE LIMITS OF WELFARE CAPITALISM

There was a close link between Americanization and welfare capitalism (Montgomery, 1980: 32). The meaning of welfare shifted over time, emphasizing family values at one time, regular employment and some security another time. The promotion of loyalty to the company may have been one common underlying characteristic of all welfare programs; its manifestations included panic-struck reactions to labor unions and industrial unrest, the necessity of creating some medical and educational provisions where even the most elementary ones were lacking, and employee representation and stock ownership. Also, the workers affected might include the skilled worker, the women and children, the new immigrant, the even more recent black worker, or some combination of all of them. Services provided could cover medical facilities; language courses; housing; education and religion; sickness and accident, old age and death, and even unemployment benefits; and profit sharing and stock ownership.

Welfare capitalism was dominated by the larger firm of 250 employees and over. Among them, the large corporation took the lead, directly or through organizations such as the National Civic Federation. This is how it was in the beginning, when Pullman, for instance, captured the imagination until the great strike of 1894 cooled the optimism. It was the same in the middle when Standard Oil and U.S. Steel were in the forefront, trying to build a benevolent image after the brutal suppression of the strikes of 1914 and 1919. It was also like that in the end, during the late twenties, when companies like General Electric carried the gospel further. The welfare capitalist movement did spread. Investigations conducted on the 1926 situation indicated that 80 percent of the larger firms had invested in welfare capitalism, and more than 4 million industrial workers (which represented between one-fourth and one-third of the total industrial population) experienced its effects. The average expenditure on welfare measures was $27 per worker per year, 2 percent of annual wage income (Brandes, 1976: 28; Nelson, 1975: 116; Bernstein, 1960: 171).

In view of the variety of its functions, services, institutions, and clients, two themes may help to place welfare capitalism in perspective. The first is the relation of welfare capitalism and the trade unions, the second the relation of welfare capitalism and the personnel department. Welfare capitalism did not prevent strikes, as the case of Pullman demonstrated. But it could serve as an attempt on the part of the company to rebuild labor morale after a strike. More generally, welfare capitalism may have been inspired by the urge to undo the attraction of trade unions (Bernstein, 1960; Coriat, 1981). Welfare programs were initiated and expanded in favorable economic weather, the same climate in which the chances of the unions grew. Likewise, welfare programs were diminished or even dismantled during recessions and crises, when their costs became burdensome and, also, when the unions faced difficulties. Welfare resembled banking; the umbrella was granted when the sun was shining, withdrawn when the rains started. There surely was such a "welfare cycle," although it was seldom a matter of all or nothing. More or less is a better description. In however small a measure, the union function of economic support in financially hard times was undercut by means of a series of company benefits. Also, the presence of the union in the shop was countervailed by employee representation, or the "company union."

In particular during the early twenties the attack on the power of the unions ranked high on the employer's list of priorities. Union membership had risen to 5 million by 1920, mainly due to the growth in union bargaining power during the war and the attempts of the federal government to pacify labor relations by promoting "responsible" AFL unions and their demands for collective bargaining and grievance arbitration. The employers were determined to regain the lost terrain and their resolution to do so grew after the passing of the conflict-ridden year of 1919. They revived the open shop campaign that had served them so well in the prewar years. In late 1920 a nationwide network of open shop organizations had sprung into being. Early in 1921 twenty-two state employer organizations met in Chicago, drew the local organizations together, and launched a national campaign under the ominous banner of the "American Plan" (Bernstein, 1960: 148). The union shop, or for that matter the union itself, now was branded an un-American institution. Little did it matter that the open shop was tightly closed to any union member or that the closed shop might be considered a defensive weapon against union busting and discrimination of union members. Yellow dog contracts, court injunctions, industrial espionage, and company violence thrived as never before. The campaign, if measured by the precipitous drop in union membership, was very successful. At the end of the decade the AFL unions counted 3.5 million members, a loss of about one-third of its membership at the start of the decade. In 1920, 18.5 percent of all nonagricultural workers were organized; in 1930, a mere 11.5 percent (Bernstein, 1960: 335; Troy, 1965).

There was more to worry the unions. Employment in industry stagnated, gains in the automobile industry being more than balanced by losses in coal mining and the textile industry. Moreover, the automobile industry was far beyond the grasp of the AFL, while mining and textiles had been among the sparse AFL-affiliated industrial union bastions. Viewing the decade as a whole, the period after 1925 showed a decline of growth, notably in construction. Finally, the employers fought the unions with their own weapon of "industrial democracy." The difference between the open shop drive of the early century and the American Plan of the twenties was precisely the slogan of industrial democracy, epitomized in employee representation or the company union. Here the open shop and welfare capitalism fused on "the problem of government in the shop" (Bernstein, 1960: 170). Employers had come to recognize that the disorganization of their workers—to save them the interference of the unions—had to be complemented by some form of representative reorganization of the workers. This, employee representation set out to do. By 1928 more than 1.5 million workers were represented through company unions, two-thirds of them in very large companies of 15,000 workers or more (Bernstein, 1960: 171). The mass-production industries (meatpacking, electrical equipment, textiles, steel, among them) led the way.

In spite of the slogan of democracy and the use of the name of "company union," employee representation was a toothless appearance. Although representatives had to be chosen, many workers declined the invitation to vote. In the vital areas of wages and conditions, the representation either had no voice at all or was used in the bad-messenger style. Indeed, the coincidence of employee representation and wage cuts was more than coincidence. Workers were too well aware that the choice was not between union representatives or company unions. Consequently, the representatives elected were not that representative. Surveys held disclosed "that they were more likely than other employees to be married, native-born American citizens who owned property and were employed by their companies for several years" (Brandes, 1970: 132–133). When, during the thirties, employees in a Rockefeller mine were allowed the choice, granted them by the early New Deal legislation, between the United Mineworkers or the representation plan, they outvoted the company union by more than three to one (Bernstein, 1960: 164).

When emphasizing the personnel wing of welfare capitalism, it should be noted that, along with a change of means, the worker involved assumed a character different from the skilled worker or his union. Stock ownership, pensions, insurance facilities, and the like had been directed mainly at—and, insofar as they were successful, followed mainly by—skilled workers (Brandes, 1970: 90ff., 102, 108ff.). Personnel measures had a wider range and were often motivated by the problem of semiskilled labor. When work in itself was without intrinsic satisfaction, the argument ran, it might help to show interest in the worker (Bendix, 1956: 389). The worker in this instance was semiskilled. Unskilled work as usual was not included for the simple reason that the bargain the unskilled had to offer was not as interesting as the bargain the semiskilled controlled. The development of work-related qualities of the semiskilled worker was no automatism, and the on-the-job training that introduced workers to the ins and outs of the specific machine system of their plant was more informal than formal. Without the cooperation and the goodwill of the worker involved, the potential gains of the work-related skills could not be tapped. On the other hand, the sanctions the worker possessed in a mechanically integrated labor process could cause considerable damage. To promote the one and to prevent the other became the major objective of the personnel movement. The initiatives taken in the field of employment stabilization, the layoffs and seniority provisions, and the priority schedules when rehiring was at stake at times were indistinguishable from welfare work. On the other hand, all of company welfare might be subsumed under this one personnel imperative. The case of Ford's Sociological Department, in connection with the $5 day, proves the point.

The personnel measures were the only ones to survive the Great Depression. Their limited effectiveness in the twenties, especially in regard to the semiskilled worker, was improved during the decade of the Great Depression. In that sense, it is erroneous to suggest (Brody, 1980; Piore and Sabel, 1984) that the Depression finished welfare capitalism. Many welfare provisions were indeed discontinued or trimmed down to insignificance. When comparing data on 1927 with those of 1935, the most striking phenomenon is the large reduction in benefit programs (such as bonus systems and profit sharing but also cafeterias, employee magazines, etc.) and the continuation of programs systematizing employment (Baron, Dobbin, and Jennings, 1968: 374, table 5).

The development of industrial relations departments in the thirties, being the company's organ to deal with the incipient industrial unionism, affirmed rather than weakened the hand of the personnel departments. The personnel departments signaled a growing professionalization and bureaucratization of the employment relationship, and they tended to play down the moralistic and outdated overtones of welfare capitalism.

The same holds, though with considerable less emphasis, for the voluntarist streak of welfare capitalism. The welfare benefits in the insurance field had come about partly as an attempt to forestall governmental, obligatory regulation. These benefits were financed through company and worker contributions, sometimes solely through company contributions. Not all were soundly administered. but even those that showed a favorable record had to be highly selective in allowing claimants, and moreover, the benefits promised alleviation of trouble only for a relatively short time. The benefits simply were not up to prolonged unemployment and all it entailed. The period after 1929 soon brought the lesson home. The final result, though, achieved during the New Deal, did not discard voluntarism as much as it undergirded it with a public insurance policy.

6

FORD AND FORDISM

Technologically, the new science-based chemical and electrical industries were much more in the vanguard than the automobile industry during the first decades of this century. Economically, however, the automobile industry surpassed them all. In the year 1900 the total number of automobiles produced was a mere few thousand. Twenty-five years later millions of cars were produced, and the automobile industry ranked first in terms of output value, costs of materials used, share in the industry as a whole, and wage sum (Chandler, 1964: xii). Relative to other industries, the greatest leap forward came during the second decade of this century, the years when Henry Ford introduced and perfected the system of "progressive production," or mass production, as it is usually called (Chandler, 1964: 5, table 3). The twenties consolidated the primary position of the automobile; the product became the core of an expansive market for construction and new electrical home appliances (Kindleberger, 1973: 60–61; Mattick, 1978: 118; McCoy, 1973: 119). The twenties, indeed, were the years of the consumer durable, which accounted for four-fifths of the increase in gross national product between 1919 and 1929 (Fearon, 1979: 29). At the same time, the automobile created a huge market for steel, rubber, plate glass, nickel, aluminum, tin, copper, felt, leather, paint, and so forth. New products and services, from roadmaps to consumer credit and insurance, were called for as well. The very growth potential of the science-based industries, petroleum refining included, was critically dependent on the automotive industry (Noble, 1977: 19; Schumpeter, 1939: 235–240).

In the early years of the century the automobile had been a fad for the few. Even in 1907 the American pattern hardly diverged from the European one. But after 1908, the year Ford introduced the Model T and started experimenting with assembly-line production, a new era came about (Bardou et al., 1982: 20, table 2-1, and 47). In 1927 one of every five Americans possessed a car, more than eight times as many as in France and Britain, and about forty times as many as in Germany (Bardou et al., 1982: 112, table 6-1). Like the case with the microprocessor of today, the car's sales had skyrocketed and its price had consistently gone down. At the heart of both was the strategy of Ford's Model T. The price of the Model T in 1909, its first full year on the market, was $950. Ford sold 12,000 of them, and with that he controlled a small 10 percent of the market. In 1925 the price of the Model T was down to $290, and Ford sold 1.5 million cars, a market share of 40 percent (White, 1982: 139, table 2). This remarkable accomplishment earned Ford a lasting name: Fordism.

FORDISM

The first American attempts to produce automobiles took place in the New England region. Powered by electricity or steam, the peak in production of these vehicles, 1,600 of them in one year, was reached in 1900. Electricity and steam necessitated either very complicated and heavy machinery or, as in the case of the electrical car, time-consuming and expensive battery charging. Slowly, the gasoline-driven car captured the market and the future of the automobile. In this case it was not New England that reigned but the Midwest, where from the 1890s on experiments had been undertaken with gasoline combustion, following in the footsteps of the Daimler example. The manufacture of cars, buses, and trucks was concentrated in the so-called auto triangle in the Midwest. The Midwest combined several advantages for automobile production. Due to the mechanization of the bicycle industry, trained mechanics were amply available; because of the relatively low entry barriers of the young automobile industry, many entrepreneurs tried and entered the new field. Mortality rates were high, but so were profits for those that managed to survive (on entries and exits, see White, 1982: 138, table 1).

Easy entrance was made possible by the nature of the early industry. Capital requirements were relatively low. The Ford Company in 1903 started with a mere $150,000 of capital in shares, of which only $28,000 was actually paid up in full. Assembly was the main activity. Auto producers purchased, usually on credit of sixty to ninety days, the parts and materials required; assembled them; sold the resulting automobile cash; repaid creditors; and began a new round. Capital, thus, largely resembled its original shape of a stock out of which wages were advanced. Production was mainly on order. Since the demand for the automobile regularly was larger than producing capacity, sales were easy, and the problem confronting the industry was not how to get rid of the cars but how to get more of them. Standardization of parts and procedures for assembly were one part of the answer to the problem; the revolutionizing of the whole process of assembly, the other. The first years of the industry were characterized by developments concerning parts and procedures, and the typical producer started manufacturing in series; when Ford stepped in, the assembly process itself became the major influence on the development of the industry, and the industry became on of mass production.

A truly industrial method of producing automobiles depended on the "democratization" (Weber 1961: 230) of this luxury item of consumption. This is what Ford set out to accomplish. Soon after the founding of the Ford Company in 1903, he acquired a majority interest and decided to discontinue the focus on the expensive Model K (Galbraith, 1964: 166–168). Instead, Ford complemented the earlier standardization effort by insisting on the prior importance of a rigorous and uncompromising standardization of output. The aim was no longer to produce the given output at as low a cost as possible but to produce an output as large as possible, lowering costs and prices along the way as a result of maximum feasible standardization. This, a strategy based on the rigid assumption of a market that would automatically expand through a low-cost and a low-priced car, was the main mark of distinction separating Ford from, for instance, Chrysler and Leland (the manufacturer of the Cadillac). The strategy was also markedly different from the one William Durant followed. Durant, as convinced as Ford was that automobiles should be counted in millions rather than thousands, built an empire buying up existing productive capacities and organizing them into one corporation. Soon, for instance, the Chevrolet and the Cadillac were divisions of General Motors. A stratified market was integral to the approach, just like the Ford strategy assumed a uniform market.

The Model T became the embodiment of the Ford strategy. There was to be one car, standardized to the extreme, including the paint. The Model T could be ordered in any color as long as it was black. This notorious Ford dictum on the color black is telling. Why black? "Black paint dried the hardest and the fastest. It was the easiest to apply. It was the most efficient. Red, green, blue, or yellow Model T Fords required different machines, different men with different skills, and different processes to paint and to dry them" (Meyer, 1977: 23). Suppression of differences was the major precondition for reaping optimal profits from standardization and efficiency. The impact of the strategy of product standardization was readily acknowledged by contemporaries (Meyer, 1977: 20ff.). The design of the product was the logical first step in the attempt to achieve maximum feasible standardization. Standardization of parts, materials, and machines was next. Specialized, single-purpose machinery (drilling machines, lathes, grinding machines, planers, and so on) was either bought on the market or, if not in existence, developed within the company. By 1914, 95 percent of the work in the Ford factory was done with specialized machinery, supplied with an advancing number of automatic and semiautomatic devices, such as controls to change and reverse speeds. It enabled a faster and more voluminous production of automobiles and parts. The very reliance on specialization drove Ford more and more in the direction of vertical integration. Body shops, production of parts and machinery, the operation of foundries, even the paint used, all became part of one huge and expanding enterprise (Ford, 1927: 116–128).

With the exception of the flywheel magneto, an improved clutch, and the use of vanadium steel, the Model T did not incorporate technological novelties (Sorensen, 1962, ch. 9). The main novelty was the organization of production on the principle of sequential, or progressive, production. In the *Engineering Magazine* of September 1914 the principle was described as "the scheme of placing both machine and hand work in straight-line sequence of operations, so that the component in progress will travel the shortest road from start to finish, with no avoidable handling whatever" (quoted in Meyer, 1977: 33). The key word is *travel*. The work moves; the worker does not. The principle was not new. McCormick's International Harvester had experimented with it, and so had the Chicago meatpacking industry. The contribution of Ford was the completeness with which the principle was applied. Whereas sequential production usually had stopped short of the adaptation of machinery to the principle, this was one of the first problems the Ford engineers tackled. The aim was to break the custom of grouping machines generically, for this meant a lot of moving about of workers from machine to machine and department to department. Also, it involved many helpers, trucking parts and components from one place to the next. The use of helpers had been a first cost-saving measure, since a helper was an unskilled worker who, by freeing the mechanic of the task of collecting his materials and tools and of trucking his product, substituted inexpensive helper time for expensive mechanic time. The place of the helper, however, was only temporary. Soon, the conveyor would take over.

The helper system was preliminary to more thorough reorganization. Starting from the machine shop and the production of parts, the whole process of production became the object of the principle of progressive production. Machine tools were no longer grouped together but grouped by function of the movement of the product. The internal transportation of hand tools, raw materials, parts, and components was taken care of by a gradually expanding series of slides, rollaways, power-driven belts and chains, cranes, and carriers. Also, the design of the factory was adapted so as to accommodate the demands of progressive production. Throughout, the Ford factory gained in productivity.

The largest gains were made when, beginning in 1913, the Ford engineers systematically started to work on the moving assembly line: "Instead of having a group of workers assemble a flywheel magneto, an engine, or a chassis at a single location, they decided to move the individual parts past each worker. That worker carried out a single step in the assembly operation" (Chandler, 1964: 26). When the experiments started with the moving assembly of the flywheel magneto, it took twenty minutes for one skilled worker to put

Table 6.1
Average Size of the Ford Work Force

Year	Average Number of Workers
1908	450
1909	1,655
1910	2,733
1911	3,796
1912	6,867
1913	14,366
1914	12,880
1915	18,892

Source: Allan Nevins, quoted in S. Meyer III,"Mass Production and Human Efficiency: The Ford Motor Company, 1908-1921" (Ph.D. diss., Rutgers University, New Brunswick, N.J., 1977), p. 12, n.4.

together a magneto. After the work had been subdivided into its component parts and subjected to the rhythm and sequence of the moving assembly line, all it took for the making of one magneto was five minutes. The progress in the assembly of the engine was just as drastic. Again, by subdivision of tasks and by introducing the moving assembly line, the time required for the production of one engine was reduced from about ten hours to fewer than four. The application of the moving line to the assembly of the chassis crowned the effort. This was a gigantic undertaking. The chassis assembly meant the coming together of more than 4,000 parts and components. It took about twelve and a half hours of one workman to complete the chassis. After a minute division of labor had been installed and the moving line set to work, the average labor time was brought back to just under two hours, less than one-sixth of the original time (Chandler, 1964: 3–5; 1977: 280; Chinoy, 1955: 12, 15; Meyer, 1977: 38–44; Bardou et al., 1982: 59–62). The labor force employed by Ford grew with productivity, as Table 6.1 indicates.

Size was not the only change. The composition of the work force changed dramatically. Although precise figures as to the earliest days of the automobile do not exist, the 1891 occupational classification for metal workers in Detroit gives some clues, as shown in Table 6.2. Within each category sizeable differences in wages existed, none as large, though, as in the category of specialists. The machine hands, the prototype of the semiskilled worker of the nearby future and in 1891 already representing more than one-third of the specialist group, earned just over $6 a week, which was about two-thirds of the average income of the remaining specialists and lower than the wages of unskilled labor. Yet the analogy with the coming machine era should not be overstressed. As the low number of foremen suggests, the average size of the metal industries at the time will have been small, and much of the work performed was in the nature of assembly work, without, however, the methodical application of interchangeable parts and single-purpose machinery.

Table 6.2
Detroit Workers in Metal Industries, 1891

Occupation Group	Number	Percent	Mean Weekly Income
Foremen	9	2	$ 19.67
Mechanics	153	39	$ 12.58
Specialists	117	30	$ 8.18
Unskilled labor	113	29	$ 6.60

Source: Michigan Bureau of Labor and Industrial Statistics, quoted in S. Meyer III, "Mass Production and Human Efficiency: The Ford Motor Company, 1908-1921" (Ph.D. diss., Rutgers University, New Brunswick, N.J., 1977), pp. 61, 313-314.

Table 6.3
Ford Workers, 1913

Occupation Group	Number	Percent
Mechanics and subforemen	329	2
Skilled operators	3,431	26
Operators	6,749	51
Unskilled workers	2,795	21

Source: W. Abell, quoted in S. Meyer III, "Mass Production and Human Efficiency: The Ford Motor Company, 1908-1921" (Ph.D. diss., Rutgers University, New Brunswick, N.J., 1977) p. 68.

In 1913, the automobile was well established as a growth industry, and Ford was in the middle of experiments with the moving assembly line. The occupational distribution in the Ford factories at that time is shown in Table 6.3. A complete classification of Ford workers is available for 1917, and it shows a reinforcement of the tendencies of the 1913 distribution (see Table 6.4). The tendencies referred to are threefold. The first is the virtual disappearance of the mechanic and his replacement by the technical worker. The second is the impressive rise of the specialist or operator. The third is the decline of unskilled labor and, with it, the short career of the helper in the automobile industry.

In the 1891 survey the mechanic dominates the metal trade. Somewhat smaller are the semiskilled and unskilled groups. The survey shows that the specialist group comprises machine tenders as well as subordinate activities off the more highly skilled occupations. A definite division of labor of the skilled occupations has set in, yet not at a scale large enough to constitute a real threat to the dominance of the mechanic's skilled occupational status. This dominance is reflected above all in the fact that the mechanic is a directly productive worker. Also, the ratio of mechanics to helpers is about 7 to 1. In 1913 the picture changed substantially. The ratio of mechanics to helpers

Table 6.4
Ford Workers, 1917

Occupation Group	Number	Percent
Salaried supervisors	198	.4
Foremen	2,523	6.2
Clerks	1,710	4.2
Inspectors	1,533	3.7
Technical workers	5,391	13.2
Skilled trades	1,003	2.4
Specialists	22,652	55.3
Unskilled workers	5,986	14.6

Source: Ford Company Archives, quoted in S. Meyer III, "Mass Production and Human Efficiency; The Ford Motor Company, 1908-1921" (Ph.D. diss., Rutgers University, New Brunswick, N.J., 1977), pp. 71, 315-317.

had become about 4 to 7 (Meyer, 1977: 315), and the number of semiskilled operators included more than half of the total work force. The data, however, are crude and the classifications continually shifting. More precise are the 1917 data. There the erstwhile mechanic was labeled the technical worker, and the operators were called the specialists. The latter were directly connected with the process of assembly, the former only indirectly. The mechanic was no longer directly productive. As Ford had it, his new skilled technical workers "do not produce automobiles—they make it easier for others to produce them" (quoted in Meyer, 1977: 73). The ratio of technical workers to helpers has been redressed and is now more than 2 to 1 (Meyer, 1977: 316–317). Since the introduction of the moving assembly line, thus, the mechanic has been pushed out of direct productive activities to become functionally if not formally part of the technostructure of the company, and the numerical rise of the helper has been shortcircuited by the wide application of the system of conveyors. The only group to keep on growing, absolutely as well as proportionally, was that of the operators, the semiskilled specialists.

The large majority, about four-fifths of their total number, of the specialists in 1917 were machine hands (by far the most numerous group) and assemblers (Meyer, 1977: 71, 317; Reitell, 1924: 181–189). They were employed either at the main assembly line of the chassis or at other lines, like those of the engine or the magneto. This means that about one-third of all Ford workers in 1917 were employed at assembly lines. This was a very high proportion, for even during the twenties the average was not above 20 percent in the Detroit automobile industry (Fine, 1963: 13). It showed the high degree of mechanization of the Ford factory and the extension of the technical division of labor. In fact, few auto companies achieved the standard of minimum efficiency size set by the Ford example, a standard that kept creeping higher to reach 100,000 cars annually by 1930 (White, 1982: 149).

With the coming of the moving assembly line, the process of production "had become almost as continuous as those in petroleum and other refining industries" (Chandler, 1977: 280). The problem of optimizing throughput had been mastered. Technically, the assembly of a car is a muster example of the heterogeneous manufacture. The organizational revolution of the labor process through progressive production and the use of the moving assembly line transformed the industry into a virtual standard of organic manufacture, the more so since Ford completed the development of the assembly line by introducing the chain drive, regulating the pace of production in the factory. The Taylorist standard time, calculated for specific performances, now could be replaced by mechanically imposed time, independent of and external to the worker (Coriat, 1980: 51–52). Fordism in this respect was the Taylor system completed. Its organizational makeup was organic; standardization was at levels unprecedented, and the process of production defined the appropriate worker, not the other way around.

THE EMPLOYMENT RELATIONSHIP

F. W. Taylor had pleaded for the formation of an Employment Bureau (Taylor, 1903: 118–119). The tasks of this bureau were several. It had to keep records of each individual employee on punctuality, absence without excuse, violation of shop rules, spoiled work or damage to tools, skill at various kinds of work, average earnings, and so on. The bureau also had to take charge of hiring and of lists of people fit for internal transfers and promotions. Finally, Taylor did not wish to deny the beneficial effects of medical services, kindergartens, healthy surroundings, and the like. But there were two major provisos in his advocacy of an improved employment relationship. First, the measures relating to welfare capitalism had to be recognized as being of secondary importance only; the problem of work and wages was primary, and any suggestion otherwise could only lead astray. Second, the Employment Bureau was not projected as an independent source of advice, expert opinion, and decision. Rather, Taylor saw it as a section of the Planning Room. It was to be a part of the grand design of the organization of production and, in fact, subordinate. Rate setting, and thus the matter of training for and codification of required skill, and the establishment of standard times for all tasks performed necessitated a translation from the designated function to the specific individual. Also, changes in rates and skill requirements and changes in standard times could wreck an unstable social balance in the shop, unless precautions were taken to prevent this from happening. Taylor was acutely aware of the dangers the prerogatives of the foreman in this field spelled for his system as a whole. The Employment Bureau would have to forestall these dangers. It robbed the foreman of some of his previous competencies. At the same time, it ensured the further hegemony of the engineering point of view.

Centralization of the employment function and the introduction of forms of scientific management indeed often came together (Baritz, 1960: ch. 2; Schmidt, 1974; Slichter, 1920; Jacoby, 1985: ch. 4; Littler, 1982: ch. 7; Kochan and Cappelli, 1984). Hardly a linear development, the organizational locus of the employment department proved the most difficult and conflict-ridden problem to be solved. Taylor, as we saw, was clear on the subject. The foremen, from their side, tried to retain hiring, firing, training, transfer, and promotion within their competence. When that did not work, they were more ready to accept some form of advice, even obligatory, rather than give up discretion in the employment field altogether. Moreover, welfare benefits, medical and hygiene provisions, and employment practices often overlapped.

The case of Ford is one example. Ford, presumably responding to the 1912 Michigan Workman's Compensation law, could boast of a medical department already before the experiments with the final assembly line had started (Meyer, 1977: 130). This department was not just charged with taking care of the medical needs of Ford workers. It also registered lateness and absenteeism of workers, a practice that was in no way unique for the Ford plants. The problems for Ford, nevertheless, were urgent. Turnover had reached very high levels and was costing the company considerable money. Estimates were that the replacement of a semiskilled worker cost, in 1913, somewhat over $70 and of an unskilled one somewhat less than $10 (Meyer, 1977: 102; Sward, 1948: 49). The company employed roughly 14,000 employees in 1913, but with more than 50,000 men actually working for a shorter or longer period, the company losses because of turnover must have been between $3 million and $4 million for that year only. Actually, Ford got off easy, thanks to his relatively large proportion of semiskilled workers. Average retraining costs in industry as a whole were higher and fluctuated between $50 and $200 per worker (Nelson, 1969: 33). Yet it cost, and the time for some action apparently had come. In the same year of 1913 a central Employment Department was established, largely as the product of Ford's personnel executive of the time, John R. Lee. This department was to take over many of the employment functions the foremen once possessed and also to institute new employment practices, such as job analysis and a wage-classification system. It revolutionized the Taylor proposals, mainly by lifting the bureau out of the decisionary discretion of the production staff. Yet the Employment Department hardly had been installed when Ford, in the first days of 1914, announced the $5 day.

Wages and Turnover

From a middle-sized town Detroit rapidly grew into a large industrial city in the first decades of this century. Between 1910 and 1920, the years of the major Ford innovations, its population doubled, from 465,000 in 1910 to 993,000 in 1920 (Leggett, 1968: 45). With the growth of the population, its origins changed. Around 1900 Germans and Americans had formed the majority of the population. Fewer than fifteen years later Poles and Italians were the majority groups in Detroit. The change was reflected in, and had been brought about to an important degree by, the automobile industry. Ford data report that by 1914, the year Ford introduced the $5 day, the work force of the company consisted of about three-quarters foreign employees, with Poles being the largest group (Leggett, 1968: Meyer, 1977: 94).

The fast industrial expansion of Detroit, centered around the automobile industry, was depending on a continuous influx of new labor power. Personnel practices, however, were initially rudimentary and added to, rather than solved, the problem of labor recruitment. Conditions in the automobile industry were not very inviting. Although the wages were relatively high, employment was irregular, and in the Ford factories in particular, the work might change from day to day. The transformation of the process of production to one completely integrated process of assembly took years of experimentation with new sequences, tools and machinery, divisions and subdivisions of labor, and so forth. The experiments meant that for several years every new day brought new machinery and equipment and thus new modes of work and changed working conditions (Sward, 1948: 49 n.; Meyer, 1977: 20–22).

All along the intensity of the work increased. The speedup system was not new in the Ford plants, but a system in which "all noses pointed in the same direction," as one Ford engineer had said, and in which the work moved while the men were frozen at their spot made control of the time and performance of the men much easier. Control also became more imperative, every time the amount of fixed capital grew in the plant and every time more mechanical links between the jobs of workers were added. The number of foremen per operative grew steadily. In a three-year time span the number of workers under one foreman was reduced from fifty-three to fifteen (Meyer, 1977: 78). The chain drive eventually magnified the possibilities of control of pacing, since it embodied the impossibility of escaping from the line. Then there was the work itself. Much of it was repetitive. It had to be performed in isolation, and the closer one was bound to the line, the more isolated one became. It consisted of one or a few movements only, to be performed for long stretches of time without a break. The surroundings were extremely noisy, and much of the work was dirty. It often required some dexterity, and it demanded physical strength but only of a one-sided and unchanging nature. Mental attention was needed but only of a surface, nonintrinsic character. It is remarkable how enduring these characterizations proved over time (Walker and Guest, 1952; Chinoy, 1955; Widick, 1976).

The lack of regular employment and job security created a situation, in the case of Ford, in which wages were of considerable influence. Ford paid the usual piece-rates, but since in 1911 operations had started in Highland Park, people had to spend more time and unpaid time to move to and from work. This already put Ford at a comparative disadvantage. His rigorous insistence on mass-production methods only added to his labor troubles. Finally, just before the introduction of the final moving assembly line, Ford did away with piece-wages and introduced a time-wage system. This, in 1913, actually reduced the wages people received (Sward, 1948: 48), and they responded by leaving in large numbers. Jobs were plentiful in Detroit in 1913, and the effective wage cut added to the already very considerable turnover rate at the Ford factory, which was nearing 400 percent annually. With that, Ford was in the lead, and it caused considerable difficulties for the continuous use of plant capacity, a consideration that grew in importance along with the outlays in fixed capital.

Just a few months after Ford's decision to introduce time-wages, the Employment Department began its work under Lee's direction. One of the measures taken was a wage raise of 15 percent, apparently to produce some stability in the ranks of the shifting Ford working population (Meyer, 1977: 138). The raise was part of a comprehensive new labor program, prepared by Lee and based on his findings in a 1913 investigation of the turnover problem. The investigation would indeed prove fundamental for Ford's new labor policies. First, the existence of the Employment Department itself promised to curtail the influence of the production staff (foremen, superintendents) on recruitment, discharge, transfer, and promotion. The role of the production staff was reduced to an advisory one. Second, the advice forwarded had to be objective. The major instrument in promoting this end was a new wage-classification scheme, which reduced the hodge-podge of existing classifications to a six-tiered skill-wage classification. The six grades again were subdivided into three or four levels. The whole classification had been developed on the basis of extensive job analyses. Lee's intention was clear; he wanted objective and easily applicable standards by which both jobs could be ranked and performances evaluated. Also, he wanted to see a job ladder established, allowing for internal promotions within and between job categories, the main criteria being merit and seniority (Meyer, 1977: 140–147). Third, Lee proposed and effected an Employees' Savings and Loan Association, bent on guaranteeing general economic security for the Ford employees and on strengthening the ties between company and workers.

Combined, the Lee program had immediate effects. In a few months turnover dropped considerably, reaching the average Detroit level of the time, which, incidentally, still was well over 100 percent annually (Meyer, 1977: 150). The main influence reportedly was the Employment Department itself, with its authority on discharge especially. How stable these first effects would prove, however, we will never know. Three months after the Lee reforms, in January 1914, Ford was in the headlines with his announcement of the $5 day. This plan incorporated many of the features of the Lee proposals, but its architect had not been Lee, but Couzens, Ford's sales manager (Sward, 1948: 51).

The $5 Day

The $5 day was a profit-sharing plan. Taking the day wage rate for common labor at the then usual level of about $2.50, Ford promised to add the same amount to the income of the worker, provided the worker would prove worthy of the honor. Thus the worker would share in the profits of Ford. Moreover, Ford stated that by far the large majority of his workers would start receiving the $5 immediately. Also, the workers could rely on fair treatment. Nobody would be discharged, and thus excluded from the bonus, without the possibility of appeal. In fact, firing people was reduced to a last-resort solution, after all attempts at internal transfer and the like had failed or the worker had simply proved unmanageable.

The problem to which the $5 day was an answer was a big one. Symbolized by turnover and absenteeism, it went beyond these things. As Ford and Couzens realized, the moving assembly line lodged potential productivity gains that were as yet untapped. After the technical problems of the assembly lines had been mastered, in late 1913, productivity and speed of the line had become synonyms. The important question now was to reduce quits and absences of workers while speeding up the work. An enlarged labor market would help in the effort, but the more safe road was to forge substantial economic links between the workers and the company. Wages were only a short-term consideration in this respect; more important was the bonus. Higher wages as such would have rewarded the work; the bonus rewarded the loyalty to the company. Ford was not just after the best men; he wanted the best and the most reliable men. Reliability was conditional upon dependency on the company. Therefore, Ford restricted the bonus to those workers whose dependence on the company was easily ascertainable. Married workers with dependent wives and children had fewer options than young, unmarried ones. Consequently, the latter were excluded from the benefits of the program. Workers with domestic problems, boarders defined as one potential source of trouble, workers with drinking habits, workers without adequate housing or the ambition for it were supposedly more prone to the seductive forces of turnover and absenteeism than workers without such deficiencies. Consequently, the former type, if allowed at all to share in the benefits of the program, faced penalties up to and including discharge.

On the other hand, Ford promised, besides the $5 day, easy loans to buy homes, furniture, and so forth. To make sure that the loans got to those workers for whom they were intended, saving was stimulated, provided the savings were held in an American bank and not in one of the many mutual associations the new immigrants had formed for themselves (Meyer, 1977: 230–231). Again, the objective is clear. Savings had to be traceable and, presumably more important, had to be stripped of all possible association with the home country and the option of return. Nobody was forced to go along with such savings recommendations, however. As long as Ford controlled the penalty of withdrawing or curtailing the bonus, force was an outmoded gesture.

It proved a paying proposition. Hardly had the announcement of the $5 day been made, when 10,000 men crowded at the gates of Highland Park, scrambling for jobs. Many of them were from Detroit, but many others came from the larger Wayne County or more distant places. The labor market swelled, and after the first few riotous days, the speedup could be effected (Montgomery, 1980: 102). Rates of turnover and absenteeism were scaled down enormously. Turnover, near 400 percent in 1913, was reduced to 15 percent in 1914. Absenteeism, 10 percent in 1913, was less than 0.5 percent in 1914 (Sward, 1948: 56; Beynon, 1973: 24–25; Lee, 1916: 194; Meyer, 1977: 214). Losses incurred because of training, hiring, and introducing new men evaporated into thin air. If only from that perspective the $5 day was almost from the beginning a largely self-paying program. Almost $4 million had been lost on account of turnover in 1913, and the $10 million, reserved for the profit-sharing fund in 1914, was not paid out in full simply because not all of the men qualified, one reason being that the criteria for benefits were defined and applied more or less leniently, depending on the state of the labor market.

When the labor market had turned favorable for Ford, mainly as a result of the $5 day, residence requirements were introduced, a seniority (six months) clause was added, and the age threshold defining a young worker was raised. When, with the coming of World War I, the labor market grew tight, the criteria were loosened (Meyer, 1977: 177ff.). But the main gains were due to increased productivity, resulting from the intensification of effort on the part of the Ford workers. Unit costs per automobile fell, brought about by the raised efficiency standard that was as integral a part of the program as the bonus was. Higher standards were translated to the Ford worker as the necessity of strictly conforming to the demands made on him by foremen and superintendents. A 1914 company pamphlet to the workers made this clear: "The Ford Motor Company does not believe in giving without a fair return. So to acquire the right to participate in the profits a man must be willing to pay in increased efficiency" (quoted in Meyer, 1977: 176). Clarity was never a weak point of Henry Ford.

Suspicion was a weak point. Ford wanted to be more than sure about the character of his workers. The newly (1914) formed Sociological Department, led by Lee, was charged with taking care of character, just like the foremen, superintendents, and Employment Department took care of access to the job and behavior within the plant (Meyer, 1977: 192–193). The sociological investigators were recruited from the Medical Department mainly and further from the ranks of foremen and other junior managerial personnel. The whole job was done by company men (Meyer, 1977: 169, 194–196). Especially in the first year, when all of the Ford employees had to be investigated, the department was large, counting more than one hundred investigators, who were supported by an office staff, interpreters included, of about the same number. Later, the department shrank somewhat, its personnel oscillating with the needs of the moment (Meyer, 1977: 195–198).

After a short while the investigators worked along formalized lines. For every worker investigated, a "record of investigation" was composed, which, together with data on entry, eventual rehires, and work performance, became part of a complete file existing for every Ford worker. The investigation record, the completion of which was the specific task of the sociological investigators, contained detailed data gathered from churches, fraternal organizations, government agencies, passports, savings accounts, neighbors, relatives, and the personal impression of the investigator. Even the presence of a family Bible was an item of interest (Meyer, 1977: 201). When something questionable was found, warnings were issued or penalties imposed. Probation periods were not uncommon, and the improvements to be made were faithfully written down and checked at a later date. The investigators took no half measures in rubbing in the penalty. A nonconforming worker was fired only in the last instance—at least officially—but his bonus was withheld for a definite period. The amount withheld was noted on his pay envelope. Week after week the penalized employee saw the amount of lost profit grow, carefully calculated and registered on his envelope. Sometimes, the investigators tried to buy compliance by offering a part of the lost bonus as a lump sum in back payment, the part growing smaller as the employee took longer in achieving the requisite conduct. This, too, was an entry on the pay envelope. Change had to be noticeable within six months at most. If not, it "was deemed that the employee had duly qualified himself for discharge" (Meyer, 1977: 165).

With Rev. Samuel S. Marquis, who took over Lee's job in 1916 and changed the name of the department to the Educational Department, the assault on the new immigrant's style of life entered a new phase. Americanization became the outspoken objective. It is not enough, said Marquis in 1916, that "a man thinks right, he must be able to will what is right, and feel what is right as well" (quoted in Meyer, 1977: 223). To these objectives the educational effort, especially that of the Ford English School, was geared. The English School had started at the beginning of the $5 day program. The assumption was that it would do no harm if the foreign Ford employees would spend the one hour they had gained by a shorter workday in the classroom. Ford had good reasons to promote such an end. Three-quarters of his employees at the time were foreign born. Many of them mastered English; yet more than one-third of the entire 1914 Ford work force did not speak English (Meyer, 1977: 241). However mechanized the assembly of the automobile had become, this situation spelled danger for the continuity of the line every time some unforeseen interruption came about. Compulsory attendance in the English School for foreign non–English-speaking workers was supposed to be the appropriate remedy. Between 1915 and 1920, 16,000 workers graduated from the school (Meyer, 1977: 243). Graduation itself always took place on the Fourth of July, labeled for convenience as Americanization Day. Graduation was a ritual, marking "the transition from immigrant to American" (Meyer, 1977: 249), and successful it was. The Ford program became the model for Detroit, and Detroit became the Americanization model for many other cities (Meyer, 1977: 251). A unilateral success it was not, however. Sociology in itself had bordered on espionage. With the English addition, the border was crossed.

On the eve of and during America's participation in the First World War, the tasks of the Sociological or Educational Department became indistinguishable from the chase after the enemy within. Naturalization became a patriotic duty as did the buying of war bonds and working overtime. Conspiracies were everywhere and, thus, had to be overheard before they could materialize. The Educational Department became enmeshed in networks of citizen clubs and governmental or paragovernmental agencies bent on curbing the influence of anti-Americanism. The Educational Department never recovered from this association. At the end of 1920 it lost, after having been reduced to a few men, its independent organizational status. The profit-sharing plan was discontinued; Marquis left the company (Meyer, 1977: 305ff.). From 1921 on, a new Service Department, a private police power, commanded the company side of the employment relationship.

Summing up, then, the $5 day for several years was an outstanding success. Its weaknesses, nevertheless, were conspicuous. The high income it promised was only of short duration; yet it took Ford five full years to go from $5 to $6. In the meantime, inflation had eaten away everything that smacked of higher than average income. The Detroit cost-of-living index rose by more than 100 percent between 1914 and 1918, a national high (Meyer, 1977: 306; Sward, 1948: 60–61). Ford did respond to these higher prices by raising wages and lowering the bonus proportion of the $5 day. The income advantage slipped away, and Ford's payments neared the Detroit average. The question as to why Ford did not raise the $5 to a higher level at an early date remains unanswered, but it is at least likely that the situation in the labor market, the relatively short but exceptional war period excluded, was of major influence. In the twenties the easy labor market allowed for the dismantling of the Educational Department, together with profit sharing. Ford's answer to the strong recession of 1921 in the automobile industry was even more telling. He just fired thousands of workers from one day to the next, however qualified the men may have been from the point of view of loyalty to the company, thrift, sobriety, or whatever.

Another weakness of the program was its total lack of all elements of social security. Some seniority was built into the program, for to become eligible for the bonus, at least a few months with the company were a requisite. Discharge, on the other hand, was not so regulated, nor was there even a semblance of unemployment compensation. Seniority and age were much less of a problem for the skilled worker, but, again, the $5 day did not hold much promise for them. The reason is all too obvious. Their wage rates were relatively high, yet under $5. Their bonus was, accordingly, low (Meyer, 1977: 162). It was the semiskilled worker who featured in the $5 day. It was the loyalty of the machine tender that Ford was after, and it is the search after loyalty of the operator and assembler that the $5 day exemplified. Profit sharing, to be sure, was just a name. The relation between effort and profits was denied from the beginning. The bonus was a private attempt at an income policy, a political company reward, based on the knowledge of who effectively held the strings of the company. Its leveling effect on the distribution of income within the skill ranks betrayed the influence of mechanization on the wage structures. Yet here the Lee wage classification had already set the tone in the company. The $5 day rubbed it in. The semiskilled found, through their pay envelope, a recognition of their organizational centrality. It was a halfway recognition only, however, a gift instead of a bond. In the twenties the labor market became favorable for the employer, and the project was discontinued.

7

CRISIS, DEPRESSION, AND THE NEW DEAL

After the mid-twenties economic growth tapered off. Much of the growth of the period had been due to the phenomenal rise in the production and purchase of consumer durables and housing (see Table 7.1). This was the other side of Fordism; it was not only mass production but mass production of consumer goods and its forward and backward linkages (Hacker, 1970: 281–282). The automobile itself was its most conspicuous specimen. The expansion of the market for automobiles depended directly on its price and thus its economy of production, on the distribution of income, and on employment. As far as price was concerned, the Ford policy proved successful. Yet this policy had its limits. For many people the purchase of a new automobile was simply beyond their means. If they wanted a car they had to buy a used one. On the other hand, for those who could afford a new car within the prevailing distribution of income, the limits of the market had been reached by the mid-twenties, and replacement demand became more important than new demand (Chandler, 1964: 95). To stimulate replacement demand, the annual model came into vogue, eating away the advantages of the extreme Ford standardization of output. It, indeed, did effect a huge inroad into the predominance of the Ford Company and was set up to do so (*Fortune* quoted in Chandler, 1964: 153). It did not, however, expand the market so much as restructure it. When the "mass market" of the Ford project was saturated, a "mass-class market," represented by the series of different priced General Motors (GM) models, took its place. When A. P. Sloan, the GM president of the twenties and thirties, evaluated the coming of the "mass-class market," he enumerated four points. The first was the system of buying on installment; the second, the "closed" car; the third, a systematic policy on occasions; and the fourth, the annual model (Sloan, 1963: 150).

Table 7.1
Consumer Durables and Housing, 1920–1929

	Increase from 1920 to 1926	Decrease from 1926 to 1929
Housing construction	215%	37%
Consumption of durable goods	66%	5%

Source: M. Aglietta, *A Theory of Capitalist Regulation: The U.S.*
Experience (London, 1979), p. 95.

Actually, the picture of the twenties should be painted in somewhat darker colors. Although real income grew, that of wage labor included, the distribution of income became more unequal. Profits increased much faster than wages. Between 1923 and 1929 wages increased 11 percent and profits 62 percent (Leuchtenburg, 1958: 193). Relatively, the share of labor diminished (Steindl, 1952: 74–75). These are aggregate figures, and they hide as much as they reveal. Not all groups fared well in the new era of the twenties. Some areas were chronically weak, notably textiles and mining (Bernstein, 1960). Agriculture also was depressed during the twenties. In other areas employment was stagnant or highly irregular or both. The introduction of the annual model in the automobile industry—to which Ford gave in only belatedly— since the mid-twenties enhanced irregular employment (Fine, 1963: 4–6, 14– 15).

A period of unemployment for two or three months—during which the changeover from one model to the next took place—was the rule rather than the exception. Although it was a high-wage industry, high wages were more a reward for the long and forced waiting periods in between models than an indication of true prosperity. Also, the share of wages in the automobile industry declined after Ford lost the hegemony and the industry assumed the characteristics belonging to an oligopolistic market (Steindl, 1952: 84, 106). Overall, also, industrial employment did not increase, in spite of the huge productivity increases of the twenties. White-collar and service occupations, in contrast, grew and kept total unemployment figures, or rather their estimates, on a tolerable average (Bernstein, 1960: 55; Hacker, 1970: 287; Kolko, 1976: 100ff.; Tawney, 1979: 104; table 5). On the other hand, the number of industrial establishments continued to decline, although the average number of workers per establishment did not change. As might be expected, these tendencies became even more pronounced during the Great Depression of the thirties (Clough, 1953: 24).

The tendencies point to a number of imbalances in the American economy of the time. The declining number of industrial establishments was an effect of the merger wave and the rise of the holding company, especially prominent in the second half of the decade (Leuchtenburg, 1958: 190–192; Aglietta, 1979:

222; Hicks, 1960: 230ff.; Galbraith, 1954: 194ff.). The declining market for industrial employment led to, on average, barely rising wages for blue-collar workers, even allowing for the fact that the pattern was highly diversified between industries and for the degree of their concentration (Steindl; 1952: 80ff.; Stricker, 1985: 300ff.). The rise in real wages in the twenties advantaged white-collar workers much more than industrial blue-collar workers, although the argument may lose some of its edge, depending on the parameters of the estimates on unemployment and its distribution (Stricker, 1985: 299, table 2; 302, table 3). Nevertheless, and allowing for some imprecision, there is a growing consensus that unemployment of about 10 percent for industrial workers is a reasonable estimate (Nelson, 1969: 24–25).

Unemployment estimates of the twenties, because of sheer lack of data, are imprecise. Unemployment statistics were gathered as part of the census data. The ten-year rhythm of the census was totally insensitive to the ups and downs of the business cycle. Data, therefore, were gathered sometimes at peak times (for instance in 1920), sometimes in depressed years. The questions asked were often vague, based not on existing data but on the memory of the respondent. Also, many questions were simply not posed at all. The 1930 census, for instance, did not inquire about lay-offs. Yet for the automobile workers and the steelworkers, lay-off was a regular experience of unemployment (Nelson, 1969: 25). Not accounting for it in the unemployment statistics of the census was certain to produce grave inaccuracy of results (Garraty, 1978: 168; Bernstein, 1960: 267–269). Only since 1937 did the United States manage to gather systematic and reliable data on the size and distribution of employment and unemployment (Hauser, 1975: 107–109).

The distribution of income within the wage-dependent population tended to become more unequal during the twenties. The wage distinctions between high and low concentration industries grew; several labor-intensive industries were in chronic difficulties; agricultural employment fell considerably, contributing to a large migration of impoverished farmers and share-croppers from farm to city, and the major industry forcing up the wages of the great mass of semiskilled workers, the automobile industry, has reversed this tendency since the mid-twenties, concomitant with the decline of Ford and the rise of General Motors. The differences within the blue-collar group, accordingly, tended to widen. The unskilled worker faced a shrinking market for unskilled labor and had to incur a real wage loss between 1923 and 1929 (Stricker, 1985: 296, graph 1). The semiskilled and skilled gained a little, though the more semiskilled jobs the industry offered, the lower the relative gain (Stricker, 1985: 297, graph 2). That is, in those industries, like the automobile and iron and steel industries, in which the semiskilled had leveled off some of the distance that separated them from the skilled, the trend was reversed after 1923 and especially later in the decade (Bernstein, 1960: 68). No wonder, then, that the mass market for cars dried up. The rosy figures about the spread of automobile ownership in the United States at the end of the twenties presumably say more about the victory of the occasion and the success of installment buying than about the expansive capacity of the market as such. After all, a used car could be purchased for $60, an amount that, granted a little credit, made the car indeed a feasibility for many people. Buying a new car, however, was not possible for large masses of working people (Stricker, 1985: 314–315). For production to continue unabated, the limits of the prevailing distribution of income and its trend toward growing inequality would have to be lifted (McCoy, 1973: 168ff.; Hicks, 1960; Galbraith, 1954).

There are other indicators pointing to the halt in the spread of the mass production–mass consumption dynamic. Since wages and especially profits increased, much of the increase in productivity was not passed on to the consumer (Fearon, 1979: 32). Only after 1927 did prices start to fall a little (Fearon, 1979: 30) but less than in Europe and not at all in line with the productivity gains. In fact, the decline in prices was a result of federal monetary policy rather than of a changed pricing policy of industry (Fearon, 1979). One measure of the resulting discrepancy is that unit labor costs, despite the small real wage increase, fell in the twenties, while prices remained relatively constant. Prices tended to become "sticky," the typical expression of an oligopolistic market (Steindl, 1952: 88). Investment outlets were declining because of increasing surplus capacity, the capital-saving technology of the twenties, and the slowing down of the expansion of the consumer markets (Gillman, 1957: 146ff.; Steindl, 1952: 160, table 28). One estimate is that almost half of all the households remained outside the market for the new consumer goods that propelled the 1920 developments (Aglietta, 1979: 87, 94; Stricker, 1985). The latter was a force in its own right, because the mass-production industries "became so large relative to the total market that the propensity to invest in manufacturing plants was determined by the prospective level of capacity utilization, rather than by changes in the costs of inputs" (Piore and Sabel, 1984: 76).

As especially the policy of GM proved, major industrialists by the mid-twenties no longer relied on a fast rate of expansion in markets. Instead, replacement demand became the focus and with it the magic device of "planned obsolescence." This was a far cry from Ford's policy of maximizing output through full capacity utilization and standardized output and low prices. The opposite became the new rule (Baran and Sweezy, 1966: 232–233). The slack in the growth of the market produced both sticky prices and underutilization of capacity in a self-reinforcing movement (Steindl, 1952: 191–192). Depressed investment outlets were the result. Moreover, investment outlets in the producer goods industries had become vitally dependent on the rate of growth of the consumer industries, and once this rate faltered, the producer goods industries were struck as well.

Severe imbalances thus characterized the American economy in the twenties. Imbalances cropped up between producer and consumer industries, between expanding and contracting ones, in the distribution of income, between wages and profits, and between capacity and capacity utilization. Added to these were financial and monetary problems. The United States after World War I was no longer a debtor nation. It had become, to the contrary, the largest creditor nation. It financed, through loans, much of Europe's postwar debts. Foreign investments had increased substantially also (Hacker, 1970: 292, table). On the other hand, the U.S. tariff policy made it practically impossible for the European countries to repay their debts through increased exports to the United States, calling for new loans, and so on (Hacker, 1970: 287–288; Fearon, 1979: 17–20). Moreover, the international gold standard, although superficially restored during the twenties, proved unable to stabilize currencies and their rates of exchange (Fearon, 1979: 21–25). Finally, the monetary and financial situation in the United States itself was far from perfect. The Federal Reserve System was still highly decentralized and was unable to check or regulate the expansion of the stock market or the explosion of bank loans, the latter for both international and domestic purposes. The growing number of bank defaults in the late twenties, especially in the agricultural states but not confined to them alone, testified to the shaky foundations of loans (Fearon, 1979: 29). The supply of money, thus, could not be effectively controlled. The problem was not that no one saved any longer. Private savings stayed relatively stable during the twenties (Steindl, 1952: 170). Stock ownership, on the other hand, was concentrated in relatively few hands. Only 8 percent of the population owned stocks. Also, most of the stock issued did not contribute to capital formation but to the expansion of the holding companies (Fearon, 1979: 34).

In itself, none of these developments had to precipitate the crisis. Combined, however, they triggered the major depression of the century. When inventories rose dramatically in 1929, together with falling prices, production, and incomes (Fearon, 1979: 31, 33), new investments were postponed or cancelled, the stock market fell, a run on the banks followed, and the crisis was a fact. Its nature soon became clear, for whereas personal consumption in 1930 dropped by 6 percent, the purchase of consumer durables fell during the same year by 20 percent (Fearon, 1979: 34). These simple figures indicate the degree to which mass consumption of consumer durables had remained a luxury. Mass consumption, apparently, had not been for the masses. It had become a basic for the maintenance of the economic system at the same time that the income of many Americans prevented the purchase of mass-produced consumer durables. Fordism, the mutual development of mass production and mass consumption, was yet to be realized.

THE DISTRIBUTION OF UNEMPLOYMENT

Between 1929 and the end of 1932 national income fell by almost one-third. Industrial production in the same period was almost halved. Whether by 1933 one-fourth or one-third of the nation was unemployed is a matter of unending debate, but even the conservative estimate of 25 percent unemployment is appalling. Hardest hit were the boom industries of the twenties. Construction declined by 85 percent; consumer durables, by 50 percent; and the immediately related industry of durable producers' equipment, by 75 percent (Bernstein, 1960: 316ff.; Tawney, 1979: 103, table 4; Fearon, 1979: 35; Rayback, 1959: 320; Rothbard, 1983: 290). Among the producers of durables, the automobile sector incurred disproportionate losses. Factory sales of cars and trucks in the period fell by 75 percent; total wages paid, by almost two-thirds; employment, by 45 percent. Ford, the champion of the "high wages" doctrine, had initially responded to the crisis by raising the daily wage to $7. By 1932 he had stepped in line, and wages were at $4.

Those who worked did so for a sharply reduced number of hours per week: around forty-five hours had been usual; around thirty hours became the new average in the auto industry. This, incidentally, was the situation everywhere. U.S. Steel in 1929 employed 225,000 full-timers; in 1933 it counted zero. Full-timers had become part-timers; yet their numbers, too, were halved in this four-year period (Leuchtenburg, 1963: 2). Also, the instability of employment in the auto industry became more pronounced in the early Depression. Typically, prices fell only by 14 percent. Many of the independents of the industry, apart from the Big Three, were wiped out during the Depression, thus contributing involuntarily to the industry's further concentration. Of the Big Three, Ford experienced the most severe setback; Chrysler and GM did much better. Yet even GM lost in 1932 on its car divisions (Fine, 1963: 17–18; Jacoby, 1985: 209; Bernstein, 1960: 255).

Unemployment was unevenly distributed. Among the male white working population, central to our study, especially the young and the old worker ran a comparatively high risk to become unemployed. Nor was this a completely new phenomenon. Already during the twenties older workers were laid off faster than younger ones, and the older worker often was flatly refused a job because of age. New technology and its training requirements were sometimes cited as a cause, as was the negative relation between physical strength and age (Graebner, 1980: 49–51, 202–203). Moreover, the situation worsened during the Depression. The average age of workers in the manufacturing sector remained on the decline between 1930 and 1940. Workers over 45 years of age were especially hard hit (Graebner, 1980: 39–40, 50; Jacoby, 1985: 219). The older worker was not replaced by youth. Youth unemployment reached alarming heights during the Depression years. A full one-third of total unemployment during the Depression was put on the plate of youth between ages 16 and 24. Forty percent of the young were unemployed (Krug, 1972: 310), and even these figures are too optimistic.

An increasing number of young people opted for prolonged schooling or returned to the high schools. Between 1930 and 1932 high school enrollments increased almost twice as fast as between 1928 and 1930. In view of the generally aging population at the time, the increase may be ascribed to the towering threat of youth unemployment (Krug, 1972: 218). This situation undoubtedly softened the unemployment rate for the age group of 16 to 20. For youth unemployment figures as a whole, however, it mainly indicated the shift of the burden to the somewhat older age group. Not surprisingly, then, a Labor Department committee reported in 1938 that unemployment was concentrated especially in the 20 to 24 age group (Graebner, 1980: 212).

The uneven distribution of unemployment among the different age groups does not mean that old inequities, based on skill for instance, had become outdated. Many skilled jobs had developed into the kind of "support" jobs Ford boasted of for his skilled work force. These jobs tend to be "overhead"; they are needed also when capacity utilization is low. In addition to this situation in the automobile industry, such circumstances could also be found in the iron and steel industry (Steindl, 1952: 81; Jacoby, 1985: 217). Moreover, skill differentiation coincided with ethnicity. Since the twenties, more and more unskilled jobs had become the province of blacks and Mexican immigrants (Jacoby, 1985: 170–171; Bernstein, 1960: 68–69), whereas the semi-skilled showed a preponderance of the former new immigrants and the skilled of the old immigrants. Yet it is difficult to disentangle cause and effect. It may be skill, rather than national origin, that explains the difference in unemployment. For instance, in a comparison of the employment difficulty of workers in Philadelphia's metalworking industries and its radio industry between 1931 and 1935, it was found that once skill-level effects were controlled, immigrant–native differences in employment difficulty disappeared. Differences did exist apart from skill, but they were mainly related to industrial opportunity and its stability (Miller, 1981: 297–325).

The line between unemployment and poverty was very thin. That, however, was not new. The major new element during the thirties was not poverty but the fact that escapes from wage dependency were virtually nonexistent. Traditionally, three escape routes had existed: the family, migration, and the land. The family was lost as a resource for hard times during the thirties. One sober assessment of the family's position in the strenuous decade is the number of married women, adding to an already voluminous labor supply. Between 1930 and 1940 the number of women in the labor market increased by 22 percent, a rate unparalleled either before or after the Great Depression (Kolko, 1979: 95ff.). Noting the generally falling level of wages during the period, we have the classic Keynesian situation of involuntary unemployment. It was not rising but falling wages that emptied the family's resources of support and produced the growing labor supply. Return migration on an international scale had fallen away with the immigration restriction acts of the twenties. In fact, the immigration balance became negative between 1931 and 1936 (Taeuber and Taeuber, 1958: 54, table 12). Internal migration also fell dramatically during the Depression (Taeuber and Taeuber, 1985: 99; Thompson, 1937: 19ff.). Former depressions, during the heydays of the new immigration and during the agricultural depression of the twenties, had led to high return migration, thus softening the problem of domestic unemployment and poverty, and to the gigantic South to North move from farm to city in which tenants and share-croppers, many of them black, tried to escape from further rural impoverishment. These escapes, whether from North to South, America to Europe, or vice versa, were out of order. Wage dependency had been generalized. It was simply everywhere.

SOCIAL SECURITY

The slow history of the coming of unemployment compensation in the United States is best written if it is considered under a double angle. One of them is the insistence on prevention of unemployment by the business community and the associated emphasis on voluntarism. State or federal interference with prevention, accordingly, would, in the best of cases, be a supplement to private, company-sponsored, unemployment insurance plans and reserve pools and, in the worst of cases, a sanction against noncomplying companies. In the business community, in academic circles, and among politicians, Hoover and Roosevelt included, prevention was a popular, even dominant theme. The second angle is the demarcation, old as Jeremy Bentham's plea for a reform of the English Poor Law, between the "working poor" and the "destitute." For the people involved, the line may have been thin between income loss because of unemployment and poverty and its relief, but politically the line was monumental. Relief was one thing, unemployment compensation another. Some, like Hoover, rejected both, at least as a federal obligation. Others, like Roosevelt acted much swifter in the field of relief than in the field of unemployment compensation. When, finally, in 1935 the Social Security Act was signed, it was a federal act in name only, at least where unemployment compensation was concerned (Perkins, 1946: 289–292). More appropriately, it was a federal act calling for a "federal–state" system and leaving to the states practically all the action in determining who was to receive unemployment benefits and for how long and at what level. It also left to the states the discretion to transform unemployment insurance into a selective device to attract new employers or, for that matter, to reward employers' efforts at prevention. Voluntarism was not killed by the Social Security Act; rather, its foundations were rebuilt through the act, proving that the supposed antagonism between voluntary and state regulation was a false issue.

Workmen's Compensation and Health Insurance

Several reasons may be cited to explain the relative ease with which voluntarism and state regulation were deemed compatible on the subject of workmen's compensation. The first, stressed by the National Association of

Manufacturers (NAM) and the National Civic Federation (NCF) alike, was that the legislation involved would help to curb the influence of employer liability laws and thus the unpredictable financial outcome of a court decision and the heavy burden of the lawsuit itself. Compensation laws made costs predictable and might in the end be much cheaper than the costs of liability insurance. Moreover, the change from liability to compensation meant a change from court to administration, its being expected that the relevant administration would look after the needs of industry at least as much as after the needs of the injured workmen (Lubove, 1968: 49ff.; Weinstein, 1968; Orloff and Skocpol, 1984). The second reason is the premium placed on company prevention of accidents. Promotion of safety regulations and precautions became quite a fad. The Wisconsin law of 1911 set an example of the combination of accident prevention and its incentive through manipulation of the premium rates (Nelson, 1969: 105). Obviously, this benefited the employer more than the worker, for the worker, with the passing of compensation acts, often lost his right to sue the employer. Labor organizations insisted on this right since they assumed that it was needed to keep eligibility, benefits, and benefit periods at an acceptable level. They were proven correct in their fears. Benefits were low, sometimes not half of wages; periods were short even in the case of total disability, often compensated by a lump sum not surpassing a fixed amount of weeks; waiting periods were usual; medical requirements for eligibility were often raised (Lubove, 1968: 60–61). Need, obviously, counted less than predictability of costs (Leiby, 1978: 205). Moreover, the effect of prevention on accident rates was far from clear, allegations by J. R. Commons to the contrary notwithstanding (Lubove, 1968: 64–65; Davis, 1986: 440).

The voluntarist takeover of state workmen's compensation legislation did not mark the start of a trend. The 1915–1920 campaign for compulsory health insurance, considered by promoters of labor legislation and reform to be the second step to social security for the worker, never left the planning stage, although enactment came close in New York and California. Employers resisted it, because it meant another tax. Workers supported it but in a lukewarm fashion caused by their experience with workmen's compensation. Also, there was a constitutional problem. Health had been a political concern before, and it could be defended as such because of the "police" power of states and the federal government. Was an insurance, partly paid for by taxing the employer, defensible under the "police" clause? It might be argued that the health of his employees warranted such an interpretation. But could the argument be stretched so far as to include the employee's children? (See Leiby, 1978: 208.)

The constitutional problems were serious but, as the Social Security Act was to prove, surmountable. The Constitution indeed was not the major obstacle. Actually, the most vehement, and very successful, opposition came from the medical profession. The American Medical Association (AMA) was, when the failure of the health campaign had been recognized by all interested parties, the only victor in the struggle. What it objected to was not some clause in the insurance idea but the idea as such: "Health insurance meant the universalization of contract practice, and a loss of freedom (including the right to determine fees and therefore the level of clientele served)" (Lubove, 1968: 89). For like reasons, it objected to private insurance schemes. It took the AMA some twenty years before, in the middle of the Depression years, it consented to the principle of voluntary, private health insurance (Lubove, 1968: 90). By then the idea of collective health insurance had completely fallen into disrepute.

The relief measures of the first New Deal administration could include costs of medication. Under no circumstances, however, were costs of hospitalization to be paid for out of relief, nor were they to be integrated into the "comprehensive" system of social security Roosevelt wanted enacted (Hopkins, 1936: 74; Perkins, 1946: 297). Roosevelt, in 1934, stated solemnly: "I am confident we can devise a system which will enhance and not hinder the remarkable progress which has been made in the practice of the profession of medicine and surgery in the United States" (quoted in Perkins, 1946: 289). It may be that Roosevelt, as an afterthought, wanted to recall the original impetus of his administration's quest for social security—which had been a compulsory health insurance system (Trattner, 1974: 241). The 1939 Wagner Bill on health insurance was not even accorded a hearing in Congress. Nor was any state health legislation passed during the New Deal (Witte, 1957: 262, 1963: 173–189; Altmeyer, 1966: 115–117).

Relief and the Military Pension

Difficult as well was the question of relief. Following the English example, outdoor relief was as suspect as its claimants. Accordingly, the main legal arrangement, at the start of the Depression, "for the care of the destitute was incarceration in almshouses or workhouses. In some places the care of the paupers are still contracted to the lowest bidder, and destitute orphans were indentured to those who would feed them in exchange for whatever labor they would perform. The constitutions of fourteen states denied the franchise to paupers" (Piven and Cloward, 1979: 42). This, then, was loyal to the standards of the 1834 English Poor Law Amendment Act, predicated on the distinction between the destitute and the working poor, the employables and the unemployables.

Much of relief had been, by necessity but also voluntarily, of private origin. It had ranged from the 1816 American Bible Society to the endeavors of Jane Addams and Lilian Wald. Slowly, in progressive circles, the conviction had become established that poverty was a social and an economic problem, rather than a moral and psychological one. This apparently opened the door to state regulation, and indeed, some initiatives for state-sponsored outdoor relief did materialize in the early decades of the century. Mother's pensions legislation, forerunner of the present-day federal Aid to Dependent Children, came first. In the name of the family, help was being forwarded to widows and dependent mothers whose husbands had deserted or divorced them, had been imprisoned, were in a mental hospital, or were permanently disabled. The home, thus, was preferred to the institution.

Relief funds for outdoor help were explicitly legalized. State acts in the field started in 1911; by 1919 thirty-nine states already had passed such an act. In the ten states that contributed financially to mother's pensions, the benefits were somewhat better than outright poor relief. On the other hand, the similarity with poor law practices was larger than the difference. Local administration, mainly by a juvenile court or a county commissioner, and local financing were still characteristic (Lubove, 1968: 96–99; Leiby, 1978: 212–213). Comparable to mother's pensions in the pre-Depression years were other new slices of relief, leading to a progressive broadening of the scope of outdoor relief. Legislation was passed concerning aid to the needy families of veterans, the needy blind, and to old-age assistance (Lubove, 1968: 124–127, 136–137; Witte, 1957: 242; Leiby, 1978: 214–215). Many of these schemes were optional, subject to far-fetched scrutiny of claimants, and locally administered and financed. Also, the federal government was conspicuously absent from them, with, however, one major exception. This concerned military pensions. After the Civil War funds for disabled veterans were appropriated. Later, in 1890, the reach of the military pension was widened considerably. A federal law authorized pensions to disabled veterans. Whether or not the disability was service related was to be of no concern. The law was generously applied. In 1907 a general service pension, extending coverage to old age, was enacted. It continued the practice started since the 1890 law to supply wives and dependent children with benefits as well.

After the Civil War generation had died out, the pension act was not renewed. The suggestion (Orloff and Skocpol, 1984) that renewal was not tried in the overall attack on the spoils system, and that regulation rather than spending was the vogue in the Progressive Era is well taken. But one should not overstress the argument. Regulation, in social security, may be just another name for selective spending and its administration. Also, the attack on the spoils system was an attack on the political presence and potential leverage of the new immigrant rather than an attack on spending as such. Yet whatever the final reason, the pension act was discontinued, leaving the United States at the start of the Great Depression with an old and outdated relief system, mainly consisting of private initiative and local responsibility, with some patches of newly added specified types of outdoor relief. No wonder, then, that this system failed soon after it was severely tried by millions of unemployed workers and their families. Expenditures increased immediately after 1929 and soon reached the financial limits of the cities concerned. From 1929 to 1933 relief expenditures by cities increased about sevenfold (Piven and

Cloward, 1977: 130, table 1). More than two-thirds of the relief came from public sources (Piven and Cloward, 1977: 127). That was, in itself, a remarkable achievement in a period when the tax receipts were dwindling. On the other hand, it was not enough by a long stretch. Most people received nothing; those that did received so meager an amount that it was not enough to live on—not even on the most parsimonious principles.

With the onset of the Depression, the days of voluntarism in relief were numbered. Soon, what went beyond charity burdened the cities and counties; when their means were exhausted, states stepped in; after the states the federal government had to act. Reluctantly at first, the 1932 Reconstruction Finance Corporation was willing to advance loans to the states to combat unemployment. Repayment of the loans, however, was to follow in a few years, and the loans bore interest. Few states responded to the invitation. It took the New Deal to complete federal involvement. Among its early measures was the Federal Emergency Relief Administration, which began immediately with the distribution of federal aid—food and clothing, work projects, and cash. Relief expenditures skyrocketed from somewhat over $1 billion in 1933 to more than $2.5 billion in 1935. More than two-thirds of the total expenditure came directly from the federal government (Piven and Cloward, 1977: 142, table 2). Again, benefits did not reach all who needed them, and benefits were dismal to live on (Schlesinger, 1959: 294; Piven and Cloward, 1977: 141–142). Selectivity in relief, after all, is a built-in property. However generalized poverty may be, needs are met only to the extent that individual eligibility for relief has been proven. H. L. Hopkins, head of the Federal Emergency Relief Administration (FERA), was painfully aware of the situation—and knew that it was beyond his power to change it: "Hence we have to admit that relief investigators have entered the front door of millions of private homes hitherto holding themselves sacred against intrusion, and have pried into painful matters" (Hopkins, 1972: 73). But the FERA did more than had been done before, and although the name of the agencies involved kept changing, it continued as one of the most important New Deal achievements. Its most difficult task was possibly not even relief itself. It was maintaining the distance between unemployables and employables. The unemployed had, through the sheer magnitude of the unemployment problem, become by far the largest group of relief dependents. By sheer necessity labor market policy entered the relief issue.

Work Relief

In 1935 Roosevelt stated that the federal government "must and shall quit this business of relief...work must be found for able-bodied but destitute workers" (quoted in Davis, 1986: 464). Actually, work relief had been a constant feature of the FERA since 1933, and what Roosevelt announced was not so much a new departure as a reorganization of work relief in combination with the expected unemployment insurance. His logic was clear. Organization of work relief was to be scheduled along the projected path of the unemployed worker: "When he leaves the unemployment insurance rolls, he gets a green ticket and is told he can make another application at another office on this green ticket for work benefits. The job will come to him. First a cash benefit, then use up his savings, then a work benefit" (Roosevelt, quoted in Perkins, 1946: 189). This was to become the famous Works Progress Administration (WPA), the heir of the former FERA-bound Civil Works Administration (CWA), again headed by Hopkins.

In the peak year of the WPA more than 3 million unemployed received work relief. The rates they earned were a little higher than the usual relief, yet below regular employment rates. Projects were not to compete with private enterprise or to be a substitute for the regular duties of government. Jobs included community services, music, theater, painting, writing, and so on. Costs for materials, machinery, and so forth were not to be compensated, leading to the recreational overtones reminiscent of the WPA (Leuchtenburg, 1963: ch. 6). This, indeed, was a difference with the CWA, under which many schools, libraries, playgrounds, airports, and so on were repaired or constructed (Sherwood, 1950: 70–71). These public works tasks, however, were lifted out of the WPA and were, on the whole, scaled down. Now, on a more modest scale, the already existing Public Works Administration distributed jobs and assignments to private industry leading to new jobs or the conservation of old ones. Combinations of work and education sprang forth from the National Youth Administration and the Civilian Conservation Corps, recruiting more than 2.5 million young men during its existence (Leuchtenburg, 1963: 171ff.).

There is no doubt that the combination of relief and work was an important characteristic of the approach to unemployment during the New Deal (Mattick, 1978: 132). At the same time, the administration did its best to separate relief and unemployment. With the introduction of the WPA the federal government wanted to withdraw from direct relief and pass it on to the states and localities. Its involvement would be financially supportive, but the actual execution of direct relief was given up in order to concentrate on work relief. Reality turned out to be somewhat removed from this intention, but the motive was clear. The federal government recognized the imperative of separating the unemployables from the employables, those dependent on direct relief from those dependent on work relief (Leiby, 1978: 228). Next to the organizational design of splitting the executive tasks of relief between the federal government and the states and local governments, it was clear from the beginning that work relief was not to be distributed to the unemployables, for instance the elderly (Leuchtenburg, 1963; Leiby, 1978). On the other hand, it was an impossible task to screen the employables. The magnitude of unemployment and its duration had turned many people into marginal workers with a highly irregular, or even nonexisting, employment record. The idea of, first, unemployment benefits and, then, work relief simply could not work, even if we set aside the sober consideration that the first unemployment benefits were not distributed before the winter of 1937–1938 (Witte, 1957: 260). Moreover, the subordination of work relief to budgetary considerations twice, almost overnight, led to an enormous slashing of appropriations for work relief. Finally, despite the millions of people who received work benefits, it was principally only a temporary affair, for each individual worker and many workers were never even touched by it. During the heyday of the WPA, only one out of four to five unemployed was helped temporarily. Most remained dependent on the dole (Piven and Cloward, 1979: 83).

Unemployment Compensation

Unemployment was a problem the WPA could not solve. But it was not its task to do so. Politically, its major duty in the field of unemployment was to be in agreement with the incumbent Social Security Act and especially unemployment compensation and pensions. This it did by means of the bifurcation it ordered between employables and unemployables, the same bifurcation that characterizes the Social Security Act. The hierarchy in support of the needy went from a top of unemployment compensation and pension legislation for those with an employment record via an intermediate and, in principle, temporary category of those on work relief to the bottom layer of the unemployables who were to have special federal programs to alleviate the burden of their disabilities. The Social Security Act was to take care of, in different clauses and classes, the top and the bottom. The intermediate category, on the other hand, was excluded from the act; its existence as a consequence remained political. Just like unemployment compensation needed to be differentiated sharply from relief, both in politics and in administration, so pensions for retired workers were to be differentiated from old-age assistance for the poor. The need for this differentiation was so urgent, apparently, that many working people, in agriculture for instance where low incomes were endemic, were exempted from pension legislation (Leiby, 1978: 230; Altmeyer, 1966: 25; Lubove, 1968: 179–180; Conkin, 1967: 61–62; Graebner, 1980: 181ff.; Witte, 1963: 258–259).

Yet the fact that such a thing as unemployment insurance had come was in itself a small miracle, for before and after the passage of the Social Security Act, unemployment compensation was difficult to establish. That unemployment compensation was late in the line of social security is not surprising. In most European countries, too, unemployment compensation was preceded by workmen's compensation and health insurance. The reason why is not hard to find. Unemployment compensation is not a final form of support but a causal one. The unemployed does not have to prove that he needs the compensation; the fact of being registered as unemployed will do, for involuntary unemployment is the cause of the claim for compensation. The administration and control of unemployment appropriations and eligibility for compensation are a matter for bureaucrats who apply uniform rules to uniform situations. On the other hand, final support, defined by the finality of the specific need in question, calls for an individual approach of each claimant, administered and controlled by the professional rather than the bureaucrat. Obviously, as Max Weber knew, bureaucratization can be the consequence of democratization, and in the area of financial support for needy people, so much the better.

Hoover, Unemployment, and Relief

Hoover's position and the tenacity with which he clung to it are of more than passing interest. He had been, during the Harding and Coolidge administrations of the 1920s, a successful secretary of commerce, much admired by Democrats and Republicans alike. Most of the admiration was due to Hoover's many efforts to spread the gospel of economy and efficiency among the business elite of America. Trained as an engineer, Hoover saw many unused opportunities to combat inefficiency and waste. Regulation of competition through trade associations was one of his major themes, next to the conviction that irregular employment, characteristic of many industries, could effectively be challenged. Standardization through active governmental policy was vigorously pushed. Business statistics were not just gathered but also used in Hoover's effort to make planning of production and employment a feasible ideal. Unemployment, in his view, definitely was a form of waste.

Hardly installed as secretary, Hoover in 1921 organized and convened an unemployment conference. The conference came up with the recommendations Hoover wanted. By means of the United States Employment Service bureaus, the planning of public works, and the regularization of employment, unemployment was to be reduced. Unemployment insurance, voluntary efforts excepted, were rejected (Nelson, 1969: 36–39; Bernstein, 1969: 263–265; Rothbard, 1970: 165–167; 1983: 172–177). Voluntary planning would keep unemployment low; the practical effects of the doctrine of high wages would keep employment high. In these opinions, then, Hoover shared the world view of the large majority of the political and business elites of the time.

Hoover's successful bid for the presidency has been explained as the last time the country checkmated the city. To the extent that Hoover's gains were Al Smith's losses, it cannot be denied that the rural vote did contribute to four more years of electoral powerlessness of the new immigrant urban vote (Lubell, 1951; Bernstein, 1960: 508ff.). On the other hand, there is no doubt that the opinions Hoover had held during the twenties and the practical actions Hoover had undertaken as secretary of commerce to lend substance to them were important in securing his victory in the 1928 presidential elections. They were, after all, the "conventional wisdom," shared by the majority of Democrats and Republicans. His parochial views on relief and his refusal on unemployment insurance legislation were not at all at odds with the prevailing concepts of the role of government and the responsibilities of individuals and private initiative.

These views may be summed up in the one word of voluntarism. In sticking to it during his presidency, in the face of mounting opposition because of the Great Depression, Hoover proved himself a politician rather than an administrator. It was, no doubt, a politics against all the odds. To praise local relief during a period of collapse, was bound to evoke protest (Bernstein, 1960: 287ff.; Rothbard, 1983: 239–240). But it lasted until 1932 and the coming of new presidential elections, before Hoover allowed the Reconstruction Finance Corporation to lend federal money to prevent the total breakdown of state and city finance. His resistance against federal intervention in the issues concerning unemployment grew rather than diminished during his presidency. He fought, vetoed, or delayed the Wagner proposals of 1931 on the federal collection of unemployment statistics, the extension of public works, and the strengthening of the employment offices (Nelson, 1969: 132–133; Schlesinger, 1957: 233). These, paradoxically, had been Hoover's remedies of 1921. Then, however, they had been part of a voluntarist message and had been presented in a climate of withdrawal of federal powers over the economy, as exemplified by the War Industries Board. Now, they could be considered only the first signs of an ever-widening circle of federal interventions.

Hoover not only rejected federal compulsory regulation, he resented private compulsory regulations just as much. The champion of the voluntary trade association was strictly opposed to a privately concocted cartellization of the economy, suggested in the so-called Swope plan of 1931, named after the president of General Electric (Nelson, 1969: 140–144; Rothbard, 1970: 176–177, 1983: 245–249). This plan, calling for compulsory restriction of production, raising of prices, and codes of fair practice was supported by both the corporate world and the NAM and was revived by the National Recovery Administration during the early New Deal. To Hoover, it was unacceptable and indistinguishable from fascism; it led to a growing estrangement between him and the business world (Rothbard, 1970, 1983: 245–249). Voluntarism, indeed, became a matter of principle; the more it was attacked, the more Hoover defended it. The imperative of balancing the budget added to Hoover's reluctance to get involved in federal relief or federal solutions to the unemployment problem. Even the use of public works was sacrificed in order to balance the budget. Yet on the necessity of a balanced budget, Roosevelt and Hoover did not differ. Roosevelt did criticize the lack of budgetary discipline under Hoover—and promised a truly balanced budget and a reduction of federal expenditures by 25 percent (Fearon, 1979: 55; Davis, 1986: 97; Leuchtenburg, 1963: ch. 1). It did not prevent Roosevelt, however, from introducing relief measures on a grand scale and starting to tackle the problem of unemployment insurance.

New Deal

The issue was no longer the principle of unemployment compensation. The Swope plan had demonstrated how far the business community had gone in the direction of planning and regulation, explicitly calling for the sanction of government. The plan included promises of employment stabilization or, if this was to fail, unemployment insurance (Nelson, 1969: 141–142). It had become a matter of pragmatics; the dividing lines had shifted. Federal regulation versus voluntarism had been transformed into the difficult question of federal regulation imbued with a more or less system of voluntarism. This held for social security as much as it did for federal intervention in the economy.

From several sides the New Deal administration was pushed to substantiate its promises on social security. The rumblings and manifestations of discontent in the later half of the Hoover presidency got somewhat subdued during the first actions of the FERA and the CWA in 1933; yet when in late 1934 the relief budget was lowered for budgetary reasons, protests were quick to follow, and this time they took on a far more organized form than they did in 1931 and 1932. The unemployed broadened their organization to reach national proportions in 1935 and 1936. At the end of 1936 the Workers' Alliance of America (WAA), as the national organization was called, had a network comprising forty-three states, 1,600 locals, and 600,000 members (Piven and Cloward, 1977: 169–175, 1979: 75–76). The organization existed until 1941, when, for obvious reasons, it was dissolved (Piven and Cloward, 1979: 90). With the growth of organization, the character of protest changed. The FERA, and later the WPA, used the WAA to canalize the forms of protest. Cooperation between officials of the WAA and of the government relief organizations developed, and many WAA officials joined the relief administration in cities, states, and even the federal government. The unemployed, by the logic of the situation, became the clients of a new relief system, whereas before they had been a driving force in the attack on the old one (Piven and Cloward, 1979: 76–82, 85ff.; for a different appraisal, see Mattick, 1969: 107–109). Partly, their new role was due to the practical merging of the unemployment organizations with the relief organizations. But also, and possibly more important, they were not accepted as affiliates of the labor movement. Even the Congress of Industrial Organizations (CIO), although more sympathetic to the movement of the unemployed than the AFL, declined the request of joining forces (Piven and Cloward, 1979: 72).

The successes of the organizations of the unemployed were local, rather than national. The local organizations, especially in the early thirties, did succeed in getting more relief—even to the extent of exhausting local financial resources and of adding to the pressure for state or federal funding. At higher levels of government their influence waned. Sometimes the WAA was heard by federal officials of the Hopkins' bureaus. More often, they were not. Also, the WAA was conspicuously absent in the writings of important Roosevelt officials like James Farley and Frances Perkins. They did, however, report on other movements bent on achieving social security, and they had every reason to report. The organizations of the unemployed were concentrated in the cities, and in the cities the Democratic vote was strongest. A poll, conducted by the Democratic party in 1935, showed that an eventual reelection of Roosevelt was guaranteed more in the cities than in the country at large. More alarmingly, however, the poll showed that Roosevelt's popularity among those Americans dependent on relief was comparatively low (Brinkley, 1983: 207–209, 284–286). What Farley, Roosevelt's campaign manager in 1932 and 1936, especially feared after studying the results of the poll was the weak and possibly losing position of the party in New York State (Farley, 1948: 51). Apparently, the political potential of the movement of the unemployed was tapped not by the WAA but by other, more explicitly political organizations.

The Compromise: The Social Security Act of 1935

Already in 1933 the ubiquitous senator Robert Wagner had proposed action on social security. On the one hand, he pleaded anew for a coordinated system of government employment offices. This idea was almost immediately taken over during the hectic first hundred days of the 1933 New Deal. Second, he introduced a bill on unemployment insurance. This bill somehow was not taken seriously. From the point of view of Frances Perkins, its purpose was educational; she assumed that it was a first step in the direction of "a satisfactory and typically American measure" (Perkins, 1946: 278). It did not work out that way. The bill was simply "forgotten" (Nelson, 1969: 196–197). The main reason for not pushing the Wagner bill, presumably, was that it was not inclusive enough, that is, that Roosevelt had decided that unemployment, pensions, and relief would have to be presented in one package (Davis, 1986: 448–449). Health insurance had been included in Roosevelt's list also but was dropped (Perkins, 1946: 289). On the other hand, Roosevelt wanted the act on social security passed before reelection (Perkins, 1946: 281).

It seems likely that Roosevelt's decision on an inclusive package and his timing of the approval of the Social Security Act in 1935 indeed were a response to the electoral danger presented by the Francis Townsend and Huey Long movements (Brinkley, 1983). There, however, their influence stopped. For Roosevelt, the programs of Share Our Wealth and the pension plan of Townsend represented the dole—and that was exactly the thing he did not want. The dole, if there was to be any, should be kept separate from social insurance, and it was only Hopkins who defended a fusion of relief and unemployment or old-age compensation (Perkins, 1946: 284–285). This, in effect, would abolish relief, too, for it meant that relief would become a matter of right, rather than a consequence of need. This view conflicted with the economic function of unemployment insurance. As Roosevelt thought, recovery of industrial vigor had to be placed ahead of a program of social reform. Also, the unemployment funds, if centrally held by the federal government, could be used as a means of stabilization (Perkins, 1946: 288–289). More important was the objection that relief and unemployables and unemployment compensation and employables should not be thrown together. That, it was felt, was the main drawback of the British system (Nelson, 1969: 167). Relief might be permanent; unemployment compensation in principle was for each individual applicant a temporary affair. Its assumption was not the continuity of need but the easing of the period in between one job and the next and thus the cushioning of the effects of cyclical unemployment (Perkins, 1946: 285; Nelson, 1969). This assumption was solidified in the act. Its function, then, was to simplify the movements and mobility of labor due to involuntary unemployment, not to give security (Miller, 1954: 60).

The inclusive approach of Roosevelt was detailed by the new Committee on Economic Security. Key members, notably A. J. Altmeyer and, as director of the program for social security, E. E. Witte, were adepts of the "Wisconsin" school. Wisconsin in 1932 had been the first state to adopt an unemployment compensation law. The law reflected the combination of voluntarist and compulsory elements that had earlier typified the workmen's compensation issue. Each employer, having ten or more employees, was obliged to send 2 percent of his total payroll to a centrally administered state fund. The fund would put each contribution on individualized company accounts. Once an employer had paid an average $55 per employee, the levy would become 1 percent. Once $75 per employee was registered, no more contributions were due, unless withdrawals because of actual compensation payments were made. Benefits to the unemployed workers were 50 percent of the last wage, not exceeding $10 a week, for a maximum period of ten weeks per year (Nelson, 1969: 128; Lubove, 1968: 169–170). Eligible for benefits were only those who had lived for two consecutive years in Wisconsin before becoming unemployed or who had worked for at least forty weeks during the period of the two preceding years (Nelson, 1969: 227). Migrant workers, unemployables, and workers in small shops were effectively excluded. Prevention was central; the individual company accounts and the ceiling in contributions testified to this. Also, the dividing issue of pooled versus individual reserves had been ingeniously avoided. In fact, it was an "unemployment reserve" more than unemployment insurance. The employer's liabilities were strictly limited to his own employees and to the sum available in his own reserve fund. The company accounts were a reserve for bad times; the more preventive the policy a company followed, however, the less the reserve would be a burden for it (Leiby, 1978: 209–210; Lubove, 1968: 170). Merit or experience rating therewith had become an integral part of compulsory legislation on unemployment compensation. By the same token, the "socially least fit," as one architect of the Wisconsin plan named them, would be punished under the system, since they would continue to contribute and worsen their terms of trade with more prevention-minded competitors (Nelson, 1969: 193).

The federal requirements with which to launch social security were a problem in themselves. What legal title could the federation use for a social security system in which many obligations were to be discharged by the states and which might be interpreted as an intrusion in the political prerogatives of the states? The federal government had the power to tax, but the use of that power was not enough to guarantee the compliance of the states. Also, if the program should be self-financing, taxes were a mere means to an end, and ways would have to be found from the federal government back to the states. The answer to this problem was the combination of taxing and a tax-offsetting device that would do the trick.

There was a precedent for this solution. When Florida in the early twenties banned all inheritance taxes, the federal government retaliated by imposing its own inheritance tax and at the same time promising repayment of the tax to states that had their own inheritance taxes. On trial, the Supreme Court, including Brandeis, found the federal tax constitutional. This, then, was the example (Davis, 1986: 447–448; Nelson, 1969: 198). It had been part of Wagner's 1933 proposal, but now it was worked out in more detail and with the backing of at least two judges from the Supreme Court, for Judge Stone had pointed to the device of taxing as well (Perkins, 1946: 286). Thus the Social Security Act, in regard to unemployment compensation, was framed. When Roosevelt signed it in August 1935, national standards were all but lacking. A 3 percent tax, beginning in 1938, on payrolls was included; yet depending on specific state legislations and their exemptions, the actual imposition and collection of the tax might diverge considerably from the stated percentage. States that enacted unemployment compensation would get their taxes repaid. Benefits, duration, and eligibility were completely within the discretion of the states. Indeed, what the federal law did contain in specifications was not in the field of standards but in the field of premiums or "credits" for experience rating (Witte, 1963: 140; Nelson, 1969: 218–219). The much publicized wish of Roosevelt that unemployment insurance would have to include employee contributions was silently buried and not heard of again. The federal act did not, like the Wisconsin one, provide for individual company accounts. What it did provide for was the possibility for states to do so, since it did promote the opportunity for states to use the unemployment compensation legislation as a competitive weapon in the struggle to attract business and employment (Advisory Council on Social Security, 1948: 528–540).

8

THE NEW STATUS OF LABOR

DEVELOPMENTS IN EDUCATION

Within two years after the passage of the Social Security Act all states had adopted unemployment insurance laws. The main common denominator of the laws was the effective exclusion of those without employment records, with intermittent records, or with records of prolonged unemployment (Trattner, 1974: 239–241). The percentage of those unemployed for three or more years remained high after the passage of the act (see Table 8.1).

All of this was not caused by the act. What the act effected was a clearer separation of those on relief, those with pensions, and those with unemployment compensation. The eligibility qualifications for unemployment compensation demanded in most states either specified minimum earnings in a base period or a minimum number of weeks worked during a base period. Whether earnings or weeks worked were used, the result was the exclusion of marginal workers (Slichter, 1940: 322–323). Moreover, since many state laws put a premium on prevention of irregular employment, the proportion of marginal workers employed was to decline rather than to be augmented, and accordingly, their chances of becoming eligible for compensation dwindled. They were on their way to becoming unemployable, combining at best temporary work and relief or, through the Works Progress Administration (WPA), temporary work as relief. Finally, the pension part of the act was a stimulus to many companies to get rid of their older workers. The act did not directly favor private, company-sponsored pension plans, because an amendment to that effect, although adopted in the Senate, proved too difficult to administer (Witte, 1963: 105–108; Altmeyer, 1966: 40–42). Its importance was, rather, that it forbade pensions to persons who weren't

Table 8.1
Percentages of Unemployed for Three Years or More

	Males	Females
1931	2.8	1.8
1932	3.3	2.2
1933	7.9	4.9
1935	34.9	19.6
1936	34.4	27.3
1937	37.7	26.1
1938	25.7	17.5

Source: S.H. Slichter, "The Impact of Social Security Legislation upon Mobility and Enterprise," in *Potentials of the American Economy: Selected Essays of Samuel H. Slichter* (Cambridge, Mass., 1940), p. 326.

retired. Soon it was found that companies without their own plans kept on their older workers, whereas companies with pension plans discharged them (Miller, 1954: 55ff.; Slichter, 1940; Jacoby, 1985: 254). Again, labor market considerations and elements of social security were intermingled, a fact of which the framers of the act were completely conscious (Graebner, 1980: 184–190).

Certain polarizing tendencies, already visible during the twenties and early thirties, became more noticeable after the passage of the act. Earlier retirement cleansed the market of older workers. At the same time it proved difficult for young workers to obtain regular employment (Rayback, 1959: 335). The 20 to 24 age group was especially hard hit by unemployment, whereas the 16 to 20 age group used the easiest accessible escape from unemployment: a prolonged stay in the schools. The participation in the labor market of young men and women and of persons over age 65 fell considerably during the Great Depression, as shown in Table 8.2.

It must be emphasized that these changes in participation were not principally caused by changes in the age structure of the population at large. The Depression did cause a sharp drop in the age group from zero to 5 years, with a delay in the later age groups; yet the proportions of those between 14 and 45 years remained relatively constant. The population, on average, was aging, however; the population of 45 years and over grew relatively, and the growth of the 65 and over age group was most marked (Taeuber and Taeuber, 1958: 28, figure 10, 31, table 6). Clearly, the rate of growth of the diverse age groups, for school enrollments a decisive factor, showed a distinct slowing down for the young. Actually, the absolute number of young males competing in the most heavily industrialized regions of the country may even have contracted, although, as the table shows, this was counteracted by the growing rate of participation of young females. The contracting factor was

Table 8.2
Sex and Age Rates of Labor-Market Participation

	1920	1930	1940	1950
Both Sexes, Totals	54.3	53.2	52.7	53.6
Men:				
14 years and over	84.5	82.1	79.7	78.9
14-19	51.5	40.1	35.4	40.0
20-24	69.9	88.8	88.5	81.1
25-34	95.7	95.9	95.7	92.6
35-44	95.4	95.7	95.4	94.1
45-54	93.5	93.8	92.7	91.3
55-64	86.3	86.5	84.6	83.0
65 years and over	55.6	54.0	42.2	41.3
Women:				
14 years and over	22.7	23.6	25.7	28.9
14-19	28.3	22.8	18.9	23.2
20-24	37.5	41.8	45.6	42.8
25-34	23.7	27.0	33.4	31.5
35-44	19.2	21.7	27.3	34.6
45-54	17.9	19.7	22.4	33.4
55-64	14.3	15.3	16.6	22.7
65 years and over	7.3	7.3	6.0	7.9

Source: J.G. Lulofs, De Amerikaanse Arbeidsmarkt: een onderzoek naar arbeidsmobiliteit in de Verenigde Staten (Meppel, Neth., 1960), p. 48.

due to two interrelated developments. First, population growth in the Northeast and North Central regions had slowed considerably since the 1890s, compared to the growth in the West and in the United States as a whole (Taeuber and Taeuber, 1958: 15, figure 4). Second, the younger age groups increased much more slowly (and in some cases even declined absolutely in the group younger than 25 years, with the North Central region since the thirties being an example) in the industrialized sections of the country than elsewhere (Taeuber and Taeuber, 1958: 45, figure 16). These were, with California, precisely the regions hit hardest by unemployment (Rayback, 1959: 321).

The high participation rates of young people between 20 and 24 years, in the face of exceedingly high unemployment concentrated in their age group, testify to their total lack of escape. Most of their jobs were unskilled or at best semiskilled. The younger that one started in the labor market, the greater the chances of becoming unemployed and the greater the chances, if a job could be obtained, of finding unskilled work. Higher age gave better access to better jobs (Kaehler and Hamburger, 1948: 37, table 3; Lulofs, 1960: 96–97). Acquiring extra vocational education in evening schools, part-time schools, or continuation schools might lead to better and more secure jobs, but in view of the fact that the larger—and growing—part of training took place on the job itself, this strategy, too, was not very promising. Also, the amount of training on the job for most jobs in the semiskilled range tended to fall rather than to rise, with the automobile industry as the most extreme example (Kaehler and Hamburger, 1948: 158–165). Insofar as educational credentials were becoming a ticket for access to jobs, the general high school diploma was at least as good a certification as a vocational one. Research on admission criteria for training in skilled occupations indicated that high school was a prerequisite everywhere, vocational training nowhere. But previous experience was essential, again excluding newcomers in the market (Kaehler and Hamburger, 1948: 188–190). As a preparation for trades, thus, the vocational school was an almost complete failure (Kaehler and Hamburger, 1948: 149–150). Only for white-collar jobs did vocational qualification promise rewards. The rise in vocational educational enrollments during the thirties logically reflected, then, the premium on the commercial curriculum (Collins, 1979: 115; Kaehler and Hamburger, 1948: 60–63). Yet the commercial arts curriculum was a development within the general high school; it was not its substitute like vocational education in principle could be. The major boost to vocationalism had to await the preparations for the war, when the vocational schools and the Depression-born National Youth Administration trained as many as 12 million people for essential war jobs of a mass-production character (Kaehler and Hamburger, 1948: 88–91; Krug, 1972: 319–327).

For the young in the age group between 14 and 20 years, and in particular between 14 and 17 years, the schools at least partly offered a way out. Although the growth in their numbers stagnated in the thirties, high school enrollments continued apace. The proportion of the relevant age group in high schools during the thirties increased from about 50 to 70 percent (Trow, 1961: 110, figure 1; Kaehler and Hamburger, 1948: 56; Krug, 1972: 218; Greer, 1972: 128–129). Budgets, however, did not increase. Especially in the early Depression years, the school budgets were slashed vigorously, and during the Depression, they never got back to their 1920s level (Krug, 1971: 208ff., 221). The growth in enrollments therefore did not represent the effects of a national policy to enhance the possibilities of youth in an unfavorable labor market (Heidenheimer, 1981: 291–292). Classes grew in size; subjects deemed too expensive were sometimes dropped (Krug, 1972: 212–214; on elementary education, see Zilversmit, 1976: 260). Many entering did not graduate; nor did the higher enrollment stop the dropout phenomenon (Greer, 1972). It took the youth off the street; it did not contribute to the solution of the problem of youth unemployment. As such, it was recognized at the time, contributing to the confusion not only over the utility of vocational education but also over the aims of secondary education as a whole (Krug, 1972: 309–314). The twenties had shown that unless economic growth was at a permanently high level, unemployment would tend to become concentrated among the young and the old. The thirties, when economic growth had become a far-away dream, documented the hardening of the unemployment pattern among age lines. Social security in the United States confirmed these lines, instead of attenuating them. So did education. Neither of the two exerted influence on the ongoing bureaucratization of the employment relationship, except, where unemployment insurance and pensions were concerned, to strengthen it.

BUREAUCRATIZATION OF THE EMPLOYMENT RELATIONSHIP

In the late twenties personnel departments and centralized employment practices had become a common feature of many of the larger firms with 250 or more employees (Baron, Dobbin, and Jennings, 1986: 351; Jacoby, 1985: 191, table 6.7). The first response to the crisis was a scaling down of personnel work, but soon it picked up again and was extended at a very fast rate (Baron, Dobbin, and Jennings, 1986; Jacoby, l985: 233, table 7.2). The reasons for the flourishing of personnel work during the crisis were twofold. First, there were more or less internal developments in industry itself. Second, there were the responses of business to the growing number of government regulations surrounding the employment relationship, the most important of which are the National Industrial Recovery Act of 1933, the Social Security Act and the National Labor Relations Act of 1935, and the Fair Labor Standards Act of 1938.

Internal Developments

Developments in industry relating to personnel were mainly concentrated on testing for employment and promotion, the use of formal rating systems for promotion, centralization of selection, and dismissal. These developments were accompanied by an upsurge of job analysis and time and motion studies. All over, the major tendency was the further centralization of personnel practices and policies, and the larger the company, the more so. Apparently, the larger firm was busily rationalizing its personnel function. The trend was especially marked in the mass-production industries (Baron, Dobbin, and Jennings, 1986: 357–358; Baritz, 1960: 119ff.; Jacoby, 1985: 233, table 7.2). The optimization of throughput, which represented the specific organizational problem in mass production, required standardization of tools, materials, machines, and operations. Each job, accordingly, had to be broken down into its constituent parts and each part had to be analyzed. Job analysis, time and motion studies, and the centralized personnel department thus grew side by side. To some, this was the true era of scientific management (Gordon, Edwards, and Reich, 1982: 170ff.; Edwards, 1979: ch. 5).

Job analysis is the twofold activity of job description—the tasks involved in each job—and job specification—the skills required to perform the job. It was not just indispensable in planning the optimal design of production;

it also could help to rationalize wage structures, grouping jobs together in classes and remunerating them according to more or less objectified criteria (Jacoby, 1985: 150ff.). Job analysis, thus, was one foundation of job evaluation, although here most companies deferred action until, after 1935, industrial unions got a foothold in collective bargaining. Job evaluation then became a managerial attempt, like merit rating, to ward off too strict an application of the seniority principle (Jacoby, 1985: 250–253). But even apart from that, as the popularity of job analysis shows, the development toward attaching a price tag to the job rather than the worker was definitely speeded up during the thirties. As Elton Mayo indicated: "where we once were dependent on 'established' skills, we now depended on 'adaptable skills'" (Mayo, 1975: 28).

Skills and Qualifications

The nineteenth-century problem of unskilled labor had led to the adaptation of the work to the men; the twentieth-century predominance of the semiskilled job led to the reverse adaptation of the men to the work. Training, a more polite expression for "adapting" the men to the work, became a key issue. Indeed, once skill is defined by the job, rather than by the men, the actual skills of people take on a signal value at most (Thurow, 1975: 75ff.). The labor market, then, is not a market in which skills are traded for wages. Skills are not an independent factor of supply, since they are primarily defined by the job, that is, by demand (Thurow, 1975: 79). Job skills and job-related skills have to be acquired on the job itself, whether in formalized sequences or in informal training. This explains the at-first-sight paradoxical situation that a decreasing average period of training for the large majority of semiskilled jobs coincides with a heavier emphasis on access requirements for training and an enhanced importance placed on training as such. Most of the training, according to a representative survey of 1937, was informal and took less than two months (Kaehler and Hamburger, 1948: 152–153, 157ff.; Baritz, 1960: 133ff.; Lulofs, 1960: 56–58). Actually, the amount of training could be underestimated. Many semiskilled jobs were learned in a short time; on the other hand, acquiring not just the technique of a job but also its speed and its margins did require much more time (Kaehler and Hamburger, 1948: 156).

Standardized jobs make for standardized requirements for applicants. The jobs are no more "homogeneous" than a table is relative to a chair. But the basic demands they made on people performing them could easily be subsumed under a few main headings—dexterity, punctuality, knowledgeable in reading charts and symbols, work experience, and so on—with each particular job broken down according to much finer and much more varied criteria. The latter, to be sure, is what in actual practice is called "on-the-job training." When actual job skills can be acquired only on the job itself, behavioral characteristics will determine the recruitment process. High school certification, but also age, marital status, country of origin, and so forth, may be and have been used as crude behavioral signals. Tests, although more applied to white- than to blue-collar workers in the thirties, served the same function (Baritz, 1960: 129; Lulofs, 1960: 92–101). Screening prospective employees via tests or reified behavioral characteristics does not, evidently, establish their competence or even their behavior. These devices are risk minimizers. Their role is not to give every job applicant a fair chance but to reduce the enormous and unsurmountable complexity of measuring competence to manageable proportions and to transform recruitment from a once and for all decision into a graded series of steps (Thurow, 1975: 170–177). Again, training and its access conditions are of paramount importance, for training is not—at least in many cases—a one-time affair. Jobs may be changed for organizational reasons or for reasons of technological change, changes in the prices of the factors of production, changes in the possibility of their mutual substitution, or a combination of these factors. Each time, job descriptions and job specifications will have to be adapted, and training will have to follow.

Two conditions must be met. The first is that there is a pool of people who, however informal, may be entrusted to have both the knowledge and the capacity to train for a variety of job changes. The second is that these trainers will be willing to train, that is, that they have some formal or factual guarantee that they are not going to be replaced by the competition of the same people they train (Thurow, 1975: 81–85). The first condition in fact assumes that training for the trainers at least is a continuous process, whereby experience in a number of jobs gets accumulated over the years. The second condition assumes that the gathering of experience is rewarded through a career with identifiable steps. The necessity of on-the-job training and the creation of job ladders come together. It is obvious that experience is a prime determinant of climbing the ladder. But it is not the sole one. Indeed, experience is important only to the degree that it signals training capacity and willingness. Under conditions of relatively stable technology, experience—and thus seniority—will be a reasonable indicator. But such situations are the exception rather than the rule. Merit, then, comes into play. It is an elusive concept and mainly a dimension of managerial prerogative in transfer and promotion as, indeed, the whole area of job analysis and its design and redesign are a matter of management.

What one should expect, accordingly, is not a polarized structure in which many jobs hardly need training time and a few need very much but a more graded structure in which within the broad categories of semiskilled and skilled several stations may be identified (Kaehler and Hamburger, 1948: 157–161). The semiskilled train one another. The skilled not only train the semiskilled, but they partly come forth from their ranks. Especially in mass-production industries, the proportion of skilled in the work force stagnated or fell, while the proportion of semiskilled grew. Chances of advancement from semiskilled to skilled therefore diminished. On the other hand, the category of the semiskilled is far from homogeneous and allows for varied recruitment modalities and paths of advancement. In this sense, training, experience, and merit reinforce the competition for jobs in the firm, as they structure the process of selection for training facilities and possibilities of advancement. This goes far to explain why, especially for the semiskilled, the nature of the work so often is a more important consideration than the pay (Lulofs, 1960: 109ff.). The job is one step on a ladder and is viewed as such. It tells about the promises of promotion and transfer and their reality. It may become important to hold on to the job, even an unpleasant one, because of the future it may open. If, on the other hand, one loses one's job, the job-related skills and the ladder they were part of are lost as well for the employee concerned. As a logical consequence of these developments for the semi-skilled worker with skills inhering in the job, seniority in lay-offs, dismissals, transfers, and promotions became of critical importance.

Lay-offs

A worker laid off temporarily has lost his work but not his job. If trade picks up, the laid-off worker has a claim on the job he temporarily left, before newcomers on the job will have a chance to obtain it. For any worker with a semiskilled job, regulation of lay-offs is of obvious importance. For the employer, the advantage is clear as well, at least as long as lay-off priority and seniority are not totally identified. Regulation of lay-off was on the move during the thirties, especially in industries in which the semiskilled predom-inated in the total work force (Slichter, 1941: 304, 1939: 216). Yet it is difficult to determine how much of this growth was due to internal developments or whether the major variable was the rise of the industrial unions and the effects of governmental legislation in the field of labor relations and unem-ployment insurance. The timing of lay-off regulation leads us to suspect that outside occurrences were decisive, since the main progress in this field dates from 1935 and after; on the other hand, the option itself in all likelihood stems from more internal developments within industry (Harbison, 1940: 312–314). Lay-off reduction as a unilateral managerial initiative was part of the struggle for higher efficiency and against uncontrollable labor turnover (Slichter, 1929: 202–203). Nor was seniority absent in managerially led reg-ulations of lay-offs, these being strictly departmentalized and valid only for workers who already had been employed for five years or more (Jacoby, 1985: 196). The period of the Great Depression did not, then, invent regulation of lay-offs. It ended the unilateral managerial prerogative in the endeavor. The dual emergence of both seniority provisions and merit rating corrobo-rates this view. Seniority and merit, after all, are answers to the common problem of the contingent relation between the job and its worker.

And Outside Interference

The first federal regulation causing change in company labor policies was the National Industrial Recovery Act of 1933 (NIRA), especially its famous section 7(a). The NIRA promised employers exemption from the antitrust laws if they in their respective branches would conclude agreements on pricing, ceilings of production, and codes of competition. The latter included rules on minimum wage rates, maximum hours, and the prohibition of child labor. Also, employers had to bargain collectively with organizations of the workers' own choice. This was the substance of section 7(a) of the act. It read that employees "shall have the right to organize and bargain collectively through representatives of their own choosing, and shall be free from the interference, restraint or coercion of employers ... in the designation of such representatives or in self-organization or in other concerted activities for the purpose of collective bargaining" (quoted in Jacoby, 1985: 223). It was an invitation to unionize, and as such it was understood by workers and companies.

Within two years after the passage of the NIRA, unions had grown with more than 1 million workers, the growth being especially strong in industrial unions, newly formed through AFL federal charters; independents; long-standing unions like the United Mine Workers; and, since 1935, CIO unions (Tawney, 1979: 101; Jacoby, 1985: 224; Troy, 1965; Taft, 1942: 133). The employers were busily organizing as well. Between 1933 and 1935 the number of employee representation plans or company unions rose to a historic high. In 1935 more than 2 million workers, around 60 percent of the number organized in trade unions, were covered by company unions. Moreover, the company unions were numerous especially in the large-scale mass-production industries (Tawney, 1979: 104; Jacoby, 1985: 226–227; Taft, 1942: 133–134; Wilcock, 1957: 288–290; Brandes, 1976: 143). Collective bargaining, apparently, was on the agenda; the question of representation of workers was still very much in the open. Section 7(a) had not brought what the unions (AFL president William Green's exclamation about labor's "Magna Charta" notwithstanding) expected of it. Lay-offs, in conjunction with seniority, were usually part of the collective-bargaining sessions; yet the hesitating steps taken toward honoring seniority were limited to a few giant industries, as yet unorganized (Jacoby, 1985: 235–237). They were no concession to unions. Rather, companies took measures to screen prospective employees more thoroughly, since the NIRA had made it more difficult to get rid of union men, once they were in (Jacoby, 1985: 234). At General Motors, for instance, the creation of a centralized labor relations office in the thirties coincided with an intensive company effort to strengthen its intelligence network, Pinkertons included (Serrin, 1973: 105ff.; on antiunion expenditures and measures see Boyer and Morais, 1955: 278–282). Nor did the federal government, at least initially, try to prevent these events from happening.

When the NIRA was declared unconstitutional in 1935, it looked as if everybody was relieved. Labor was relieved, because business interests had dominated the formulation and the enforcement of the codes of competition, production ceilings, prices, and working conditions. Many codes, moreover, simply ignored the labor sections of the NIRA (Conkin, 1967: 35–37). Business was relieved, because after the first formulation of the codes the federal representatives became more precise in their controlling quality. Therewith the fundamental problem of the NIRA—whether it was to improve conditions of fair competition or to restrict competition—came to the fore. The existing codes reflected the dilemma. In industries in which labor costs were among the major company outlays—like textiles and mining—improved competitive conditions seemed at stake, especially in the relations between northern and southern states and their diverging wage rates. Unionization helped the cause, since unions demanded uniform wage rates industrywide. In the larger mass-production industries like petroleum refining and automobiles, the codes clearly restricted competition. As could be expected, unions were fought much harder in these industries. The fight, however, went both ways, for workers struck for the right to organize, and even though many of the strikes were lost, by business leaders as well as by everybody else, they were seen as a product of the NIRA and its elusive labor section (on strike activity in 1933–1934, see Edwards, 1981: 134ff.; see also Rubin, Griffin, and Wallace, 1983: 330; Milton, 1982: 31ff.).

Even in the labor-intensive industries enforcement of the codes proved difficult. Ceilings for production were often inaccurately established and thus had to be bargained over again (Kolko, 1976: 129–138). On the other hand, the automobile code suffered from the refusal of Ford to cooperate and was, accordingly, hampered in its effectiveness. When, temporarily, in 1934 the economy improved, the business community turned against the NIRA and its codes, thereby proving the truth of the old dictum that cartellization may work in bad times but never when recovery seems incipient. Even those who merely wanted to get back from the present open collusion to the former secretive arrangements now rallied behind the cry for free competition (Conkin, 1967: 35–37). Finally, there was the government itself. Administration of the codes had proved difficult all along, and the frequent violations of codes, or allegations to that effect, brought administrative breakdown nearer (Emerson, 1983: 208). The 1935 decision of the Supreme Court to declare the NIRA unconstitutional saved the administration the more difficult step of killing the NIRA through its own initiative (Katz, 1983: 122–123; Jones, 1979: 91–92).

Fair Labor Standards Act and National Labor Relations Act

Not all of the National Recovery Act (NRA) period was lost. The Agricultural Adjustment Act, after being found at fault by the Supreme Court, returned with a few amendments. The code for the coal industry came back under the so-called little NRA. Nor did the disappearance of the NRA stop federal intervention in the monetary and banking systems and in the branch of public utilities (Leuchtenburg, 1963: 157–163; Hacker, 1970: 310–311). Finally, section 7 of the NIRA returned in more vigorous form in the shape of two acts: the National Labor Relations Act of 1935 (dealing with section 7[a]) and the

Fair Labor Standards Act of 1938 (dealing with sections 7[b] and 7[c] on minimum wages, maximum hours, and the abolition of child labor). The Fair Labor Standards Act (FLSA) was one more attempt to create comparable competitive conditions in the states. For obvious reasons, the southern interests, always strongly represented in the Democratic party, objected to the act. Although the act was passed eventually after a three-year struggle, the uniform and low standards did not survive the fight unscathed (Brandeis, 1957: 217ff.). Although the act directed that "no minimum wage rate shall be fixed solely on a regional basis" (quoted in Brandeis, 1957: 228), enough loopholes were present so as to make everybody happy, except those workers needing protection the most. Many of the service and commercial occupations, for instance, catering to local or state-bound markets, fell beyond the reach of the act, since only interstate commerce could be subjected to federal intervention. Also, agricultural labor was largely exempted from the act, thereby creating a huge black labor reserve "that was available on call to the manufacturing sector at the prevailing industrial wage rate" (Piore and Sabel, 1984: 85). The inescapable consequence is easy to guess: the labor reserve acted as an effective brake on upward movement of the minimum wage rate.

The impact of the FLSA on the employment relationship in the important industries of the country was limited. Possibly its major assets in the field of the bureaucratization of the employment relationship were the requirement that companies keep records on wages and hours of all their employees and the clause on rewards for overtime. Much greater was the shock of the National Labor Relations Act (NLRA). It is a matter of debate how far the CIO was, via the act, created by the federal government. On the other hand, the impact of the NLRA on the employment relationship in American industry has been enormous, whatever the standard of assessment used. Partly, this resulted from the new wordings of the act, when compared to the NIRA. Partly, also, it resulted from the powers of the administrative arm of the act, the National Labor Relations Board. The NLRA provided that in industries affecting the flow of interstate commerce, workers should be left free to unionize and to bargain collectively. This was no different than 7(a) had been, but the NLRA also specified some unfair labor practices, forbidden under the act. Any intervention of the company in a union, financial or otherwise, was forbidden. The yellow dog contract was outlawed. Workers on strike—for union recognition, for instance—did not fall beyond the sphere of action of the act and were accordingly entitled to its protection. Finally, employers, if faced with a majority union, were compelled to bargain "in good faith" (Douglas, 1937: 432–438; Rayback, 1959: 341–346). Therefore, the purpose of the act "was not to mediate in industrial disputes, but to ensure that workers had complete liberty to organize and that employers dealt, in good faith, with their organizations" (Tawney, 1979: 13–14; see also Harris, 1940: 149).

The National Labor Relations Board

Part of the act consisted of directives to the newly created National Labor Relations Board (NLRB), headed by three independent persons, appointed by the president. The NRA had had a Labor Board and even a Labor Relations Board. Yet both lacked powers to enforce the labor parts of the NRA codes. The NLRB, in contrast, had effective powers. It could ward off the crippling effects of the injunction, so often used in the early decades of the century. This could be done in the case of all unfair labor practices. The implementation of the act and its enforcement were—an important difference from the NIRA labor clause—taken seriously from the start (Goldman, 1984: 131ff.; Gould, 1982: 31ff.). According to the act, one of the tasks of the NLRB was the decision on the bargaining unit (Harris, 1940: 173; Thomson, 1981: 159).

The text of the act is vague on the issue of the bargaining unit (Goldman, 1984: 42, 52). All that is stated is that workers in a unit must have a "community of interest" (Gould, 1982: 43). The relevant bargaining size could be a company, a plant, several plants grouped together, a department, a group of workers defined by an occupational demarcation, and so on. The act was clear on whom it excluded from any bargaining unit, but it is silent on whom should be included in any specific bargaining situation. Excluded were, among others, foremen, for they did not belong to the category of "employees" for which the act was relevant (Goldman, 1984: 41). It was clear as well that the act thought of collective bargaining on an employer-by-employer base, although local, regional, or even national associations of manufacturers were formally not excluded as bargaining parties. In general, the bargaining units did not exceed the one-employer confines, but they could be considerably smaller than that (Pullman and Reed Tripp, 1957: 325–333; Clegg, 1983: 47–48).

The bargaining-unit problem was indistinguishable from another issue: that of the representative and, therewith, exclusive bargaining agent. The agent could not be a company union, but it could be union or organization limited to one company. The agent could be affiliated with the AFL, the CIO, or an independent. Again, the act left the initiative, when doubts arose, to the board. The board could order and organize secret elections to determine the majority preferences of the employees. The act itself did not state who could ask for elections; the first board, until 1939, decided that it was the employee (Harris, 1940: 195). Union busting, through employer requests for new elections and thus the testing of certified bargaining agents, was not the intent of the act or the board during the thirties. Yet the interpretation of the intent of the act was hardly patterned by the act itself. It was the board that took the decisions about the intent of the act and decisions could be, and have been as the recent past shows, revoked simply by a changed personnel of the NLRB. The act was not clear about the certification of a once-chosen representative bargaining agent.

The certificate was exclusive, but how long it would last, when it was due for renewal, and who could initiate a request to that effect were not part of the act. To all of these questions the board had to provide answers. What it did, in case of doubt between industrial or craft organization, was something that amounted to the holding of two elections, "one based on a craft unit and one based on a more inclusive industrial unit. If the craft workers voted for the craft union, it would be certified for the craft union only, but if they voted for the industrial unit, they would become part of the larger industrial unit" (Thomson, 1981: 1960). In the process, industrial and craft boundaries tended to become blurred, even more so since AFL unions, after the passage of the NLRA, started organizing and competing along industrial lines. The introduction of collective bargaining thus broke the strict lines between external structure—the historical boundaries erected by craft principles—and internal structure—the actual mode of governing the union organization (Clegg, 1983: 33, 40).

Collective Bargaining

The NLRA prepared the ground for collective bargaining. What collective bargaining stood for was not specified in the act (Selznick, 1980: 141). It seems obvious that hours and wages were to be part of the negotiations. But what about seniority, promotions, and fringe benefits? These things were left open, at least in the act. The board, following the examples set by contracts deemed representative, had to do the job. It soon created a situation in which some leading contracts became the prime reference for all others (Piore and Sabel, 1984: 97ff.). The NLRA did not sanction industrial unionism, at least not in terms of law. But it did deal a hard blow to the AFL unions, because the act made the chartering policy of the federation almost worthless. A charter from now on was determined by the NLRB. The exclusive character of the AFL charters was destroyed by the exclusive bargaining rights, certified by the board. This was a loss for the AFL, and it opened up the possibility, though not the certainty, of industrial unionism. Chartering continued, both by the AFL and the CIO, but it now was a mechanism to adjudicate conflicts over organizational jurisdiction within a federation, rather than the legitimate and exclusive base of bargaining as such.

The federal support for collective bargaining was of immediate importance for the employment relationship in American industry. When Roosevelt had signed the NLRA, be it with some hesitancy, the first response of the business community was to put its constitutionality in doubt (Fleming, 1957: 127–128; Wilcock, 1957: 290–294). In April 1937, however, the constitutionality of the act was upheld by the narrowest of margins, five to four in the Supreme Court. It was just two months after the victory of the automobile workers over General Motors. Yet obstruction had not been the only business response to the act, although especially the first section of the act gave every reason for this to happen. There, it was said that the act sought to redress "the inequality of bargaining power between employees who do not possess full freedom of association or actual liberty of contract, and employers who are organized in the corporate or other forms of ownership association" (quoted in Selznick, 1980: 140). Labor would be provided with a new substantive right: to be certified as an exclusive bargaining representative. Through a redefinition of the status of the employee, the employment relationship was to be reformed. No longer was the employee the atomized individual, presupposed in the practice of the purposive contract. Instead, it was recognized that the purposive contract in labor was merely the thin veil hiding the prerogative variety that gave management every right that the worker was denied. Limited liability had saved corporate owners the fate of personal bankruptcy in case of company failure. Social security set out to do likewise for the unemployed worker. Now, the same was about to happen for the employment contract. Managerial prerogative was not ordained to disappear. Rather, it had to be reconstructed, provided the new legal status of labor was acknowledged.

A New Status of Labor

The assumption of inequality in bargaining power between capital and labor was not merely the standard story of the giant enterprise and the tiny employee. The assumption was a recognition of the fact that the employee held no property that was independent from the employment contract. An employee might have skills that were in great demand. But these skills did not constitute "property" in any meaningful sense of the word. Property is always an option to exclude. When skills have become the property of the job, rather than of its incumbent, there is, as far as the worker is concerned, no longer an object of property. This was the case with semiskilled work and also of large parts of skilled work in the mass-production industries.

The NLRA and the Social Security Act (SSA) responded to the fact of the expropriation of skills, although not in the sense of the "deskilling" of work but in the much more fundamental sense that skills, whatever their level, no longer inhered in the worker but in the job. Accordingly, in the internal labor market the character of labor mobility had been changing from a voluntary to a forced movement, and the obstacles to movement between employers were increasing (Slichter, 1940: 317–318). As a result, the relation between the worker and the job could no longer be determined through skills and the exclusions they permitted. At first, managerial prerogative had filled the gap, leading to the struggle against turnover, increased attention for access requirements in on-the-job training, attempts at employment regularization, and a slowing down of lay-offs. After 1935, the relation became the object of potential financial gains or losses through the tax-offsetting device of the SSA and of negotiations under the NLRA.

Public Law and Private Contract

The SSA and the NLRA did not replace voluntarism so much as underwrite it with a few collective guidelines. The net effect of the SSA was the hardening of the lines between the regularly employed worker, finding protection under the act, and the marginal, irregularly employed worker (Slichter, 1940: 317–318). The NLRA, once in motion, worked to the same effect. Internal developments had led to more emphasis on screening potential employees. Training necessities had led to an emphasis on the complexity of the balance of merit and experience. At first, the NLRA pushed the business community into the direction of measures assumed to forestall unionism. Personnel departments were further centralized and internal promotions and development of grievance mechanisms encouraged (Jacoby, 1985: 242). Job-evaluation programs, to substantiate the prerogative of merit rating, were initiated or expanded.

Once the NLRA had been found constitutional, these programs were not discontinued but were adapted. The personnel department had to be supplemented by industrial relations expertise, and the union's claim on job security had to be integrated into the exigencies of workplace organization and centralized personnel administration (Wilcock, 1957: 294; Kochan and Cappelli, 1984: 140). A compromise solution often resulted, combining merit, especially in promotion, and seniority, especially in lay-offs, and transfers and rehiring (Baron, Dobbin, and Jennings, 1986: 364; Pullman and Reed Tripp, 1957: 338–339; Taft, 1942: 140; Bernstein, 1970: 775). The temporary character of lay-offs under seniority provisions was thus enhanced. Unemployment compensation, geared to a short benefit period, thus tended to become a collective insurance for temporary lay-offs (Slichter, 1940: 324). The compromise union–management solution, however, made entry for newcomers into the labor market more difficult. It was, for example, not uncommon that the collective-bargaining contract stated that seniority began only after six months or more of continuous employment. Before that date the employer should be free to end the employment contract, a consideration that grew in importance with the stricter application of the seniority principle (Slichter, 1940: 320–322; McPherson, 1940: 123).

These were the results of contract, not of the prescriptions of the NLRA. The NLRA, once accepted as the frame for labor policy, was no obstacle. Within the broad parameters set by the act, parties were to devise their own contracts and to make them as specific as the occasion required. Indeed, the fact that collective bargaining should lead to contracts, enforceable by law and modeled after the usual private contract, is significant. The elaborate grievance machinery in collective-bargaining contracts is definitely not the product of federal regulation. It is the result of a contractual relationship in which it is understood that in case of differing interpretations of the contract, further negotiations between the parties are called for (Gould, 1982: 135; Brody, 1980: 200ff.). Again, it proved that the NLRA was not out to create a zone of public law at the expense of the realm of private law. What public law exists is facilitative, rather than prescriptive (Selznick, 1980: 212). The NLRA is therefore best understood as an attempt to establish reasonable conditions for negotiating in the field of the employment relationship; granted that it was up to the negotiating parties to make their own private law. But the act was not taken for granted. It took a series of protracted struggles before the NLRA became the accepted law governing the employment relationship.

THE RISE OF THE CIO

Roosevelt announced the end of the New Deal in his 1939 presidential address. The time for social reform was up; it was time for recovery (Hofstadter, 1948: 342). The passage of the FLSA in 1938 had been the last major New Deal achievement (Lubell, 1951: 13; Conkin, 1967: 101). The act had already been part of the original NIRA legislation, and the fact that it took three years, after the NIRA was declared unconstitutional, to get it through Congress illustrates the little support it could muster. Labor, for example, had accepted only the wages and hours clause of the NIRA, because without it, section 7(a) would have fallen also (Brandeis, 1957: 205–206). When in 1935 the NLRA was adopted, labor felt no need to push the wages and hours bill. The CIO, or actually its few leading figures, was somewhat divided; John Lewis was lukewarm; Sidney Hillman, on the other hand, was positive about the act (Brandeis, 1957: 223, 230). No doubt this reflected their respective backgrounds and histories. Lewis had his "little NRA" for the coal operators and the United Mine Workers (UMW). Hillman, coming from the needle trades and its many sweatshops, had nothing of the sort. Also, Lewis feared too close a relationship between organized labor and the New Deal, whereas Hillman had few qualms about a more intimate relationship with the administration (Dubofsky and Van Tine, 1977: 319–323; Milton, 1982: 107ff.).

Throughout, the AFL voiced its fears that minimum wages in practice would prove to be maximum wages. Also, loyal to its long history of voluntarism, the federation objected to governmental intervention in the realm of collective bargaining, a position not that different from the stand Lewis had taken (Rayback, 1959: 359; Brandeis, 1957: 220ff.). What the AFL favored was a stronger position for collective bargaining. It apparently assumed that with collective bargaining a separate legal arrangement, and especially its administrative machinery, for the protection of the weakest workers was not needed. This was something of a heroic assumption, for one important function of the FLSA was to fill the gap created by the very limited worker coverage of the SSA. It should be remembered that in the first years of its operation only about half of the total number of employed workers fell under the protection of the SSA (Rayback, 1959: 338–339). The blunt idea that those not covered— those working in small sweatshops for instance or working for short times, those working in service occupations, and so forth—did not need the FLSA as much as they needed effective collective bargaining was no more than an insult. In this, the AFL was for some time supported by the NAM, and "for the first time in years Congress was treated to the spectacle of the AF of L and the NAM fighting cordially on the same side" (Perkins, 1946: 262). Yet it is of significance that the CIO, too, during its stage as a "committee" abstained from forcefully endorsing a law that was in the interest of many unskilled workers—those, that is, who were least likely to become organized and who most likely were black and living in the South.

The AFL and Unemployment Insurance

The AFL was, with Hoover, the champion of the opposition to unemployment insurance. The publication, in 1930, of its "Labor's Unemployment Program," meant to be an answer to the economic crisis, did not contain one word on the issue (Nelson, 1969: 154–155). Instead, it advocated public works, reduced hours, improved employment exchanges, vocational retraining, and better management. These recommendations were consonant with the Hoover approach to the crisis and reflected the closeness of the AFL to the Taylor society (Nelson, 1969: 75). They underscored the point that workers wanted jobs, not charity. If charity was in order, workers would have to take care of their own, and the government should stay out. Voluntarism, said Samuel Gompers, is the "cornerstone" of the house of labor (quoted in Nelson, 1969: 67). Accepting unemployment compensation automatically included for the AFL a further loss in its jurisdiction of defining skilled work and its conditions. The threat that union members would be forced to accept work in nonunion industries was far from imaginary (Nelson, 1969: 155; Bernstein, 1960: 348). On the other hand, such fears might have prompted the AFL to take a more active stand on eventual legislation. From this it refrained until the very last moment.

The passivity of the AFL during the thirties on the topic of unemployment compensation illustrated the stalemate in the organization. After 1932, when the United Mine Workers had declared itself in favor of unemployment compensation, the AFL wavered in its view. By then a series of affiliated unions, both craft and industrial, had already supported the issue, as had scores of state federations and city labor organizations (Nelson, 1969: 156; Bernstein, 1960: 350–351). Sheer necessity had forced them to embrace the cause of unemployment compensation. Most unions had no funds of their own to protect their needy members (Nelson, 1969: 66, 77). The old pride of the craft unions had been that their skills permitted them enough mobility to escape prolonged unemployment. Over time, this had become a half truth at best, although the indifference of the craft unions to the seniority principle is evidence from a closely related field (Slichter, 1941: 304ff.). The impact of the Depression destroyed what was left of the "economic freedom" of the skilled union men, although the AFL conventions were still filled with the rhetoric of its memories (Bernstein, 1960: 347–350; Nelson, 1969: 155ff.). The louder the rhetoric, however, the less it convinced anyone. In mid-1932 the AFL finally opted for unemployment compensation, to be financed through employers' contributions. The AFL had four representatives on the advisory board on social security, a

Table 8.3
Union Membership and Affiliation

Year	All Members (thousands)	AFL	AFL%	CIO	CIO%	Other	Other%
1930	3,393	2,745	81			648	19
1931	3,358	2,743	82			615	18
1932	3,144	2,497	79			647	21
1933	2,973	2,318	78			655	22
1934	3,609	3,030	84			579	16
1935	3,928	2,300	58	1,050	27	578	15
1936	4,575	2,500	56	1,500	33	575	13
1937	7,159	2,861	40	3,718	52	580	8
1938	8,240	3,023	44	3,788	46	835	10
1939	8,311	4,006	48	3,700	45	605	7
1940	8,642	4,375	51	3,624	42	643	7

Source: R.H. Tawney, The American Labour Movement, and Other Essays (Brighton, Eng., 1979), p. 101.

key organ in the wording of the SSA. Nothing much was heard of them, and in fact: "It was assumed by just about everybody . . . that whatever the administration might propose, labor would go along with it, so long as it assured increased protection against the personal hazards of life" (Witte, 1957: 252). The AFL had consented to unemployment insurance when the pressure had become too strong to resist it.

Organizing

The craft unions were not pleased with the new balance of power that accompanied the membership gains in the wake of the NIRA. Moreover, the more formidable strongholds of mass production like automobiles and steel were still hardly organized. The weak attempts of the AFL, in fact, soon discouraged the few gains made in the automobile sector. The gains of 1934 were not lasting. Nor were the losses limited to the automobile organization. All over, the year 1935 showed losses for the newest AFL organizations, and it was not hard to guess its causes (Brody, 1980: 90; Piven and Cloward, 1979: 116ff.; Davis, 1980: 49). Union membership and its affiliation showed a remarkable pattern in the thirties, strongly determined by the AFL's unwillingness to organize by industry until 1938 and its eagerness to do just that after 1938 (see Table 8.3).

When in June 1935 the NLRA was signed by Roosevelt, containing the renewed promise of a federal government favorable to collective bargaining and union representation, the stage was set for a showdown between defenders of craft principles and the advocates of industrial unionism. It came at the October 1935 convention of the AFL. Lewis of the UMW, the leading voice on industrial unionism, reiterated the 1934 decision on organization and supported a motion to clarify the necessity of organizing the great mass of workers in the mass-production industries. In his view, organization came first, jurisdiction second. He had been defeated by the craft interests on the issue earlier in the year (Dubofsky and Van Tine, 1977: 211–212). In October the issue was restated. The industrial unionists declared that it was not craft versus industrial unionism that divided the AFL. Instead, it was organizing the unorganized. Again, the industrial point of view lost (Dubofsky and Van Tine, 1977: 219–220; Rayback, 1959: 349–350; Brody, 1980: 89ff.; Harris, 1940: 41–47).

The defeat was not unexpected. The day after the closing of the convention the group of union leaders favorable to industrial unionism met to reaffirm their determination to continue organizing the mass-production industries. Three weeks later, a somewhat extended company, representing almost 1 million trade union members, formed the Committee for Industrial Organization "as an organized bloc inside the A.F. of L. dedicated to unionizing mass-production workers along industrial lines" (Dubofsky and Van Tine, 1977: 222; see also Taft, 1942: 135). Lewis became its chairman; Charles P. Howard (of the Printer's union), secretary; and John Brophy (like Lewis from the UMW), director. The positions were unpaid, except for Brophy, whose salary was paid by the UMW. The CIO offices in Washington faced those of the UMW, showing again that the CIO and Lewis were, at least at the start, indistinguishable. The AFL was quick to retaliate. Within a year after the founding of the committee, the AFL, after a series of insincere negotiations, suspended the unions under the CIO aegis (Dubofsky and Van Tine, 1977: 232–242; Rayback, 1959: 350–351; Harris, 1940: 48–53). Dual unionism, the foe of the American labor movement, now was the reality of the day, although it would take two years before the committee was officially transformed into the Congress of Industrial Organizations.

The committee took organizing seriously. The UMW funded and staffed the Steel Workers Organizing Committee (SWOC) in 1936, luring the old Amalgamated Association to the CIO along the way. By the end of 1936 the SWOC had 100,000 members in 150 locals. Steel, it seemed, was ripe for organization (Rayback, 1959: 351; Dubofsky and Van Tine, 1977: 234–238). Viewing the industrial scene as a whole, the CIO in 1936 added half a million workers to its ranks, due to organizing efforts mainly in the steel, rubber, and automobile industries. Lewis had even dropped his familiar anti-Left policies and so profited from the organizing capacities of the Communist party. In exchange, 1935 had been the year when the Third International dropped its "social fascism" thesis and adopted the popular-front strategy, therewith giving the Communist Party of the United States (CPUSA) the leeway for a more flexible policy regarding trade unionism (Davis, 1980: 53; Klehr, 1984: 228ff.). The CIO produced a record distinctly superior to that of the AFL in the same period. Within one year the CIO controlled one-third of the organized workers (Table 8.3; Dubofsky and Van Tine, 1977: 234–238; Tawney, 1979).

The true test of the American labor movement, all the same, was not the winning of one or more battles in labor's "civil war" (Harris, 1940). The test was to get the employers to bargain collectively with union representatives. The employers remained adamant, however, and calculated that the NLRA would be defeated before the Supreme Court. The employers had not given in to the strike waves of 1933 and 1934, although both the number of strikes, the workers involved, and the duration of strikes had increased considerably (Hardman and Neufeld, 1951: 532). Strike activity, in fact, had more than doubled in comparison to that in 1932. Also, there was a huge increase in the proportion of strikes having union recognition as their primary cause (Fleming, 1957: 131, table 1, 132, chart A; Edwards, 1981: 263, tables A.8a, A.8b). The employers had not been surprised by the fact that the unions might lose their grip on the workers, although the signs, especially in 1933, did point in that direction (Edwards, 1981: 139–141; Rubin, Griffin, and Wallace, 1983: 341). Moreover, strike activity in 1935 and 1936 showed a different pattern from that of 1933 and 1934, proving again that these years were preceding a new period but with its exact shape undecided. The number of strikes kept increasing, but the number of workers involved decreased and was in 1936 just over half of what it had been in 1934 (Hardman and Neufeld, 1951: 532). There was one matter, however, that should have warned the employers of things to come. The proportion of strikes for union recognition continued climbing upward and was about 50 percent of the total, involving also around 50 percent of the striking workers, 1936 (Fleming, 1957: 131, table 1, 132, chart A). Of all data available for the period, these figures were the handwriting on the wall.

Sit-Down and the United Automobile Workers

In 1935 GM counted almost 30,000 employees in Flint, Michigan, about one-seventh of its total number. Since the industry as a whole employed about 420,000 workers at the time, Flint was an important auto town (Fine, 1969: 21, 71). Fifty-five percent of the Flint auto workers were reported as semiskilled, almost one-fourth as skilled, and not even 10 percent as unskilled (Fine, 1969: 54). The very high share of the semiskilled was typical for the automobile industry. Not so typical, however, were the national origins or backgrounds of the workers in Flint. Whereas in Detroit more than half of the semiskilled and unskilled workers were of foreign origin or black, this held for only one-fourth of the Flint workers. Foreign in Flint indicated descent from Canadian or Western European parents more than from Central, Southern, or Eastern European parents, as in Detroit. Blacks, especially, were a tiny minority in Flint, whereas in Detroit, due to the hiring policy of Ford, their presence was much more proportionate to their share in the population of the United States as a whole. On the other hand, reflecting the very irregular employment in the industry, only 30 percent of the city population in the thirties had been born in Flint itself. The large majority came from elsewhere in Michigan and from other states (Fine, 1969: 102–104).

The Depression struck hard in Flint, and as in Detroit, the population shrank. Employment fell, from a high of 50,000 in 1929 to 17,000 in 1932, the worst year. After that the trend went upward again to 21,000 in 1934 and 30,000 in 1935. Yet even in 1935 almost one in five auto workers was unemployed (Fine, 1969: 104). This was somewhat under the city average, and the prospects for further improvement were good. Economically, in the 1935–1937 period, the worst for the automobile industry if not for industry as a whole, appeared already to have happened (Bernstein, 1970: 503; Dubofsky and Van Tine, 1977: 255). In fact, in 1936 production for the first time was back at the 1929 level, at least for General Motors (Fine, 1969: 21). As a simple comparison of figures shows, the Depression was at least normal in that worker productivity increased substantially. Accordingly, complaints about the speedup were as numerous as the changes in machinery and organization of the line, and the culprits for the working conditions were easily identifiable.

GM's organizational setup guaranteed plants and divisions a wide margin of independence, which in practice boiled down to the common knowledge that working conditions, the speed of the line, and the vicissitudes of lay-off and discharge were the full responsibility of the nearest management (Bernstein, 1970: 515). Remarkable, at any rate, was the sharp increase in productivity after 1934 (Fine, 1969: 56–58). GM was not, like Ford, heavily concentrated in one city only. It possessed in the United States sixty-nine plants in thirty-five cities, spread over fourteen states (Dubofsky and Van Tine, 1977: 256). During 1935 GM started a policy of enlarging its inventories of semifinished and finished products and of diversification of plants to nullify eventual union action. As the company was to find out, however, this policy might have been stricter, for it had no real alternative for the Fisher Body plant in Flint. Of this, union organizers were better informed than, apparently, the company (Fine, 1969: 49).

The company was determined to fight unionism as long as it possibly could. It may not have expected that the union would attack in Flint. But after the United Automobile Workers, in July 1936, affiliated with the CIO, unionization of GM was on the agenda. Organization of new members in the UAW progressed in the second half of 1936, such that, at the close of the year, the most conservative estimate was that about one-seventh of the auto workers belonged to the union (Fine, 1969: 97–98). In Flint, with 1,500 members in late 1936, the figure was just 5 percent (Fine, 1969: 136). Gains still could be made in Flint, for a small conflict in November 1936, in which the UAW stood up for the workers involved, had raised membership from 150 to 1,500 at the end of the year (Brecher, 1972: 192). Still, it was low.

On the other hand, from the point of view of the UAW, GM had to be tackled, and the Fisher Body plants were the logical target. Of the Big Three, Chrysler entertained better relations with the UAW than GM did, and the impact of a fight with Chrysler would be limited. Ford, although, in size, number three in 1936, still commanded enormous public attention. Yet the Ford plants were almost completely unorganized also after the organizing drive of the UAW in 1936 (Fine, 1969: 133). No doubt, Ford's feared Service Department, numbering more than 3,000 men in the mid-thirties and made up "of ex-cops, ex-athletes, thugs and racketeers" (Serrin, 1973: 116), was one cause of Ford's resilience to union organization. But Ford's hiring policies may have been more important, specifically in relation to the position of blacks in his company (Meier and Rudwick, 1979: 16–33; Foner, 1981: 221ff.; Babson, 1984: 105ff.). It had to be GM.

So a handful of able organizers, largely from the ranks of the CPUSA, and a few more men captured the fort of GM at the close of 1936 (on the influence of the CPUSA in the Flint strike, see Klehr, 1984: 232–233; Fine, 1969: 221–223). Significantly, the CIO, though supporting the strike, had not expected it. Its own attention had been directed almost completely at organizing steel (Dubofsky and Van Tine, 1977: 255). The UAW, also, was taken by surprise, for the organization had planned the strike for 1937, when the new Democratic governor of Michigan would be in office. Lewis was of the same opinion (Dubofsky and Van Tine, 1977: 257; Bernstein, 1970: 521; Mortimer, 1972: 124). The workers themselves, and the UAW organizers in Flint in their wake, had taken over—and they had every reason to do so since GM in December 1936 had flatly refused to negotiate with the union about recognition or collective bargaining (Rayback, 1959: 353).

The strike lasted for six weeks. Estimates of the damage it would inflict on GM proved accurate. January production of GM, projected for 224,000 cars and trucks, was reduced to 60,000. In the first ten days of February a meager 151 cars were the total result for the entire organization of GM (Brecher, 1972: 198). GM tried everything to get the strike undone: injunctions, police brutality, turning off the heating, the National Guard, public opinion. They all failed (Bernstein, 1970: 525ff.). In this case, worker militancy increased organizational capacity, and organizational capacity increased worker militancy (Rubin, Griffin, and Wallace, 1983: 335–337). Moreover, although it is hard to evaluate in exact terms, Roosevelt had just been reelected for a second term and had been strongly supported by Lewis along the way. Alfred P. Sloan, still GM's president, had supported the Roosevelt enemies, gathered in the so-called Liberty League (Fine, 1969: 95–96; Dubofsky and Van Tine, 1977: 249ff.). Frank Murphy, again, had been elected governor of Michigan with strong labor support. This, added to the NLRA and GM's defiance of it, may explain the lenient attitude of both Roosevelt and Murphy to the fact of the sit-down. They knew it was illegal and a violation of property rights. They also knew that rights have a fringe of power, and that GM and power—under the circumstances—were, at least temporarily, not identical.

On February 16 negotiations between GM and the UAW started. They ended in an agreement on March 12. From the point of view of the UAW it was a meager agreement, and it took the UAW officials a good thirteen hours to convince the union members that it should be accepted (Fine, 1969: 326). First, the agreement held good for only seventeen of the GM plants. All of the plants that had not been affected by the strike—the identification of which was in itself a bone of contention—were not covered by the agreement (Mortimer, 1972: 144; Fine, 1969: 302; Bernstein, 1970). The no-strike pledge was maintained (Fine, 1969: 325). Seniority rules were improved, but merit and skill were not to disappear. On the other hand, the UAW made its point that in the case of reduced production (with the annual model a yearly event) temporary workers with less than six months of employment were to be laid off first (Fine, 1969: 324). Eligibility for social security and seniority, thus, were coupled through the agreement. By the same token, seniority would begin only after a six-month "probationary period" during which, in fact, managerial prerogative in discharge was complete (Mortimer, 1972: 144). On wages, hours, and timing of operations, the union did not have its way. The agreement stated that time studies, though to be made with fairness and equity, belonged to the full authority of local management (Bernstein, 1970: 551ff.; Fine, 1969: 324–325).

On one issue GM gave more and less than was demanded. The agreement provided for grievance machinery. The union had asked for one shop steward for every twenty-five workers and for the right that grievances be put before the steward first. This, GM refused, and it did not appear in the agreement. Instead, shop committees from five to nine men in each plant were agreed upon. The first address in grievances remained, however, the foreman, and only in the case of unsatisfactory adjustment could the matter be referred to the committee if, that is, the correct procedural path was followed (Fine, 1969: 323). The qualification of "unsatisfactory" denoted a procedural bias: The substance of a grievance was quick to disappear behind questions of formal competence and the like (Brody, 1980: 202ff.). It was containment of shop-floor protest rather than the recognition of its legitimacy that GM was after. The UAW dared hardly suggest that grievances could be tackled in a serious way by a maximum of nine employees in a plant with thousands of workers. But GM was satisfied and happily extended the grievance procedure to all of its plants, not just the seventeen to which the rest of the agreement was limited (Fine, 1969: 323).

For all of its defects, the agreement confirmed that the largest corporation in the world had been forced into collective bargaining with the representative union of the workers. The union had been recognized, and its representatives could and did take action in the day-to-day operations of the company. Within half a year after the agreement was concluded, the UAW was among the largest unions in the country, counting in October 1937 almost 400,000 members (Bernstein, 1970: 554; Fine, 1969: 327). The growth was so fast that it put the organization under considerable strain. Internal dissension and competition from the rival AFL union threatened to wreck the union. In the end, the CIO stepped in, reorganized the union, and defeated the AFL contender (Bernstein, 1970: 566ff.).

Soon after the end of the Flint strike, Chrysler consented to collective bargaining. Then U.S. Steel gave in—without any sit-down or other labor action. In April 1937 the Supreme Court enhanced the value of these concluded contracts through a verdict declaring the NLRA constitutional. Then the tide turned. In May the UAW tried to organize Ford. It got a severe beating by the Service Department. At the very same day of the Ford brutality, the SWOC started organizing "Little Steel." It ended in bloodshed, and the organizational attempt failed. Unlike before, the federal government did not move to stop company violence or the use of the National Guard. Power, the CIO learned, was an unstable balance and an unpredictable one at that. In the later half of 1937 Roosevelt cut spending drastically, leading to a severe recession and mounting unemployment. The pace of unionization was interrupted, and the CIO lost its headstart, relative to the AFL, in industrial unionism (Bernstein, 1970: 773ff.).

Results

The NLRA was not again subjected to a constitutional test. State Labor Relations Acts, sometimes restrictive concerning unionization, made the effectivity of the NLRA optional on location. Industry therewith had a choice (Killingsworth, 1948: 499–508). The postwar Labor Management Relations Act (LMRA) of 1947 amended the substance of the NLRA somewhat, but its principles on workers deciding about their representatives and on the necessity of collective bargaining were upheld. The sit-down had been outlawed since 1939, but that had never been part of the NLRA. The closed shop was forbidden under the LMRA. Yet seniority had become a standard part of collective-bargaining agreements, and seniority is, whatever else it may be, one functional equivalent of the closed shop (Slichter, 1941: 308).

Together with seniority, the development of elaborate grievance machinery stands as the most conspicuous achievement of union recognition and collective bargaining (Gordon, Edwards, and Reich, 1982: 179ff.). On wages and hours, the influence of unions is harder to determine. Hours were shortened, to be sure, but federal intervention had been very near. Some leveling of wages took place after 1937, but this may have been in the air anyway (Bernstein, 1970: 774–775; Hacker, 1970: 290; Kolko, 1976: ch. 5; McPherson, 1940: 149). This is not to state that hours and wages were unimportant, for they were not. The unions did influence the timing and the spread of new regulations on hours and wages. Without them, it might have taken longer. More generally, the industrial unions enforced the formal recognition of the position of the semiskilled in industry. The factual recognition was already in the making under the aegis of managerial prerogative. The unions added to it and hastened its codification. The process of the bureaucratization of the employment relationship was both adapted and furthered.

But the NLRA and the collective bargaining practice that grew out of it did not change the dominant characteristics of the American pattern. The legal framework of collective bargaining was public law; the collective-bargaining contracts, on the other hand, were issues of private law. Again, voluntarism and federal intervention were projected as sustaining, rather than mutually exclusive, principles of regulation. Collective bargaining was not merely forced on the corporation. It was geared to its mode of functioning and integrated into its internal developments already under way in the fields of training on the job, attempts to reduce voluntary turnover, and stabilization of employment. The rise of the unions, from this perspective, was more a compromise with, than a defeat for, the corporation. Voluntary turnover had been on the wane for the majority of workers after the First World War, together with the stagnation of industrial employment opportunities and the shift of skill from the jobholder to the job. The emphasis on seniority was a more worker-oriented translation of the loss of exit than the emphasis on merit. These were shifts in emphases, however, not pure seniority to the detriment of unadulterated merit. In promotions, merit remained prominent; in discharge and lay-off, seniority became the prime criterion. But the price was a higher rate of forced mobility on those excluded, like the young and the old, the women, the blacks, and, in the postwar era, the "newest" new immigrants. In this, corporate interest, union accommodation, and federal intervention came together.

9

CONCLUSION

Until well into this century the corporation resembled a total institution. The corporate mode of organizing company towns or city politics and the practices relating to the employment relationship were distinctly premodern: "A basic social arrangement in modern society is that the individual tends to sleep, play, and work in different places, with different co-participants, under different authorities, and without an overall rational plan. The central feature of total institutions can be described as a breakdown of the barriers ordinarily separating these three spheres of life" (Goffman, 1968: 17; see also Walzer, 1983: 295–303).

Socially, the total institution can be identified along a few dimensions. First, there is the fact that the supervision of persons entails surveillance rather than a mix of guidance and inspection. Second, one may expect to find a basic split between the supervisory staff and the workers of the institution. Mutual stereotyping is common; direct interaction is negligible and formal, limited to strategic behavior rather than to communicative actions. The social distance separating the two groups is therefore great. Third, total institutions plan not just the work of their subjects but their needs as well; the relation of authority connecting institution and worker does not stop short of work. Instead, the compensation given to the workers derives from its use in reproducing the statuses of worker and staff (Goffman, 1968: 18–21).

The period of American welfare capitalism, Ford's $5 day included, demonstrated the proclivity of American corporations to develop into total institutions—but only to a degree. The concept of a total institution is an "ideal type" (Goffman, 1968: 17). It serves to highlight characteristics of developments, and it is an option in identifying salient differences, but it is neither the essence of developments nor coterminous with developments. There are, in this sense, no total institutions, only contextually defined degrees of correspondence. The context of the corporation includes, in our case, the labor contract, that is, both the ascendancy of the prerogative contract interpretation during the heydays of welfare capitalism and a high rate of voluntary mobility. Workers left in droves, possibly for economic reasons but also because they were completely free to do so. The contract, in the end, was private and terminable at will by the employer as well as the employee. The prerogative indicated that the employer was master in his own house. Termination at will indicated that the employee, too, had property: "in himself." Accordingly, the employee was free to take it elsewhere. It was a strenuous relationship nevertheless, and the rise and fall of welfare capitalism show it. By means of overt and covert provisions, the employee was promised, in exchange for his discretion in matters of voluntary mobility, a more inclusive existence. The obnoxious sides of the trade-off were due to its implicit character. Checking the moves and behavior of employees had to be tinged with some secrecy, because ultimately the employee in matters beyond the shop was his own master.

The resentment that welfare capitalism produced and the apprehension of the corporation in stressing its voluntary and moral character signal the fact that welfare capitalism was not an extension of relations of authority. It was an attempt to solve the problem of company order, without the authority to impose it. It was a product of relations of power—and employees and employers alike were well aware of it. When during the twenties the theme of technological unemployment dominated the industrial scene, the employers had little to fear from voluntary mobility. Accordingly, welfare capitalism lost its earlier character of being the appendage, and possibly even the substitute, of recruitment, and it became one of the methods of creating new hierarchies within the labor force. Employee background characteristics, the sieve in recruitment, lost some of their prominence and direct behavioral surveillance came to the fore. The concomitant development of welfare provisions and the personnel function during the twenties was, after all, not a mere coincidence. In this situation the tyrannical potential of welfare capitalism flourished, creating, in effect, the semblance of the total institution. The Great Depression, although it dissolved the welfare provisions, did not dissolve the personnel function or the policing of employees. Quite the contrary, in fact, happened.

It was an unequal bargain, but as long as not just the labor contract but wage dependency itself was treated as volitional—that is, as long as exits were upheld as realistic options in the case of, for instance, prolonged unemployment—the balance would remain unstable. A zone of indeterminacy, of which welfare capitalism itself is an expression, would command the employment relationship. The political development of the thirties changed all that. It arranged a bifurcation between the status of wage dependency and the conclusion of a labor contract. The former was recognized by public law;

the latter was to remain a private affair between contracting parties. This, obviously, was not done to vitiate the privately arranged labor contract but rather to save it from being destroyed by the policing power of the corporation. The property of the employee "in himself" was now protected not by protecting the individual employee but by public recognition of his status of wage dependency.

The Social Security Act (SSA) transformed unemployment from a voluntary solution into a social risk beyond individual control. The National Labor Relations Act (NLRA) transformed bargaining from an individual responsibility into a collective one—if the employees so desired. The federal government granted the collectivity of employees the right to choose for collective representation at the bargaining encounter. State labor relations acts sometimes emphasized the reverse: the right of employees not to be represented collectively in bargaining. Like the SSA, the NLRA and, willy-nilly, even the state laws it provoked emphasized that the employment relationship was beyond the control of the individual employee. The responsibilities of the individual employee, accordingly, became negative. If unemployment was not voluntary, compensation would follow. If employees declined collective representation, bargaining could follow its own course.

Public law facilitated; it did not prescribe. The same emphasis can be detected in the application of the Fair Labor Standards Act (FLSA): the federal government waits for complaints, filed on initiative of concerned employees, instead of actively monitoring and thus implementing the act (Selznick, 1980: 227). The facilitating approach also dominates collective bargaining. The NLRA created boundaries to managerial prerogative—provided the employees collectively demanded such boundaries and had them codified in collective bargaining. The administrative arm of the act did not assume mediating competencies. Its task was to help, with the act, create the conditions for collective bargaining. The rest was up to the parties: "the new law aimed to save freedom of contract, not to reject it" (Selznick, 1980: 140). The widespread use of grievance machinery is among its more noticeable manifestations (Selznick, 1980: 145). Grievance machinery did not eradicate managerial prerogative; rather, it corrected the situation in which the unilateral exercise of the prerogative threatened the rights of workers as citizens. Public law, in sum, stated what could be done within the confines of the law; whether it was done depended on the interested parties to a contract.

The fiction of a private contract, enforceable by law and detailed as to responsibilities and duties, was upheld, then, by the New Deal in labor relations. Even without viable exits, the employee was still presumed to offer his property "in himself" and to receive a wage in return. This is what the rule of private contract presupposes. The rule pits property owners against one another in the arena of interests and suggests a contract as the peaceful mode of playing the nonzero game. In the game, resources and strategies may be used, combinations—even across the capital–labor divide—may be entered or dissolved, ranks may get opened and closed, and so forth. The game in such an image enables the transformation of resources into strategies and vice versa, provided that in the end resources and strategies retain their distinct properties. In sociology the "arena" perspective on labor markets (refining the earlier "dualization" and "segmentation" approaches) is the major recent example along these lines (Loveridge and Mok, 1979: 173–186; van Hoof, 1987: 175ff.; Soerensen and Kalleberg, 1981: 49ff.; Schervish, 1981: 153ff.; 1983: 11–18, 38–39; Althauser and Kalleberg, 1981: 119ff.). Yet resources and strategies of labor power in the end cannot be separated.

Property in the means of production did not originally mean the privilege of command, unless the workers attracted, such as women, children, the poor, and prisoners, were bereft of their full civil and citizenship status (on the argument, see Rusche and Kirchheimer, 1974). For craft workers, on the other hand, these methods would not do. They held a stronger social and political–legal status, and they kept their skills, for these were person bound. Whole industries in the early days of capitalist Europe sometimes moved along with the migration of skilled workers. Werner Sombart, in fact, argued that the rise of English industry is due in large part to the influx of skilled artisans who were fleeing religious intolerance on the mainland of Europe (Sombart, 1921: 826). The command of capital in such instances could only be "formal." This situation ruled the early days of nineteenth-century American capitalism, and it was expressed in dreams on the frontier. But then, these were also the days of liberal immigration policies, the fast occupation of lands, and heavy governmental involvement in the construction of a transportation network. By the late nineteenth century the frontier was past tense, and labor power's exit options were practically reduced to return migration. Skills were on their way to becoming objectified in the job, leading to a growing array of attempts to bridge the gap between educationally achieved qualifications and job entry through credentialism, thus recreating the semblance of "property."

After World War I return migration and immigration were reduced to insignificance, and the possibilities of exit became smaller again. The period of the New Deal did not recreate the possibility of exit. Instead, New Deal social and labor legislation recognized labor for what it was: neither a collective commodity nor a regular, private one. This most peculiar status was clearer in the United States than elsewhere, split between a collective realm defining the status of wage dependency and its associated rights and a private realm defining the status of the employee as the junior partner in a contract. In the collective realm the employee was defined as propertyless. The SSA provides the resources the unemployed worker is not supposed to possess. The NLRA is built on the assumption that the worker has no resources that have any currency beyond the employment relationship. Again, unemployment compensation is the official recognition of the fact that the unemployed wage worker is without property that can be put "to some use or benefit."

The inference is that the only property the worker has is in his job, and jurisprudence to that effect indeed exists (Selznick, 1980: 68; Kahn-Freund, 1979: 39). But this property right flows from the collective-bargaining situation, especially its clauses on seniority and grievances, and not from the law itself (Kahn-Freund, 1979: 55). It exists only in and through a labor contract. It is not property by law but by a compromise of interests. Legally, it is an odd construction indeed. Property rights are absolutes, since they, at least potentially, exclude everybody. Contract rights are relative; they do not bind other than those mentioned in the contract (Neumann, 1936; Durkheim, 1957: 158ff.).

What gives the employment contract its distinguishing characteristic is not the fact that it enables bargaining or reflects its results. Nor is it the fact that it represents services to be rendered by the owner of labor power. Its specific difference relative to other forms of contracts on the alienation of property, services included, is exactly the relation of authority and submission it presupposes and expresses. Property and possession in labor power, accordingly, are metaphors at best. Both property and possession presuppose the power to exclude, which implies the power to put it to other use. When possessions in labor power are strictly person bound, the power of multiple use, autonomously or with a variety of employers, may be said to be probable. The crafts are one example, the professions another. For the large majority of employment opportunities, however, this does not hold true, for they are characterized by the gap separating jobs and their skills and workers and their qualifications or, more generally, their background characteristics. Qualifications, in these instances, are not "property" but screening devices.

It could be argued that qualifications resemble property in that they are both person bound and one of the independent variables in the process of "matching" qualifications and job skills (van Hoof, 1987: 183; Kreckel, 1983: 154–157; Thurow, 1975: 79ff.; Soerensen and Kalleberg, 1981: 52ff.). The argument takes qualifications or, more generally, negatively or positively privileged background characteristics as one independent variable in the matching of persons and jobs. This may lead to a run on qualifications and thus to the phenomenon of overqualification in the face of unchanged job skills (Thurow, 1975: 95–97). That, however wasteful it may be for society at large, does not detract from the issue. If the price of qualifications goes down, these qualifications suffer a fate not unlike that of other commodities in a glutted market. This, then, is not the problem. The problem rests in the assumption that companies are looking for the lowest training costs in bridging the gap between qualifications and job skills rather than that companies do not look for the better fit or match but for the smaller risk. These options, it must be emphasized, are not identical. Matching means that qualifications or background characteristics are indicators of trainability for job skills. Risk minimization, on the other hand, means that the moment of deciding on trainability is postponed until after hiring and that qualifications and background characteristics are nothing but a crude screening device, rejecting some and keeping others in the waiting room of training facilities or opportunities.

Referring to the American developments, we contend that the American practice corroborates the risk-minimization approach and not the matching one. Periods of probation, the agreements to apply seniority in case of layoff and rehiring, the counting of seniority only after the end of the probationary period, and the bracketing of seniority in promotions and transfers are so many instances of risk minimization and as many denials of the primacy of matching. Recruitment is determined by risk minimization of firms, training is determined by the combination of risk minimization and matching. The first question, then, is not one of finding ways and means to bridge the gap between qualifications and skills. The question is one of finding out about risk minimization.

Company risks may be minimized by exploiting the differential social and citizenship statuses of workers. Risk minimization, here, is not an economic so much as a political strategy. Recruitment, like the position of the employee, reflects status. This may mean the legal recognition of "alternative roles," such as mother or housewife (Offe and Hinrichs, 1977: 10, 26). Alternative roles are echoed in civil status in that for instance social security discriminates eligibility to the exclusion of persons possessing alternative roles. Migrant labor is an instance in that citizenship may be denied to it and that eligibility for social security may, regardless of the contributions made, discriminate against those without permits to stay or work permits. The young are an instance, since their civil status may be curtailed on a score of issues, citizenship being one, family accountability another. The pattern of recruitment, reinforced by the selective discretion of governments in social security and labor relations, responds to the mobility discretion of workers, even if this discretion amounts to no more than an unwanted ticket home. The discretionary mobility by now has developed into the distribution of poverty. It seals the irrelevance of property in person-bound skills and the necessity of qualifying the jobs, the skills of which are not just beyond control of the worker but which also make a joke of the cherished notion of property.

What property the worker has is above all a status conferred upon him selectively. We have been stressing, in this study, the personal nature of the labor contract. Civil leeway and citizenship rights are among the more conspicuous features of civil and citizenship statuses. Indeed, from the standpoint of theoretical economics, the situation of an imperfect market for unskilled labor is an anomaly. The usual assumption, especially about unskilled labor, is that of an unlimited supply. We have tried to substantiate the thesis that the anomaly is the key to understanding the developments in the American labor market. It has not been the frontier as such that explains the tenacious shortage of unskilled labor during the greater part of the nineteenth century. The frontier does not stand on its own, for those that were allowed to participate in its promises had to qualify as citizens. This excluded blacks, native Americans, women, and children. It included white, male immigrants.

The importance of the new immigration was exactly that here, for the first time in American history, unskilled labor and citizenship options coincided. No material market regulation limited the new immigrant's labor market—in contrast to the labor market for women, children, and blacks, for instance. It is a matter of future research to what exact degree the citizenship option of the new immigrant facilitated his movement from unskilled to semiskilled positions. The option itself, nevertheless, was of major importance. It enhanced the uncertainty of the employer's recruitment risks, since the very option was a token of the possibility of return migration. Length of stay, on the other hand, reduced the likelihood of return migration and therefore opened up the road to semiskilled work. Restriction of immigration, during the second and third decade of this century, therefore strengthened the claim on semiskilled work of the erstwhile new immigrant. The developments during the thirties in the field of labor legislation and social security completed the claim.

This has been a unique constellation. The emancipation of black citizenship, in the sixties, was followed by a shrinking market of semiskilled labor. The predicament of black workers is that by now unskilled labor is available in plentiful supply and has become again the province of persons with a weak citizenship status: the newest new immigrants as they are sometimes called in a false analogy (Piore, 1979). Yet while the movement of the new immigrant coincided with the growth of semiskilled work, a concomitant or comparable growth cannot be detected for the black worker. This, to be sure, is a hypothesis for research rather than an established fact. But it is at the very least an informed hypothesis. We believe that the relationship between citizenship and labor-market position is of fundamental importance. We also believe that its importance has been vastly underestimated in labor-market research. Discretionary mobility, and therewith the "person" in any labor contract, is deeply influenced by the dimension of citizenship. In the field of labor-market policy, then, progress consists, first, of the extension of the rights to citizenship for those who do not enjoy them fully.

One cannot help but endorse Walzer's thesis that the just principle in this respect is

that the processes of self-determination through which a democratic state shapes its internal life, must be open, and equally open, to all those men and women who live within its territory, work in the local economy, and are subject to local law. Hence, second admissions (naturalization) depend on first admissions (immigration) and are subject only to certain constraints of time and qualification, never to the ultimate constraint of closure. (Walzer, 1983: 60–61)

In itself, this does not relieve the plight of black unemployment and discrimination. Indeed, it is not a fair record of black history. It does, however, cover a good part of the new world of the new immigration, and a good case can be made for the idea that equalizing opportunities for all labor-market participants depends on Walzer's principle. One may actually doubt the possibility of achieving this ideal state of the world, without, however, renouncing the necessity of trying to reach it. The tension between ideal and attempt may produce disappointments. But for better or worse, the tension is the source of our shifting involvements (Hirschman, 1982), and in the final analysis our involvements, too, are a matter of discretion.

BIBLIOGRAPHY

Advisory Council on Social Security. 1948, 1951. "Unemployment Insurance." In *Readings in Labor Economics and Industrial Relations*, ed. J. Shister. Chicago, Philadelphia, and New York, pp. 528–540.

Aglietta, M. 1979. *A Theory of Capitalist Regulation: The U.S. Experience*. London.

Akerman, S., B. Kronborg, and T. Nilsson. 1979. "Emigration, Family, and Kinship." In *American Immigration: Its Variety and Lasting Imprint*, ed. R. Kroes. Amsterdam, pp. 32–47.

Alexander, J. W. 1963. *Economic Geography*. Englewood Cliffs, N.J.

Allswang, J. M. 1979. "Immigrants in Urban Politics: Ethnic Interest and Political Choice." In *American Immigration: Its Variety and Lasting Imprint*, ed. R. Kroes. Amsterdam, pp. 134–143.

Althauser, R. P., and A. L. Kalleberg. 1981. "Firms, Occupations, and the Structure of Labor Markets: A Conceptual Analysis." In *Sociological Perspectives on Labor Markets*, ed. I. Berg. New York, pp. 119–149.

Altmeyer, A. J. 1966. *The Formative Years of Social Security*. Madison, Wis.

Arrow, K. J. 1970. *Essays in the Theory of Risk-Bearing*. Amsterdam and London.

Ashton, P. 1978. "Political Economy of Suburban Development." In *Marxism and the Metropolis*, ed. W. K. Tabb and L. Sawyers. New York, pp. 64–89.

Babson, S. 1984. *Working Detroit: The Making of a Union Town*. New York.

Baran, P. A., and P. M. Sweezy. 1966, 1970. *Monopoly Capital: An Essay on the American Economic and Social Order*. Harmondsworth, Eng.

Bardou, J. P., J. J. Chanaron, P. Fridemon, and J. M. Laux. 1982. *The Automobile Revolution: The Impact of an Industry*. Chapel Hill, N.C.

Baritz, L. 1960. *The Servants of Power: A History of the Use of Social Science in American Industry*. Middletown, Conn.

Baron, J. N., F. R. Dobbin, and P. Devereaux Jennings. 1986. "War and Peace: The Evolution of Modern Personnel Administration in U.S. Industry." *American Journal of Sociology* (September): 347–380.

Barton, J. J. 1978. "Eastern and Southern Europeans." In *Ethnic Leadership in America*, ed. J. Higham. Baltimore and London, pp. 150–175.

Becker, G. S. 1964, 1968. "Investment in on-the-Job Training." In *Economics of Education*, vol. 1, ed. M. Blaug. Harmondsworth, Eng., pp. 183–207.

Bendix, R. 1956. *Work and Authority in Industry*. Translated from *Herrschaft und Industriearbeit*. Frankfurt, 1960.

Berg, I., ed. 1981. *Sociological Perspectives on Labor Markets*. New York.

Bernstein, B. J. 1969. "The New Deal: The Conservative Achievements of Liberal Reform." In *Towards a New Past: Dissenting Essays in American History*, ed. B. J. Bernstein. New York, pp. 203–288.

I. Bernstein, 1960, 1972. *The Lean Years: A History of the American Worker, 1920–1933*. Boston.

———. 1970. *Turbulent Years: A History of the American Worker, 1933–1941*. Boston.

Beynon, H. 1973. *Working for Ford*. Harmondsworth, Eng.

Bock, G. 1976. *Die andere Arbeiterbewegung in den USA von 1909–1922*. Munich.

Bologna, S. 1976. "Class Composition and the Theory of the Party at the Origin of the Workers Councils Movement." In *The Labour Process and Class Strategies*. CSE Pamphlets no. 1. London, pp. 68–91.

Bonacich, E. 1979. "A Theory of Ethnic Antagonism: The Split Labor Market." In *The American Working Class: Prospects for the 1980s*, ed. I. L. Horowitz, J. C. Leggett, and M. Oppenheimer. New Brunswick, N.J., pp. 73–93.

———. 1980. "Class Approaches to Ethnicity and Race." *The Insurgent Sociologist* 10, no. 2:9–23.

Bourne, R. S. 1916, 1970. *The Gary Schools*. Cambridge, Mass., and London.

Bowles, S., and H. Gintis. 1976. *Schooling in Capitalist America*. New York.

Boyer, P. 1978. *Urban Masses and Moral Order in America, 1820–1920*. Cambridge, Mass., and London.

Boyer, R. O., and H. M. Morais. 1955, 1980. *Labor's Untold Story*. New York.

Brandeis, E. 1957, 1972. "Organized Labor and Protective Labor Legislation." In *Labor and the New Deal*, ed. M. Derber and E. Young. New York, pp. 193–237.

Brandes, S. D. 1976. *American Welfare Capitalism, 1880–1940*. Chicago.

Braverman, H. 1974. *Labor and Monopoly Capital: The Degradation of Work in the Twentieth Century*. New York and London.

Brecher, J. 1972. *Strike!* San Francisco.

Brinkley, A. 1983. *Voices of Protest: Huey Long, Father Coughlin, and the Great Depression*. New York.

Brock, W. R. 1984. *Investigation and Responsibility*. Cambridge.

Brody, D. 1960. *Steelworkers in America: The Nonunion Era*. Cambridge, Mass.

———. 1968. "Career Leadership and American Trade Unionism." In *The Age of Industrialism in America*, ed. F. C. Jaher. New York and London, pp. 288–303.

———. 1980. *Workers in Industrial America: Essays on the Twentieth-Century Struggle*. New York and Oxford.

Brown, H. Phelps. 1986. *The Origins of Trade Union Power*. Oxford and New York.

Burawoy, M. 1979. *Manufacturing Consent: Changes in the Labor Process under Monopoly Capitalism*. Chicago and London.

———. 1980. "Migrant Labour in South Africa and the United States." In *Capital and Labour*, ed. T. Nichols. N.p., pp. 138–173.

Callahan, R. E. 1962. *Education and the Cult of Efficiency*. Chicago.

Calvert, M. A. 1967. *The Mechanical Engineer in America, 1830–1910*. Baltimore.

Chandler, A. D., Jr. 1962. *Strategy and Structure: Chapters in the History of the American Industrial Enterprise*. Cambridge, Mass., and London.

———. 1977. *The Visible Hand: The Managerial Revolution in American Business*. Cambridge, Mass., and London.

———. 1985. "The Emergence of Managerial Capitalism." In *The Coming of Managerial Capitalism*, ed. A. D. Chandler, Jr., and P. S. Tedlow. Homewood, Ill., pp. 396–424, ed. 1964.

———.*Giant Industry: Ford, General Motors, and the Automobile Industry: Sources and Readings*. New York and Burlingame, Vt.

Chandler, A. D., Jr., and P. S. Tedlow, ed. 1985. *The Coming of Managerial Capitalism*. Homewood, Ill.

Chinoy, E. 1955. *Automobile Workers and the American Dream*. Garden City, N.Y.

Clawson, D. 1980. *Bureaucracy and the Labor Process*. New York and London.

Clegg, H. 1983. *Trade Unionism under Collective Bargaining: A Theory Based on Comparisons of Six Countries*. Oxford.

Clough, S. B. 1953. *Histoire Economique des Etats-Unis Depuis la Guerre de Secession (1865–1952)*. Paris.

Coleman, T. 1974. *Passage to America*. Harmondsworth, Eng.

Collins, R. 1979. *The Credential Society*. New York.

Commons, J. R. 1907, 1920. *Races and Immigrants*. New York.

———. 1924, 1959. *Legal Foundations of Capitalism*. Madison, Wis.

———. 1951, 1970. *Economics of Collective Action*. Madison.

Conkin, P. K. 1967. *The New Deal*. New York.

Cordeiro, A. 1983. *L'Immigration*. Paris.

Coriat, B. 1980. "Ouvriers et Automates." In *Usines et Ouvriers: Figures du Nouvel Ordre Productif*, ed. J. P. de Gaudemar. Paris, pp. 41–76.

———. *De Werkplaats en de Stopwatch*. 1981. Amsterdam. Translated from *L'atelier et le chronometre*. Paris, 1979.

Cot, J. P. 1980. "Quel role pour la classe ouvriere?" In *"Faire": Le reflux Americain: decadence ou renouveau des Etats-Unis?* Paris, pp. 82–94.

Cremin, L. A. 1961. *The Transformation of the School: Progressivism in American Education*. New York.

Dahl, R. A. 1961. *Who Governs? Democracy and Power in an American City*. New Haven.

David, P. A. 1975. *Technical Choice, Innovation, and Economic Growth*. Cambridge, Eng.

Davis, K. S. 1986. *FDR: The New Deal Years, 1933–1937*. New York.

Davis, M. 1980. "Why the U.S. Working Class Is Different." *New Left Review* 123 (September–October): 3–44.

Dawley, A. 1976. *Class and Community*, Cambridge, Mass.

Degler, C. N. 1962. *Out of Our Past*. New York and Evanston, Ill.

Derber, M. 1984. "Employers Associations in the United States." In *Employers Associations and Industrial Relations: A Comparative Study*, ed. J. P. Windmuller and A. Gladstone. Oxford, pp. 79–114.

Dinnerstein, L., R. L. Nichols, and D. M. Reimers. 1979. *Natives and Strangers: Ethnic Groups and the Building of America*. New York.

Douglas, P. 1921. *American Apprenticeship and Industrial Education*. New York.

———. 1937, 1951. "The National Labor Relations Act of 1935." In *Readings in Labor Economics and Industrial Relations*, ed. J. Shister. Chicago, Philadelphia, and New York, pp. 432–438.

Dubofsky, M., and W. Van Tine. 1977. *John L. Lewis: A Biography*. New York.

Durkheim, E. 1903, 1983. *De La Division du Travail Social: Etude sur l'organisation des sociétés superieures*. Paris.

———. 1957, 1983. "The Nature and Origins of the Right of Property." In *Durkheim and the Law*, ed. S. Lukes and A. Scull. Oxford, pp. 192–237.

Ebner, M. H. 1985. "The Passaic Strike of 1912 and the Two IWW's." In *The Labor History Reader*, ed. D. J. Leab. Urbana, Ill., and Chicago, pp. 254–268.

Eckaus, R. S. 1963, 1968. "Investment in Human Capital: A Comment" In *Economics of Education*, vol. 1, ed. M. Blaug. Harmondsworth, Eng., pp. 208–214.

Edwards, P. K. 1981. *Strikes in the United States, 1881–1974*. Oxford.

Edwards, R. 1979. *Contested Terrain*. London.

Elbaum, B. 1984. "The Making and Shaping of Job and Pay Structures in the Iron and Steel Industry." In *Internal Labor Markets*, ed. P. Osterman. Cambridge, Mass., and London, pp. 71–107.

Emerson, T. I. 1983. "The National Labor Relations Board." In *The Making of the New Deal: The Insiders Speak*, ed. K. Louchheim. Cambridge, Mass., and London, pp. 205–213.

Farley, J. A. 1948. *Jim Farley's Story: The Roosevelt Years*. New York and Toronto.

Faulkner, H. U. 1938. *Economic History of the United States*. New York.

———. 1941. *American Political and Social History*. New York.

Fearon, P. 1979. *The Origin and Nature of the Great Slump, 1929–1932*. London and Basingstoke.

Feldstein, S., and L. Costello, eds. 1974. *The Ordeal of Assimilation: A Documentary History of the White Working Class 1830's to the 1970's*. New York.

Fine, S. 1963. *The Automobile under the Blue Eagle: Labor, Management, and the Automobile Manufacturing Code*. Ann Arbor, Mich.

———. 1969. *Sit-Down: The General Motors Strike of 1936–1937*. Ann Arbor, Mich.

Fisher, B. 1967. *Industrial Education: American Ideals and Institutions*. Madison, Wis.

Fleming, R. W. 1957, 1972. "The Significance of the Wagner Act." In *Labor and the New Deal*, ed. M. Derber and E. Young. New York, pp. 121–155.

Flexner, A., and F. P. Bachman. 1918, 1970. "The Gary Schools: A General Account." In *The Gary Schools*, ed. R. S. Bourne. Cambridge, Mass., and London, pp. 219–313.

Foner, P. S. 1965. *History of the Labor Movement in the United States, Vol. 4: The Industrial Workers of the World, 1905–1917*. New York.

———. 1981. *Organized Labor and the Black Worker, 1619–1981*. New York.

Ford, H. (with S. Crowther). 1927. *Heden en Morgen*. Amsterdam. Translated from *To-Day and To-Morrow*. Garden City, N.Y. 1926.

Fox, A. 1974. *Beyond Contract: Work, Power, and Trust Relations*. London.

Friedman, M. 1962. *Capitalism and Freedom*. Chicago.

J. K. Galbraith. 1954, 1977. *The Great Crash, 1929*. Harmondsworth, Eng.

———. 1964. *Politieke Economie*. Utrecht and Antwerp. Translated from *The Liberal Hour*, Harmondsworth, Eng., 1960.

Garraty, J. A. 1978. *Unemployment in History: Economic Thought and Public Policy*. New York.

Giedion, S. 1946. *Mechanization takes Command*. Translated from *Die Herrschaft der Mechanisierung*. Frankfurt, 1987.

Gillman, J. M. 1957. *The Falling Rate of Profit*. Translated from *Das Gesetz des tendenziellen Falls der Profitrate*. Frankfurt and Vienna, 1969.

———. 1965. *Prosperity in Crisis*. Translated from *Prosperitaet in der Krise*. Frankfurt and Vienna, 1968.

Goffman, E. 1968. *Asylums*. Harmondsworth, Eng.

Golab, C. 1977. "The Impact of the Industrial Experience on the Immigrant Families: The Huddled Masses Reconsidered." In *Immigrants in Industrial America, 1850–1920*, ed. R. L. Ehrlich. Charlottesville, Va., pp. 1–32.

Goldman, A. L. 1984. *Labor Law and Industrial Relations in the United States of America*. Deventer, Neth.

Goldman, P., and D. R. Van Houten. 1979. "Bureaucracy and Domination: Managerial Strategy in Turn-of-the-Century American Industry." In *The International Yearbook of Organization Studies, 1979*, ed. D. Dunkerley and G. Salaman. London, pp. 108–140.

Gordon, D. M. 1978. "Capitalist Development and the History of American Cities." In *Marxism and the Metropolis*, ed. W. K. Tabb and L. Sawyers. New York, pp. 25–63.

Gordon, D. M., R. Edwards, and M. Reich. 1982. *Segmented Work, Divided Workers*. Cambridge, Eng.

Gordon, M. M. 1964. *Assimilation in American Life*. New York.

Gould, W. B. 1982. *A Primer on American Labor Law*. Cambridge, Mass., and London.

Gouldner, A. W. 1954, 1965. *Wildcat Strike*. New York.

Graebner, W. 1980. *A History of Retirement: The Meaning and Function of an American Institution*. New Haven and London.

Graham, H. D., and T. R. Gurr, eds. 1969. *Violence in America: Historical and Comparative Perspectives*. N.p.

Granovetter, M., and C. Tilly. 1988. "Inequality and Labor Processes." In *Handbook of Sociology*, ed. N. J. Smelser. Newbury Park, Calif., pp. 175–221.

Greer, C. 1972, 1976. *The Great School Legend: A Revisionist Interpretation of American Public Education*. Harmondsworth, Eng.

Griffen, C. 1977. "The 'Old' Immigration and Industrialization: A Case Study." In *Immigrants in Industrial America, 1850–1920*, ed. R. L. Ehrlich. Charlottesville, Va., pp. 176–204.

Griffin, L. J., M. E. Wallace, and B. A. Rubin. 1986. "Capitalist Resistance to the Organization of Labor before the New Deal: Why? How? Success?" *American Sociological Review* 51 (April): 147–167.

Grob, G. N. 1961, 1969. *Workers and Utopia*, Chicago.

Guerin, D. 1977. *Le Mouvement Ouvrier aux Etats-Unis de 1866 à nos jours*. Paris.

Gumperz, J. 1932. "Zur Soziologie des Amerikanischen Parteiensystems." *Zeitschrift fuer Sozialforschung* 1, no. 3:278–310.

Gutman, H. G. 1977. *Work, Culture, and Society in Industrializing America*. New York.

———. 1987. *Power and Culture: Essays on the American Working Class*. New York.

Gutman, H. G., and I. Berlin. 1987. "Class Composition and the Development of the American Working Class, 1840–1890." In *Power and Culture: Essays on the American Working Class*, ed. H. G. Gutman. New York, pp. 380–394.

Habakkuk, H. J. 1962. *American and British Technology in the Nineteenth Century.*
    Cambridge, Eng.
————. 1981. *Population Growth and Economic Development since 1750.* Leicester,
    Eng.
Haber, S. 1964. *Efficiency and Uplift: Scientific Management in the Progressive Era,
    1890–1920.* Chicago and London.
Hacker, L. M. 1970. *The Course of American Economic Development and Growth.*
    New York.
Hall, P. D. 1984. *The Organization of American Culture, 1700–1900.* New York.
Handlin, O. 1952. *The Uprooted: The Epic Story of the Great Migrations That Made
    the American People.* Boston.
————. 1957. *Race and Nationality in American Life.* New York.
Harbison, F. H. 1940, 1951. "The Seniority Problem in Mass Production Industries."
    In *Readings in Labor Economics and Industrial Relations,* ed. J. Shister. Chi-
    cago, Philadelphia, and New York, pp. 312–314.
Hardman, J. B. S., and M. F. Neufeld, eds. 1951. *The House of Labor: Internal Operations
    of American Unions.* New York.
Harris, H. 1940. *Labor's Civil War.* New York.
Hauser, P. M. 1975. *Social Statistics in Use.* New York.
Hays, S. P. 1957. *The Response to Industrialism, 1885–1914.* Chicago and London.
Heidenheimer, A. J. 1981. "Education and Social Security Entitlements in Europe and
    America." In *The Development of Welfare States in Europe and America,* ed.
    P. Flora and A. J. Heidenheimer. New Brunswick, N.J., and London.
Hicks, J. D. 1960. *Republican Ascendancy, 1921–1933.* New York.
Hirschman, A. O. 1970. *Exit, Voice, and Loyalty.* Cambridge, Mass.
————. 1977. *The Passions and the Interests: Political Arguments for Capitalism before
    Its Triumph.* Princeton, N.J.
————. 1982. *Shifting Involvements: Private Interest and Public Action.* Oxford.
————. 1983. "Morality and the Social Sciences." In *Social Science and Moral Inquiry,*
    ed. N. Haan et al. New York, pp. 21–32.
————. 1985. "Against Parsimony." *Economics and Philosophy* 1:7–21.
Hobsbawm, E. J. 1964, 1968. *Labouring Men: Studies in the History of Labour.* London.
Hofstadter, R. 1948, n.d. *The American Political Tradition.* New York.
————. 1955. *The Age of Reform: From Bryan to FDR.* New York.
Holt, J. 1985. "Trade Unionism in the British and U.S. Steel Industries, 1888–1914: A
    Comparative Study." In *The Labor History Reader,* ed. D. J. Leab. Urbana, Ill.,
    and Chicago, pp. 166–196.
Holton, S. M. 1982. "Secondary Education." In *Encyclopedia of Educational Research.*
    New York, pp. 1683–1696.
Hopkins, H. L. 1972. "The New Deal and the Indigent." In *Poverty and Social Welfare
    in the United States,* ed. R. Lubove. New York, pp. 71–76.
Hovens, P. 1977. *Indianen van Noord-Amerika.* Assen and Amsterdam.
Huberman, L. 1947, 1970. *We, the People.* New York and London.
Hutchinson, E. P. 1981. *Legislative History of American Immigration Policy, 1798–
    1965.* Philadelphia.
Jacoby, S. M. 1985. *Employing Bureaucracy.* New York.
Jevons, W. S. 1871, 1970. *The Theory of Political Economy.* Harmondsworth, Eng.

Jones, E. 1979. "Der CIO–Reform zur Reaktion." In *Jahrbuch Arbeiterbewegung 6: Grenzen Gewerkschaftlicher Politik*, ed. C. Pozzoli. Frankfurt, pp. 78–114.

Judd, C. H. 1934. "Education." In *Recent Social Trends in the United States*, ed. Research Committee on Social Trends. New York and London, pp. 325–381.

Kaehler, A., and E. Hamburger. 1948. *Education for an Industrial Age*. Ithaca, N.Y., and New York.

Kahn-Freund, O. 1979. *Arbeit und Recht*. Cologne and Frankfurt.

Katz, M. 1983. "From Hoover to Roosevelt." In *The Making of the New Deal: The Insiders Speak*, ed. K. Louchheim. Cambridge, Mass., and London, pp. 120–129.

Katznelson, I. 1976. *Black Men, White Cities: Race, Politics, and Migration in the United States, 1900–30, and Britain, 1948–68*. Chicago and London.

Kerr, C. 1954, 1982. "The Balkanization of Labor Markets." In *Readings in Labor Economics and Labor Relations*, ed. L. G. Reynolds, S. H. Masters, and C. H. Moser. Englewood Cliffs, N.J., pp. 48–59.

Kessler-Harris, A., and V. Yans-McLaughlin. 1978. "European Immigrant Groups." In *Essays and Data on American Ethnic Groups*, ed. T. Sowell. N.p., pp. 107–137.

Killingsworth, C. C. 1948, 1951. "State Labor Relations Acts." In *Readings in Labor Economics and Industrial Relations*, ed. J. Shister. Chicago, Philadelphia, and New York, pp. 499–508.

Kindleberger, C. P. 1973. *The World in Depression, 1929–1939*. Berkeley, Calif., and Los Angeles.

King, E. J. 1972. *Ontwikkeling van Maatschappij en Onderwijs in de Verenigde Staten*. Rotterdam and Antwerp. Translated from *Society, Schools, and Progress in the USA*. Oxford, Eng. 1965.

Kirst, M. W. and F. M. Wirt. 1982. "State Influences on Education." In *Encyclopedia of Educational Research*. New York, pp. 1770–1780.

Klehr, H. 1984. *The Heydey of American Communism: The Depression Decade*. New York.

Kochan, T. A., and P. Cappelli. 1984. "The Transformation of the Industrial Relations and Personnel Function." In *Internal Labor Markets*, ed. P. Osterman. Cambridge, Mass., and London, pp. 133–161.

Kolko, G. 1976. *Main Currents in Modern American History*. New York.

———. 1979. "The Structure of the Working Class and the Working Wife." In *The American Working Class: Prospects for the 1980s*, ed. I. L. Horowitz, J. C. Leggett, and M. Oppenheimer. New Brunswick, N.J.

Korver, T. 1988. "Banale Politiek." In *Krisis; Tijdschrift voor filosofie (Journal of Philosophy)* 32. Amsterdam, pp. 58–63.

———. 1988. "Revival of Craftsmenship?" In *Technology and Work*, ed. W. Buitelaar. Aldershot, Eng., pp. 43–68.

Kreckel, R. 1983. "Soziale Ungleichheit und Arbeitsmarktsegmentierung." In *Soziale Ungleichheiten*, ed. R. Kreckel. Goettingen, pp. 137–162.

Kroes, R., ed. 1979. *American Immigration: Its Variety and Lasting Imprint*. Amsterdam.

Krug, E. A. 1972. *The Shaping of the American High School, Vol. 2: 1920–1941*. Madison, Wis.

Laurie, B., T. Hershberg, and G. Alter. 1977. "Immigrants and Industry: The Philadelphia Experience, 1850–1880." In *Immigrants in Industrial America, 1850–1920*, ed. R. L. Ehrlich. Charlottesville, Va., pp. 123–150.

Lee, J. R. 1916, 1964. "The So-Called Profit-Sharing System in the Ford Plant." In *Giant Industry: Ford, General Motors, and the Automobile Industry: Sources and Readings*, ed. A. D. Chandler, Jr. New York and Burlington, Vt., pp. 189–194.

Leggett, J. C. 1968. *Class, Race, and Labor: Working-Class Consciousness in Detroit.* Oxford, London, and New York.

Leiby, J. 1978. *A History of Social Welfare and Social Work in the United States.* New York.

Leuchtenburg, W. E. 1958. *The Perils of Prosperity, 1914–1932.* Chicago and London.

———. 1963. *Franklin D. Roosevelt and the New Deal.* New York.

Levine, A., and M. Levine. 1970. "The Gary Schools: A Sociohistorical Study of the Process of Change." In *The Gary Schools*, ed. R. S. Bourne. Cambridge, Mass., and London, pp. xii–lv.

Littler, C. R. 1982. *The Development of the Labour Process in Capitalist Societies.* London.

Loveridge, R., and A. L. Mok. 1979. *Theories of Labour Market Segmentation: A Critique.* The Hague.

Lubell, S. 1951, 1956. *The Future of American Politics.* New York.

Lubove, R. 1968. *The Struggle for Social Security, 1900–1935.* Cambridge.

Luebke, F. 1978. "The Germans." In *Ethnic Leadership in America*, ed. J. Higham. Baltimore and London, pp. 64–90.

Lulofs, J. G. 1960. *De Amerikaanse Arbeidsmarkt: een onderzoek naar arbeidsmobiliteit in de Verenigde Staten.* Meppel, Neth.

Lux, D. 1982. "Industrial Arts Education." In *Encyclopedia of Educational Research.* New York, pp. 859–863.

Markusen, A. R. 1978. "Class and Urban Social Expenditure: A Marxist Theory of Metropolitan Government." In *Marxism and the Metropolis*, ed. W. K. Tabb and L. Sawyers. New York, pp. 90–111.

Marsden, D. 1986. *The End of Economic Man?* Brighton, Eng.

Marx, K. 1867, 1976. *Capital*, vol. 1. Harmondsworth, Eng., and London.

Mattick, P. 1969. *Arbeitslosigkeit und Arbeitslosenbewegung in den USA, 1929–1935.* Frankfurt.

———. 1978. *Economics, Politics, and the Age of Inflation.* London.

Mayo, E. 1975. *The Social Problems of an Industrial Civilization.* London.

McConnell, G. 1966. *Private Power and American Democracy.* New York.

McCoy, D. R. 1973. *Coming of Age: The United States during the 1920s and 1930s.* Harmondsworth, Eng.

McPherson, W. H. 1940. *Labor Relations in the Automobile Industry.* Washington, D.C.

Meier, A., and E. Rudwick. 1979. *Black Detroit and the Rise of the UAW.* New York and Oxford.

Meiksins, P. F. 1984. "Scientific Management and Class Relations: A Dissenting View." *Theory and Society* 13, no. 2 (March): 177–209.

Meltzer, M. 1967. *Bread—And Roses: The Struggle of American Labor, 1865–1915.* New York.

Merton, R. K. 1967. *On Theoretical Sociology.* New York and London.

Meyer, S., III. 1977. "Mass Production and Human Efficiency: The Ford Motor Company, 1908–1921." Ph.D. diss., Rutgers University, New Brunswick, N.J.

Miller, G. W. 1954. "The Effect of Social Security on Manpower Resources." In *Man-*

power in the United States: Problems and Policies, ed. W. Haber, F. Harbison, L. R. Klein, and G. L. Palmer. New York, pp. 51–66.

Miller, R. K., Jr. 1981. "Patterns of Employment Difficulty among European Immigrant Industrial Workers during the Great Depression: Local Opportunity and Cultural Heritage." In *Sociological Perspectives on Labor Markets*, ed. I. Berg. New York, pp. 297–325.

Milton, D. 1982. *The Politics of U.S. Labor: From the Great Depression to the New Deal*. New York and London.

Montgomery, D. 1980. *Workers' Control in America*. Cambridge, Eng.

Moore, Barrington, Jr. 1978. *Injustice: The Social Bases of Obedience and Revolt*. White Plains, N.Y.

Mortimer, W. 1972. *Organize! My Life as a Union Man*. Boston.

Mosher, E. K. 1982. "Federal Influence on Education." In *Encyclopedia of Educational Research*. New York, pp. 671–682.

Nadworny, M. J. 1955. *Scientific Management and the Unions, 1900–1932: A Historical Analysis*. Cambridge, Mass.

Nelson, D. 1969. *Unemployment Insurance: The American Experience, 1915–1935*. Madison, Wis.

———. 1975. *Managers and Workers: Origins of the New Factory System in the United States, 1880–1920*. Madison, Wis.

———. 1980. *Frederick W. Taylor and the Rise of Scientific Management*. Madison, Wis.

Neumann, F. L. 1936. *The Governance of the Rule of Law*. Translated from *Die Herrschaft des Gesetzes*. Frankfurt, 1980.

Noble, D. F. 1977. *America by Design: Science, Technology, and the Rise of Corporate Capitalism*. Oxford.

Norman, H. 1979. "Emigration from the Nordic Countries: Some Aspects." In *American Immigration: Its Variety and Lasting Imprint*, ed. R. Kroes. Amsterdam, pp. 50–66.

North, D. C. 1966. *Growth and Welfare in the American Past: A New Economic History*. Englewood Cliffs, N.J.

Offe, C., and K. Hinrichs. 1977. "Sozialoekonomie des Arbeitsmarktes und die Lage 'benachteiligter' Gruppen von Arbeitnehmern." In *Opfer des Arbeitsmarktes. Zur Theorie der strukturierten Arbeitslosigkeit*, ed. C. Offe and Projektgruppe Arbeitsmarktpolitik. Neuwied and Darmstadt, W. Ger., pp. 3–61.

Okun, A. M. 1982. "The Invisible Handshake and the Inflationary Process." In *Readings in Labor Economics and Labor Relations*, ed. L. G. Reynolds, S. H. Masters, and C. H. Moser. Englewood Cliffs, N.J., pp. 212–220.

Orloff, A. S., and T. Skocpol. 1984. "Why Not Equal Protection? Explaining the Politics of Public School Spending in Britain, 1900–11, and the United States, 1880s–1920." *American Sociological Review* (December): 726–750.

Osterman, P. 1980. *Getting Started: The Youth Labor Market*. Cambridge, Mass., and London.

Parenti, M. 1969. "Ethnic Politics and the Persistence of Ethnic Identification." In *Ethnic Group Politics*, ed. H. A. Bailey, Jr., and E. Katz. Columbus, Ohio, pp. 267–283.

Parkin, F. 1979. *Marxism and Class Theory: A Bourgeois Critique*. London.

Pelling, H. 1960. *American Labor*. Chicago and London.

Perkins, F. 1946. *The Roosevelt I Knew*. New York.

Perlman, S. 1928, 1982. *A Theory of the Labor Movement*. In *Readings in Labor Economics and Labor Relations*, ed. L. G. Reynolds, S. H. Masters, and C. H. Moser. Englewood Cliffs, N.J., pp. 308–314.

Perrow, C. 1986. "Economic Theories of Organization." *Theory and Society* 15:11–46.

Piore, M. J. 1979. *Birds of Passage: Migrant Labor and Industrial Societies*. Cambridge, Eng.

Piore, M. J., and C. F. Sabel. 1984. *The Second Industrial Divide: Possibilities for Prosperity*. New York.

Piven, F. F., and R. A. Cloward. 1970. *Regulating the Poor*. Translated from *Regulierung der Armut*. Frankfurt, 1977.

————. 1977, 1979. *Poor People's Movements*. New York.

————. 1988. *Why Americans Don't Vote*. New York.

Polanyi, K. 1944, 1957. *The Great Transformation*. Boston.

Pollard, S. 1981. *Peaceful Conquest: The Industrialisation of Europe, 1760–1970*. Oxford.

Popitz, H., H. P. Bahrdt, E. A. Jueres, and H. Kesting. 1964. *Technik und Industriearbeit*. Tubingen, W. Ger.

Potter, A. M. 1955. *American Government and Politics*. London.

Poulantzas, N. 1977. "The New Petty Bourgeoisie." In *Class and Class Structure*, ed. A. Hunt. London, pp. 113–124.

Presser, J. 1965. *Amerika, van Kolonie tot Wereldmacht*. Amsterdam and Brussels.

Prude, J. 1983. "The Social System of Early New England Textile Mills: A Case Study, 1812–40." In *Working-Class America*, ed. M. H. Frisch and D. J. Walkowitz. Urbana, Ill., Chicago, and London, pp. 1–36.

Pullman, D. E., and L. Reed Tripp. 1957, 1972. "Collective Bargaining Developments." In *Labor and the New Deal*, ed. M. Derber and E. Young. New York, pp. 317–360.

Rayback, J. G. 1959, 1966. *A History of American Labor*. New York and London.

Reitell, C. 1924, 1964. "Machinery and Its Effect upon the Workers in the Automobile Industry." In *Giant Industry: Ford, General Motors, and the Automobile Industry: Sources and Readings*, ed. A. D. Chandler, Jr. New York and Burlington, Vt., pp. 104–110.

Rodgers, D. T. 1978. *The Work Ethic in Industrial America, 1850–1920*. Chicago.

Rose, M. 1975. *Industrial Behaviour*. London.

Rosenberg, N. 1972. *Technology and American Economic Growth*. New York.

Rosenblum, G. 1973. *Immigrant Workers*. New York.

Ross, H. N. 1968. "Economic Growth and Change in the United States under Laissez-Faire: 1870–1929." In *The Age of Industrialism in America*, ed. F. C. Jaher. New York and London, pp. 6–48.

Roth, K. H. 1977. *Die "andere" Arbeiterbewegung und die Entwicklung der kapitalistischen Repression von 1880 bis zur Gegenwart*. Munich.

Rothbard, M. 1970. "The Hoover Myth." In *For a New America*, ed. J. Weinstein and D. W. Eakins. New York, pp. 162–179.

————. 1983. *America's Great Depression*. New York.

Rubin, B. A., L. J. Griffin, and M. Wallace. 1983. " 'Provided Only That Their Voice Was Strong': Insurgency and Organization of American Labor from NRA to Taft-Hartley." *Work and Occupations* 10, no. 3 (August): 325–347.

Rubinson, R. 1986. "Class Formation, Politics, and Institutions: Schooling in the United States." *American Journal of Sociology* 92, no. 3 (November): 519–548.

Rusche, G., and O. Kirchheimer. 1974. *Sozialstruktur und Strafvollzug*. Frankfurt and Cologne.

Schervish, P. G. 1981. "The Structure of Employment and Unemployment." In *Sociological Perspective on Labor Markets*, ed. I. Berg. New York, pp. 153–186.

———. 1983. *The Structural Determinants of Unemployment*. New York.

Schlesinger, A. M., Jr. 1946. *The Age of Jackson*. New York.

———. 1957. *The Age of Roosevelt: The Crisis of the Old Order, 1919–1933*. London.

———. 1959. *The Age of Roosevelt: The Coming of the New Deal*. Boston.

Schmidt, G. 1974. *Gesellschaftliche Entwicklung und Industriesoziologie in den USA: Eine historische Analyse*. Frankfurt and Cologne.

Schumpeter, J. A. 1939, 1964. "Business Cycles." In *Giant Industry: Ford, General Motors, and the Automobile Industry: Sources and Readings*, ed. A. D. Chandler, Jr. New York and Burlington, Vt., pp. 235–240.

Selznick, P. 1980. *Law, Society, and Industrial Justice*. New Brunswick, N.J., and London.

Serrin, W. 1973. *The Company and the Union*. New York.

Sherwood, R. E. 1950. *Roosevelt and Hopkins, Vol. 1: The Men Who Shaped Our Lives*. New York.

Slichter, S. H. 1920, 1961. "Industrial Morale." In *Potentials of the American Economy: Selected Essays of Sumner H. Slichter*, ed. J. T. Dunlop. Cambridge, Mass., pp. 167–183.

Slichter, S. H. 1929, 1961. "The Current Labor Policies of American Industries." In *Potentials of the American Economy: Selected Essays of Sumner H. Slichter*, ed. J. T. Dunlop. Cambridge, Mass., pp. 184–212.

———. 1939, 1961. "The Changing Character of American Industrial Relations." In *Potentials of the American Economy: Selected Essays of Sumner H. Slichter*, ed. J. T. Dunlop. Cambridge, Mass., pp. 213–232.

———. 1940, 1961. "The Impact of Social-Security Legislation upon Mobility and Enterprise." In *Potentials of the American Economy: Selected Essays of Sumner H. Slichter*, ed. J. T. Dunlop. Cambridge, Mass., pp. 317–336.

———. 1941, 1951. "Control of Layoffs: Policies and Problems." In *Readings in Labor Economics and Industrial Relations*, ed. J. Shister. Chicago, Philadelphia, and New York, pp. 303–312.

Sloan, A. P., Jr. 1963. *My Years with General Motors*. New York.

Soerensen, A. B., and A. L. Kalleberg. 1981. "An Outline of a Theory of the Matching of Persons to Jobs." In *Sociological Perspectives on Labor Markets*, ed. I. Berg. New York, pp. 49–74.

Sombart, W. 1921. *Der moderne Kapitalismus*, vol. 1, part 2. Munich and Leipzig.

Sorensen, C. E. 1962. *My Forty Years with Ford*. New York.

Sowell, T., ed. 1978. *Essays and Data on American Ethnic Groups*. N.p.

———. 1983. *The Economics and Politics of Race*. New York.

Stark, D. 1980. "Class Struggle and the Transformation of the Labor Process." *Theory and Society* 9, no. 1: 89–130.

Steindl, J. 1952, 1976. *Maturity and Stagnation in American Capitalism*. New York and London.

Stevenson, J. A. 1980. "Daniel de Leon and European Socialism, 1890–1914." *Science and Society* 44, no. 2 (Summer): 199–223.

Stone, K. 1974. "The Origins of Job Structures in the Steel Industry." *The Review of Radical Political Economics* 6, no. 2 (Summer): 61–97.

Strauss, A. L. 1971. *The Contexts of Social Mobility*. Chicago.

Stricker, F. 1985. "Affluence for Whom? Another Look at Prosperity and the Working Classes in the 1920s." In *The Labor History Reader*, ed. D. J. Leab. Urbana, Ill., and Chicago, pp. 288–316.

Struik, D. 1962. *Yankee Science in the Making*. New York.

Sward, K. 1948, 1972. *The Legend of Henry Ford*. New York.

Taeuber, C., and I. B. Taeuber. 1958. *The Changing Population of the United States*. New York.

Taft, P. 1942, 1976. "Organized Labor and the New Deal." In *Readings in Labor Economics and Labor Relations*, ed. R. L. Rowan. Homewood, Ill., pp. 132–141.

Tawney, R. H. 1979. *The American Labour Movement, and Other Essays*. Brighton, Eng.

Taylor, F. W. 1903, 1972. "Shop Management." In *Scientific Management*, F. W. Taylor. Westport, Conn., pp. 17–207.

———. 1911, 1972. "Principles of Scientific Management." In *Scientific Management*, ed. F. W. Taylor. Westport, Conn., pp. 5–144.

Taylor, R. E. 1982. "Vocational Education." In *Encyclopedia of Educational Research*. New York, pp. 2002–2012.

Temin, P. 1973. "Labor Scarcity in America." In *New Economic History*, ed. P. Temin. Harmondsworth, Eng., pp. 165–180.

Thernstrom, S. 1964. *Poverty and Progress*. Cambridge, Mass.

———. 1968. "Urbanization, Migration, and Social Mobility in Late Nineteenth-Century America." In *Towards a New Past*, ed. B. J. Bernstein. New York, pp. 158–175.

Thompson, E. P. 1968, 1981. *The Making of the English Working Class*. Harmondsworth, Eng.

Thompson, F. W., and P. Murfin. 1976. *The IWW: Its First Seventy Years, 1905–1975*. Chicago.

Thompson, W. S. 1937, 1972. *Research Memorandum on Internal Migration in the Depression*. New York.

Thomson, A. W. J. 1981. "The United States of America." In *Trade Unions in the Developed Economies*, ed. E. Owen Smith. London, pp. 155–177.

Thurow, L. C. 1975. *Generating Inequality: Mechanisms of Distribution in the U.S. Economy*. New York.

Trattner, W. I. 1974. *From Poor Law to Welfare State: A History of Social Welfare in America*. New York and London.

Tronti, M. 1972. "Workers and Capital." *Telos* 14 (Winter): 25–62.

Trow, M. 1961, 1977. "The Second Transformation of American Secondary Education." In *Power and Ideology in Education*, ed. J. Karabel and A. H. Halsey. New York, pp. 105–118.

Troy, L. 1965. *Trade Union Membership, 1897–1962*. New York.

Tyack, D. B. 1972, 1977. "City Schools: Centralization of Control at the Turn of the Century." In *Power and Ideology in Education*, ed. J. Karabel and A. H. Halsey. New York, pp. 397–411.

———. 1974. *The One Best System: A History of American Urban Education*. Cambridge, Mass., and London.

van Hoof, J. 1987. *De Arbeidsmarkt als Arena*. Amsterdam.

Wachter, M. L. 1974. *Primary and Secondary Labor Markets.* Brookings Papers on Economic Activity, no. 3. Washington, D.C.

Walker, C. R., and R. H. Guest. 1952. *The Man on the Assembly Line.* Cambridge, Mass.

Walzer, M. 1983, 1985. *Spheres of Justice.* Oxford.

Weber, M. 1920, 1978. *Economy and Society,* 2 vols. Berkeley, Calif., and Los Angeles.

Weber, M. 1961. *General Economic History.* New York.

Weinstein, J. 1968. *The Corporate Ideal in the Liberal State, 1900–1918.* Boston.

White, L. J. 1982. "The Automobile Industry." In *The Structure of American Industry,* ed. W. Adams. New York and London.

Widick, B. J., ed. 1976. *Auto Work and Its Discontents.* Baltimore and London.

Wilcock, R. C. 1957, 1972. "Industrial Management's Policies Toward Unionism." In *Labor and the New Deal,* ed. M. Derber and E. Young. New York, pp. 275–315.

Williamson, H. F., ed. 1951. *The Growth of the American Economy.* Englewood Cliffs, N.J.

Williamson, O. E. 1975. *Markets and Hierarchies.* New York and London.

———. 1985. *The Economic Institutions of Capitalism.* New York and London.

Wilson, W. J. 1978. *The Declining Significance of Race.* Chicago.

E. E. Witte. 1957, 1972. "Organized Labor and Social Security." In *Labor and the New Deal,* ed. M. Derber and E. Young. New York, pp. 239–274.

———. 1963. *The Development of the Social Security Act.* Madison, Wis.

Wood, S. 1985. "Work Organization." In *Work, Culture, and Society,* ed. R. Deem and G. Salaman. Milton Keynes, Eng., and Philadelphia, pp. 77–101.

Zilversmit, A. 1976. "The Failure of Progressive Education, 1920–1940." In *Schooling and Society: Studies in the History of Education,* ed. L. Stone. Baltimore and London, pp. 252–263.

INDEX

About the Author

TON KORVER is a Lecturer at the University of Amsterdam. He has published widely in Dutch professional journals, and he is currently working on "The Concept of Equality," a study of equal opportunity and affirmative action in The Netherlands and the United States.